Self Psychology
in Clinical
Social Work

Self Psychology in Clinical Social Work

Miriam Elson, M.A., A.C.S.W.

School of Social Service Administration
University of Chicago

W · W · NORTON & COMPANY
New York   *London*

Printed in the United States of America.

First published as a Norton paperback 1988

Library of Congress Cataloging-in-Publication Data

Elson, Miriam.
  Self psychology in clinical social work.

"A Norton professional book."
Bibliography: p.
Includes index.
  1. Personality, Disorders of.   2. Self.   3. Psychiatric
social work.   I. Title.
RC554.E47 1986   616.89   86-5337

ISBN 0-393-95797-7

W. W. Norton & Company, Inc., 500 Fifth Avenue, New York, NY 10110
W. W. Norton & Company Ltd., 10 Coptic Street, London WC1A 1PU

  3 4 5 6 7 8 9 0

For Alex

Contents

SECTION IV
Broader Perspectives

Foreword

OVER THE YEARS OF LEARNING, practicing, and teaching psychotherapy and psychoanalysis I have known a small group of gifted therapists I call "therapeutic personalities." (I am not including therapists who deliberately make use of active techniques with the intent to engage, support, reassure, strengthen, etc.) No one discipline, gender, or character type has a monopoly on these individuals. They come from the ranks of social work, psychology, and psychiatry, include both men and women, and run the gamut of different manifest personality types and styles of doing treatment. (I shall come to the comparison I make to social workers as a group in a moment.)

Although my impressions have taken shape in connection with supervising and analyzing some of these therapists, my ideas about them are not based on a systematic study. However, what they have in common, I think, is that their patients very readily experience them as having unusually available, sustaining, and invigorating selfobject functions. Another way of saying this is that they are magnets for revival of thwarted needs and for the development of cohesive selfobject transferences. A core quality of their own self organization evokes this experience in patients.

Prior to Kohut's discoveries of the enormous benefit selfobject functions can have for patients with disorders of the self, these therapists were doing a kind of self psychology without really knowing it, and without knowing how. In their training they can at times feel like the centipede who has awkwardly to relearn what had already come naturally. In any event, to become analysts and analytically oriented psychotherapists they have to learn to understand and explain their transference-fostering effect and beneficial influence, and acquire the skills and capacities needed to make disciplined use of themselves. In other words, training is as necessary for them as for other therapists if the benefits of treatment are to be more than nonspecific and permanently accrue to the patient in the form of strengthened functions and capacities of his own.

Interestingly enough, Miriam Elson makes a somewhat analogous assertion about social workers as a group. Her assertion goes something like
this: In the diverse care-providing roles social workers were traditionally
trained to assume they too have been functioning as selfobjects. Because
so many individuals they see are chronically threatened by faulty or failing cohesion the workers' functions reactivate thwarted needs for the mirroring, strengthening, and self-expanding responses sorely lacking in their
present lives and in their childhood development. In other words, the
assertion is that social workers also are prime targets for selfobject transferences. I am generally in agreement with this point, although here it is
important to at least note that there is a difference between patients' attachment to therapists' selfobject functions and the deep-going, cohesive
selfobject transferences which are mobilized in intensive therapy. Be that
as it may, I am also in accord with the other two points which constitute
the underpinnings of *Self Psychology in Clinical Social Work*. First, social
workers who want to do treatment need to acquire understanding, skills,
and self-awareness commensurate with the kinds of transferences they
evoke; and second, Kohut's theory of the self and its normal growth is
the theoretical framework most suited to their treatment endeavors.

Miriam Elson brings strong qualifications to the task of demonstrating
precisely how Kohut's self psychology explains so much about the efficacy
of traditional social work methods and interventions, and how it is particularly applicable to the various kinds of growth-furthering psychotherapy social workers (and others) do. Her qualifications blend the accumulated wisdom of a seasoned social work scholar, educator, and practitioner
who thoroughly knows the past and present directions in her own field,
and the requisite knowledge of self psychology which comes from familiarity with psychoanalytic theory and long-time, serious study of Kohut's
evolving work. In fact, she was among the first social work educators to
see that the use of Kohut's contributions in social work practice augments
possibilities for resumed structural growth, and she was among the first
to learn the applications of self psychology to a broad range of clinical
problems from Kohut himself, firsthand, in the seminar where he responded to material presented by social workers, psychologists, and
psychiatrists. I personally profited a great deal from reading the unpublished 1971 manuscript *Self Esteem and Ideals*, based on seminars with
Kohut, which Elson generously made available to those of us who were
eager to learn self psychology and equip ourselves for practice by seeing
how Kohut actually worked.

The special merit of *Self Psychology in Clinical Social Work* is its rich clinical
detail presented in a clear, readable style. Because Elson paints portraits
of flesh and blood people the way they look and feel, formidable sound-

ing theoretical concepts such as selfobject transferences, the bipolar self, structural deficits in idealizing and mirroring poles, fragmentation, transmuting internalization, and more become graspable clinical realities. Because she paints portraits of real therapists at work, the often frustrating gap between theoretical abstractions and actually doing therapy is narrowed. Readers who carefully study her case histories can vicariously participate with therapists engaged in the dual task of trying to make disciplined use of themselves and their countertransferences while applying self psychology to what the patient says and does. They can begin to see for themselves such things as patients' increasing capacity for therapeutic engagement (alliance and self observation), and the decrease of confusion, defensiveness, rage, manipulativeness, etc. in an atmosphere of attunement to precarious cohesion and chronically thwarted developmental needs. They can begin to see for themselves that there are multiple and complex selfobject functions at work in the different kinds of treatment and treatment interventions described (these include a whole spectrum from therapeutic diagnosis and briefest crisis intervention to long-term psychotherapy); that there are differing consequences of the therapists' functions depending on the specific nature and extent of the patient's self disorder (these range from transient disequilibriums at times of increased stress and change to chronic and severe structural deficits); that transmuting internalization and "structure building" are neither easy nor fast nor mystical but silently go on in the subtle back and forth of the long-term patient-therapist exchange.

One of many moving illustrations of how acquisition of needed soothing and firming structures actually comes about can be seen in the case of Mrs. B. Particularly noteworthy is the alleviation of her abusiveness towards her child and her punitiveness towards herself via the experience of selfobject functions described in this way: "She often didn't really remember what the therapist said but rather her soft voice. 'Just sitting here and looking at you and knowing that you really care to take the time for me makes me feel good. No one else ever did.'"

Self Psychology in Clinical Social Work abounds in important insights into the nature of the therapeutic process and what can be accomplished in different kinds of treatment. The cases cover a broad spectrum. For example 20-year-old Andy was treated twice a week for two years. He suffered from a "vast disinterest" in his future and had lost sight of any meaningful, fulfilling goals. His treatment demonstrates the dynamic-genetic relationship between his childhood parent loss and his lack of goal structures, and the all-important point that "successful" mourning of a childhood loss is accomplished when the therapist's reinstated selfobject functions buffer the loss and begin to fill in the resulting structural deficit.

At a quite different part of the spectrum the case of the elderly, cantankerous, demanding Mrs. D. demonstrates the profound importance for "cost effectiveness" and prevention of chronic geriatric illness of the social worker's cohesion-restoring interventions.

I am sure that Miriam Elson's readers will have the pleasure and the benefits which go with discovering the many insights to be found here for themselves. This last thought—that there is pleasure and benefit in store for the practitioners from any field who mine this rewarding book—brings me to one final point. There is much to be said about the question of the acceptance of the trained clinical social worker as a full-fledged citizen of the community of qualified psychotherapists, and there is much to be said about the nature of the training, including systematic training in self psychology, which a therapist needs. *Self Psychology in Clinical Social Work* merely alludes to some of these problems in an occasional mention of the social worker's feeling demeaned or depreciated because of the uncertain status of the field, and of the necessity for disciplined use of the self and understanding of countertransference. Miriam Elson's agenda here is mainly to teach by introducing social work practitioners to the great potentiality of self psychology for more effective practice. She has left the problem of the status of the clinical social worker as therapist for another time or for other authors. However, I would expect her contribution to exert a stimulating and beneficial impact on further developments in traditional aspects of social work, since the psychological and social import of effective self psychological "supportive" interventions can hardly be overestimated. And I would expect, as well, that the publication of this book will exert a constructive and stimulating influence on the ongoing efforts of clinical social workers to establish their training and qualifications as psychotherapists. On both these scores this book does social work a real service.

Marian Tolpin, M.D.
Glencoe, Illinois
May 5, 1986

Preface

I HAVE BEEN URGED to undertake this work by students, colleagues and friends. It was their encouragement that permitted me to overcome a sense of presumption in attempting an introduction to self psychology.

Heinz Kohut was a friend of many years. He was a classical analyst whose work as a teacher and theorist had long stimulated my interest. In lectures or in seminars, he shared in an intimate way his efforts to understand the complexities of human striving: striving that led to fulfillment and productivity, and striving that, bewilderingly, led to purposelessness and defeat. He was fond of saying that without theory and ordering principles we can see nothing, but with theory alone we are closed to new experience.

As early as 1957, he described empathy and introspection as scientific tools of psychoanalysis through which clinical material enriched theory and theory provided an understanding of clinical material. It was this method of working that ultimately led to his formulating the theories of self psychology. He moved our understanding beyond drive/defense and compromise formation as the basic building blocks of the individual to a theory that encompassed the drives—that of a cohesive nuclear self which takes form from the empathic response of caretakers. Driven behavior emerges only when the caretakers seriously fail in their response to the mirroring and idealizing needs of the child's forming self.

Although his theories were to be used in psychoanalysis, their power to illuminate human striving offered broad insight to mental health professionals working in less intensive modes of treatment. Kohut recognized this.

And so I invited Kohut, under the auspices of the Charlotte Rosenbaum Fund, to conduct a yearlong seminar in the Student Mental Health Clinic of the University of Chicago, where I had been for many years the chief psychiatric social worker. It was in this setting that the insights of self psychology seemed to offer new understanding of vulnerable youth on the brink of leaving home, youth seeking to discover and professionalize their talents even as they sought new relationships.

Kohut broadened our vision by enabling us to recognize that the need for human relatedness took many forms and matured from early to late forms. Selfobjects were needed in the creation of the self, in the consolidation of the self, and in the sustenance of the self throughout life, and especially at periods of transition. From his response to the clinical material presented by psychiatrists, psychologists, and social workers, we learned that we could respond to the emotional distress and disorder of those who sought our help as new selfobjects, reactivating the point at which deficits in self structure had occurred and rekindling the urge to continue the process of growth.

Later, in teaching and consulting, I had an opportunity to explore in various settings the broader application of these theories, culminating, finally, in this effort. The cases I have selected to illustrate the application of self psychology cover a broad range of typical life situations. It is my hope that readers will find them useful and will continue their study of self psychology.

ACKNOWLEDGMENTS

Over the course of a lifetime, one has numerous teachers. The many individuals who have allowed me the privilege of entering their psychic life have enlarged my vision of the resiliency of the human spirit in turning adversity to mastery. In my chosen field of social work, Charlotte Towle infused theory with her profound belief in the dignity of the individual and the duty of society to provide the opportunity for a meaningful life. Helen Perlman, distinguished professor and longtime friend, brought to her writing in the field of social work the warmth and vitality of an informed mind and the grace to express her thoughts.

In the field of psychoanalysis, Kohut's colleagues, both through the further exploration and elaboration of his theories and through their own contributions, have expanded and enriched my understanding of self psychology. Most especially, these are Michael F. Basch, Arnold Goldberg (who read a portion of the manuscript), Anna and Paul Ornstein, Marian and Paul Tolpin, and Ernest S. Wolf.

In consultation I have come to know the work of several agencies. But two in particular gave me an opportunity to examine the treatment process by which change comes about. Evelyn E. Diers, Director of Counseling, Chicago Child Care Society, and her staff have often demonstrated their competence and responsiveness in bringing about more productive engagement in life's tasks for the individuals with whom they have worked.

Adrienne C. Kraft, Executive Director of St. Mary's Services of Chicago, and her staff have provided with skill and wisdom their special services to children.

Rebecca Cohen and Elizabeth M. Kohut, friends and colleagues, read this manuscript in preparation and offered wise suggestions with magnanimity and encouragement. Ann Rothschild, an early student and my oldest friend, posed questions that stimulated my inquiry and my efforts to clarify concepts. Christine Sussman succeeded in deciphering its many criss-crossings. To Susan E. Barrows, Norton Professional Books, whose clear eye and gentle pen improved this manuscript, I owe a special debt.

In a more intimate sense, my parents, David and Elizabeth Almond, were my first mirrors, my first ideals. Rosalind, Gabriel, and Ruth, my sisters and brother, were part of that vivid world of literature and of the mind in which our lives were steeped. But it was my husband, Alex, who first led me from the world of literature to the real world of people and their needs. His conduct in his own chosen profession continues to inspire my own. And finally, an enormous indebtedness must be recognized for the delight and affirmation that our children, Jacova Silverthorne and Karen O'Neil and their families have given us over the years.

Miriam Elson
Chicago
January, 1986

SECTION I

Theory

1

The Fit Between
Self Psychology and
Social Work Practice

M Y PURPOSE IN UNDERTAKING this book is to present and examine self psychology as a theory of human development that has the capacity to illuminate social work practice across the spectrum of human sevices. As a theory of human development, it helps us to explore in a new way a broad range of services in the mental health profession, in education, and in community work. But my focus will center on the practice of social work in child and family agencies, in clinics and outpatient departments of psychiatry, and in private practice. An understanding of the theories of self psychology improves our vision of human striving and of the manner in which, as professionals, we make our skills available to individuals and groups who encounter difficulties in their lives which distort growth and invade the capacity to enjoy life and pursue goals. It clarifies what practitioners have long observed and known—that is, the manner in which those we work with use our mature psychic structure to provide for their missing structure and in the process transmute the functions we perform into self structure.

The practice of social work embraces a broad range of services, extending from community-based action programs of social intervention to individual treatment for intrapsychic difficulties. In her work, the practitioner has only one tool and that tool is herself. She has no pharmacopeia; she has no protocol of tests and procedures; she has no more than any citizen's control of political processes, educational or correctional systems. The master's level practitioner has a broad range of methods and of community resources, and an understanding of how and with whom these may be effectively employed, but her principal tool is herself.

Social workers have long been aware of this special dimension in their

3

relationship with the individuals they serve. Indeed, the search for and development of methods of intervention arose because of their need to understand and to regulate the manner in which they responded to the needs of the individuals with whom they worked. For they found that whether the practitioner worked with an individual directly or as an agent of society extending its interventions to individuals and groups, the self of the social worker was always a crucial element in the equation.

In their efforts to understand this dynamic relationship in their work with individuals, and the dynamic relationship of those individuals with society, social workers have absorbed many theories of human development. As a profession, social work came into being during the fruitful years when Freud was formulating his theories of the tripartite structure of the mind, psychosexual development, the centrality of the oedipus complex, and the role of the defenses in conflict resolution. Hartmann (1939) expanded these theories to include the innate capacity of the individual to function adaptively, exploring both adaptive and defensive functions of the ego. Anna Freud (1965) proposed interacting lines of development and described the defensive functions of the ego. Erikson (1950) formulated a theory of psychosocial development that bridged intrapsychic development and interpersonal environmental and cultural experience in an epigenetic series extending over the life cycle. Further infused with the theories of Fairbairn, Winnicott, Guntrip, Jacobson, and Mahler and her associates, ego psychology and object relations theory were absorbed into the practice of social work.

Ego psychology and object relations theory have had the power to illuminate human development and behavior and are useful theories in ordering observation and response. Self psychology now adds to our understanding of the manner in which the self of the social worker becomes a key element in the repair and restoration of psychic structure building in the individual or individuals with whom we work. Kohut's theory of self psychology, with its concept of the selfobject, becomes the key to our understanding of why it is and how it is that the self of the social worker exerts a force in restoring an individual's self-esteem and enables him to regulate that self-esteem as he seeks to realize cherished goals.

Kohut has described, metaphorically, a *bipolar self* which comes into being through twin streams of experience: that of being mirrored, admired, confirmed and guided; and that of being permitted to merge with the power and wisdom of an idealized selfobject. As necessary to his survival as food and oxygen, *selfobjects* constitute the empathic milieu into which a child is born. We shall see that they are essential to the creation of the self in infancy, to its consolidation in early childhood, and to the sustenance of the self *throughout life*. The psychic structure of a cohesive nuclear self comes into being through *transmuting internalization*. Myriad *selfobject functions* are transmuted into *self functions* as long as they are withdrawn gradually, not abruptly or traumatically: *optimal frustration* thus allows for the replacement of selfobject functions by self functions.

The selfobjects of early infancy and childhood perform mirroring, confirming, and guiding functions, and they permit empathic merger with their idealized strength and wisdom in sufficient amounts and for sufficient duration to allow selfobject functions to be transmuted into self functions. These functions are the capacity to regulate self-esteem, to monitor stress, to define and pursue realistic goals. Deficits occur in the self of the individual when the original selfobjects have been unable to provide such functions in a consistent manner. The self emerges subject to fragmentation and enfeebled rather than cohesive, vigorous, and harmonious. It is with the social worker as *new* selfobject in the present that the individual is able to reengage himself in the process of structure building. It is this concept of the social worker as new selfobject that clarifies what we do.

The well-known sense of being "exploited" or "manipulated" that social workers experience in working with individuals with severe deficits can now be better understood as the desperate attempt of an individual to complete psychic structure by attaching the mature psychic structure of the social worker. Such an understanding removes the pejorative nature of the terms "manipulation" or "exploitation" by enabling the social worker to recognize that such feeling states and behaviors signal the depth at which deficits in self structure exist; indeed, the earlier the deficit the more blindly demanding the need. Its very intensity signals the force of the hitherto unresponded to need for the performance of selfobject functions. And these are now released in the equation of the new self/selfobject unit. This understanding, through empathy and introspection, fosters the capacity of the social worker to use herself as a diagnostic tool and then to function in a healing manner as she enables the individual to understand why the need arises in the present, as well as its origin in the past. Towle, almost 40 years ago, described social work as "a way of feeling, a way of thinking" (1946, p. 108). But Kohut provided us with an understanding of empathy—more than a way of feeling—and introspection—more than a way of thinking—as *scientific tools* through which we grasp "the essence (of another's) inner state" (Kohut, 1984, p. 102). These tools enable us to respond to the individuals with whom we work in a manner that rekindles their urge to continue development. In Chapter IV we shall examine in greater detail the concepts of empathy and of introspection as they are employed in social work practice.

Through numerous experiences of being understood in the present, the individual transmutes the selfobject functions performed by the social worker into self functions; there gradually comes into being the capacity to monitor anxiety, to regulate self-esteem. The world of selfobjects expands: the individual can undertake with renewed vigor and purpose his efforts to establish meaningful and rewarding goals and relationships.

The clinical and agency experience of social workers is predominantly with individuals struggling to achieve cohesion, to have a meaningful image of themselves reflected, to find confirmation and guidance. Such struggles arise from deficits in self structure, from an inability to cue others, both earlier and later selfobjects, to their needs and wishes, in many instances even to define these needs and wishes.

Damaged in their ability to cue others appropriately, through myriad failures of their original selfobjects, such individuals are highly vulnerable to narcissistic injury. They suffer low self-esteem, fragment readily, are subject to narcissistic rage, and respond with behavior and feeling states abrasive to others and injurious to themselves. In large numbers, individuals seen in social agencies and in clinics are unable to have or maintain sufficiently continuous selfobject relationships necessary to the sustenance of the self.

Social workers are accustomed to listening to those to whom society turns a deaf ear, from whom society often turns away. They are accustomed to having individuals with less developed structure, or with structure invaded by pathology, use them to complete psychic structure. With the emergence of self psychology, with the concept of the selfobject, a new lens has become available for clarifying these selfobject needs. Social workers may now avoid a repetition of past injury to the individual that has resulted in maladaptive behavior and failure by understanding the needs for mirroring, idealizing, or partnering selfobject functions. Most importantly, self psychology enables social workers to develop a more effective understanding of the manner in which their selfobject functions may facilitate an individual's capacity to transmute missing functions into self functions, to transmute missing structure into psychic structure which can reliably regulate self-esteem. The mature use of empathy and introspection thus allows the social worker to understand the selfobject functions which must be performed in the present in such a manner as to permit their growth into cohesive, vigorous self structure. As a new selfobject in the present, the social worker now performs the selfobject function of understanding not only the affect (cue to inner state) in the present, but, in addition, the earlier unsuccessful efforts to engage the selfobject milieu in understanding or responding to the affect of that earlier time, which then resulted in deficits in self function, in driven behavior and thought. It is this process through which selfobject functions may now become self functions: the ability to monitor anxiety, to seek out appropriate selfobjects, to cue others effectively, to establish reliable goals, to work toward them effectively, and to regulate self-esteem in the face of difficulty and disappointment.

I have found a special congruence between the practice of social work and the theories of self psychology. Although Kohut formulated these theories in the context of psychoanalysis, he recognized their explanatory power in psychoanalytically-oriented psychotherapy (Goldberg, 1977; Ornstein, P. and A., 1977) and their applicability to a broad range of problems (Basch, 1984; Kohut and Tolpin, 1980). It is my purpose in this volume to demonstrate the manner in which self psychology may give expanded meaning to work with emotionally troubled individuals who come to social agencies, outpatient clinics, the educational or correctional system, and social workers in private practice. Self psychology enhances our understanding of the manner in which the self of the social worker, as new selfobject in the present, provides and promotes the conditions for healing deficits in self structure.

I will first consider Kohut's theory of self psychology as an explanatory system of human development and behavior, and will illustrate the special insights it provides in gender definition. I will describe his approach to pathology, disorders of the self, and present a method of treatment based on the theories of self psychology. I will trace the history of transference and countertransference in social work literature, their diagnostic significance, and their broadened definition in self psychology.

In the second and third sections I will apply the theory of self psychology to clinical social work with self disorders across the life cycle: childhood, adolescence, late adolescence and young adulthood, adult years and old age.

In the final section, I will illustrate the vicissitudes of self formation and cohesion in a study of the James family. And lastly, I will suggest the possible application of the theories of self psychology to family therapy, group therapy, and community work.

2

Self Psychology:
A Theory of Human Development

LIKE OTHER PROFESSIONS, social work has sought many teachers and explored many fields of knowledge in order to define its special mission, its boundaries, and its methods. In the years that have spanned the development of social work as a profession, there have been many theories about what was helpful, many modes of being helpful (Simon, 1970; Hollis and Woods, 1981; Perlman, 1957, 1979). They were based on a prevailing theory of human development along psychosexual lines culminating in the oedipal conflict which, when resolved, ushered in mature sexuality and adulthood. Drive theory focused attention on the sequelae of oral, anal, and phallic phases coalescing in painful, unproductive, or destructive attitudes and behaviors. Since theory orders what we see and the manner in which we make ourselves available, it follows that theory may also distort our vision. The older view of the human infant as a bundle of drives, each of which must come under the civilizing influence of caretakers to be neutralized and sublimated as it achieves ascendancy, does not do justice to our current knowledge of neonates or the course of childhood. Current studies (Beebe, 1985; Brazelton and Als, 1979; Broucek, 1979; Demos, 1985; Emde and Robinson, 1979; Stern, 1977, 1983) have shown that the newborn is an assertive, seeking, responsive being equipped with a highly complex structure for cueing others to his needs. Self psychology has been able to indicate how the human infant cues an empathic selfobject milieu to perform caretaking functions which are then transmuted into self functions, the psychic structure of a cohesive self.

Thus, it is not the drives which organize the individual but the empathic response of caretakers to affect signaling the infant's emerging and changing needs. Parental response will determine whether the child will become driven or will form a cohesive nuclear self able to experience pleasure in his physical and mental attributes, capable of balancing this with his ideals in a manner which allows him to achieve goals he can define for himself. It is out of the failure of earlier selfobjects to perform these caretaking functions that unresponsiveness to affect results in deficits which give rise to driven behavior. And it is in the opportunity to engage a new selfobject and in the ability of that selfobject to understand and provide what is needed that the self can expand and maintain cohesion.

Self psychology arose out of necessity. It was from his immersion in classical analysis that Heniz Kohut began increasingly to examine a phenomenon in his treatment of individuals with narcissistic disorders. He found that individuals with these disorders did not respond to him as a target of instinctual aims, that they did not regress to earlier states as resistance to oedipal issues. Rather they sought him as they had once earlier sought and failed to find that admiration and guidance, that opportunity to merge with the calmness and competence of an idealized figure, through whom their own worth and capability could take reliable form. As long as Kohut viewed transference as signaling neurosis arising out of oedipal conflict, these individuals continued to feel misunderstood and to struggle with their difficulties. From his immersion in the psychic life of the individuals he treated, as well as his work as a training analyst and teacher, he came reluctantly but increasingly to the recognition that he was "stumped" by the difficulties he encountered in a large group of patients. To quote:

> I tried unsuccessfully to understand them on the basis of the classical assumption that they had failed to solve their emotional involvements with their parents, in particular the love and hate relationships with their parents around what is called the Oedipus complex. If I tried to explain their relationship to me, their demands on me as revivals of their old love and hate for their parents, or for their brothers and sisters, I had more and more the feeling that my explanations became forced and that my patients' complaints that I did not understand them . . . were justified. It was on the basis of feeling stumped that I began to entertain the thought that these people were not concerned with me as a separate person but that they were concerned with themselves; that they did not love or hate me, but that they needed me as a part of themselves, needed me *as a set of functions* [emphasis supplied] which they had not acquired in early life; that what appeared to be their love and hate was in reality their need that I fulfill certain psychological functions for them and anger at me when I did not do so. (Kohut, in Ornstein, 1978, II. p. 888)

These psychological functions were to respond to their need to be affirmed, admired, and stimulated, and to merge with the power and generosity of an idealized figure. It was Kohut's discovery that their immature demands for his admiration and for his calming presence were not a retreat from the complexities of the oedipal period but a legitimate, currently experienced need which led him to the concept of selfobject. For these individuals an unfolding transference reflected their need of him not as a target of incestuous aims but as a selfobject, one who performed missing intrapsychic functions they were unable to perform for themselves. And these functions, through transmuting internalization, gradually became their own, ultimately allowing the growth of a cohesive, vigorous, and harmonious self capable of monitoring stress and regulating self-esteem on their journey toward goals they could enjoy.

Kohut has set forth the history of the formulation of his theory of self psychology in his writings. In them we can trace the development of an explanatory system of human development which transcends the treatment of narcissistic disorders and provides an understanding of human growth in health and in illness. His theory of the self as bipolar, of the caretaking functions of the selfobject milieu, and of transmuting internalization through which a cohesive nuclear self takes form provides new understanding of the course of development from infancy through the life cycle. Moreover, escalating findings from infant research confirm what Kohut derived from his employment of the scientific tools of empathy and introspection in understanding the affective experience of his patients.

CREATION AND CONSOLIDATION OF THE SELF IN INFANCY AND EARLY CHILDHOOD

We are more appreciative, today, of the instructive role played by infants for their caretakers. Though differing in temperament and capacity, at birth infants have the innate ability to cue others to their needs. They are eager learners, competent in being able to observe the world in structured fashion and mentally active in organizing their perceptions (Stern, 1983). When Emerson (1885) wrote that " . . . infancy conforms to nobody; all conform to it; so that one babe commonly makes four or five out of the adults who prattle and play to it . . . ," he was unaware that prattling, mirroring, shaping and giving affect to its sounds with playful intonations, and stilling its cries are the vital responses of parents to the infant's cues (Elson, 1984).

We know now that elaborate facial muscles to express affect are present at birth and that such affect constitutes a basic alphabet of communication (Basch, 1983a). Parents as receivers of such communications empathically respond by helping the child to identify the feeling that the affect has signaled. With their mature psychic structure, parents respond empathically to the child's communications in an ascending spiral of cue/ response/further cue/redirection or intensification of the first response. Through myriad bits of such interplay between endowment and nurture, the self of the child evolves in unique fashion. For this he requires empathic selfobjects. Those who perform caretaking functions for the child in tune with his needs are selfobjects; they are prestructural selfobjects whose functions, through transmuting internalization, become uniquely his own.

From his stirrings and mewings, an empathic mother interprets the child's needs by feeding or changing him, holding him closely and murmuring to him, finding more soothing positions for his body. As she eases the child, he merges with her calmness and competence. In its simplest form, the evolution of psychic structure can be seen from the way in which, when she is delayed, the baby may need only to hear her voice from another room or her footsteps down the hall to still his cries. Within himself there is already in embryo form the expectation of comforting relief of his needs and the ability to withstand delay. This delay, this optimal—because it is not too severe or prolonged—failure on the part of the selfobject, enables the child to preserve within himself a minute bit of the capacity for self-soothing. Slight frustration in the perfect union between self and selfobject sets in motion a process—transmuting internalization—through which in embryo form the earliest beginnings of self are defined. Transmuting internalization is not incorporation, or introjection, or simply internalization. It is transmuting because it is not the identical function which is taken inside but one unique to the child; he has made it his own, much as nourishing food goes into making the unique physical structure of the child (Kohut, 1971). The self of the child expands and achieves cohesion through innumerable transmuting internalizations of selfobject functions into self functions.

Kohut has described this self as bipolar,* arising from twin streams of experience of being mirrored and of being permitted to merge with the competence and generosity of the selfobject. Thus, one pole is imbued with grandiose ambitions, our wish to display and be admired, pleasure in our physical and mental attributes. The second pole is formed of our basic idealized goals. Kohut believed that in the formation of the bipolar self the child has two chances for consolidating a cohesive nuclear self. Self disturbances of a pathological degree result only from the failure of

self = narcisism vs. idealism combined!

---

* Kohut (1978) commented that he did not believe these terms would last forever. Students sometimes have difficulty with the concept of a bipolar self, tending to reify it and imbuing it with rigidity. I am fond of the term "double helix" particularly in view of the fact that its structure, an ascending spiral in form, has in addition regular communicating rungs. This too can be reified!

both these developmental opportunities (Kohut, 1977, p. 185). If the child has been unable to elicit adequate response to his grandiose ambitions, his need for mirroring and confirmation of his perfection and greatness, then, as he turns to a second selfobject and is allowed to merge with the power and goodness of an idealized figure, the pole formed of idealized values and goals may offset weakness in the first. The order may also be reversed, with resulting weakness in the pole harboring idealized values and goals. It is the relationship between these two poles which forms a tension arc through which innate talents and acquired skills are brought into play so that ambitions can be realized in specific goals. "The patterns of ambitions, skills and goals; the tensions between them; the program of action they create; the activities undertaken toward their realization; all are experienced as continuous in space and time; they are the self, an independent center of initiative, an independent recipient of impressions" (Kohut and Wolf, 1978, p. 414).

In describing the beginnings of a cohesive self, Marian Tolpin (1971) uses two familiar experiences from earliest childhood—the blanket and stranger anxiety—to indicate the way in which cohesive psychic structure is acquired. It is the mother initially who provides the blanket. In preparation for her absence while the child naps, she tucks his blanket about him. Stirring in his sleep, the child feels the blanket about him and preserves a bit of the mother's enfolding warmth. Gradually, in infinitesimal stages, he imbues the blanket with the soothing and regulating qualities of the mother—her smell, her softness, her support. The child needs both mother and blanket, but he can endure the mother's absence by "dosing" himself with the blanket. For longer and longer periods of time he can do without mother but needs the blanket. At other times it is the mother alone who can satisfy. At periods of special fatigue or overexcitement, he searches frantically for the blanket if it is not immediately at hand. Ultimately, it is not that he outgrows it but that the function of the blanket has gone inside to become a primitive but permanent part of self-esteem regulation: that calming and soothing that the child may now perform for himself or by cueing a caretaker to his need for comforting. An example Freud gave of a small child frightened of the dark beautifully illustrates this type of cueing (Freud, 1905, p. 224):

> Child: Auntie, speak to me. I'm frightened because it's so dark.
> Auntie: What good would it do . . . you can't see me.
> Child: That doesn't matter. If anyone speaks to me it gets light!

The child's immature structure at this point requires the caretaking function of a selfobject to feel whole again—"when someone speaks to me it gets light"—on the path to transmuting the soothing self-function which can be relied on to minimize fears of darkness.

Empathic dullness on the part of the mirroring selfobject, psychological or real absence of the caretaker prevents the child from acquiring dependable structure. Rather than the capacity to soothe himself, a mild state of anxiety will flood the immature self; instead of a self-soothing function which he has made his own, there exists instead a deficit which may be expressed in any of the well-known disorders of childhood—the whole range of separation problems, such as clinging, manipulative behavior, temper tantrums, demanding behavior, impairments in development such as being unable to take new steps in learning, motor skills, etc. The child fragments easily, and such disturbances of cohesiveness may take on any symbolic expression in any phase of development as fears of darkness, noise, helplessness, illness, robbers, kidnappers, witches, insects, monsters (M. Tolpin, 1978).

Similarly with stranger anxiety, M. Tolpin (1971) uses the example of the child on the mother's knee, serenely perched with ready access to her soothing voice and explanation. When a stranger appears, the child turns to the mother and absorbs within himself those maternal functions which she performs for him. One can hear small children reassuring themselves in the words of their selfobjects; "That's the mailman," or "doggie won't bite"; the mother's reassuring sounds or comments are precipitated into self-functions. The capacity to self-soothe and monitor anxiety defines the child's unique and maturing psychic structure. The functions mother performs for him he can now, in small doses, perform for himself. With greater distance from mother and for longer intervals of time, he can respond to the signal of anxiety with the capacity to monitor his feelings, to reassure and to comfort himself, or to take those necessary steps within his developing repertoire to seek out selfobjects who will aid and protect him.

[margin annotation: incorporate maternal reassurance]

Let me illustrate from the life experience of a small child the manner in which monitoring stress and regulating self-esteem appear to have taken place. Michael, not quite two, donned a make-believe coat, picked up a bag and announced to his mother that he was going off to shop. His mother made a playful crying face, indicating her desolation at his leaving. With a beaming smile he turned to her and said, "I'll be back. You'll see. I always am!" His mother recognized this as the language she had used with him on occasions when she had had to leave him, and she caught him up in her arms with a hug as they both broke into laughter. The child played the leave-taking game several more times with pleasure in his mastery.

On another occasion, Michael, now two-and-a-half, was building a house with his blocks. He called to his mother to see what he had done, circling around it. His mother said, "That's very good, Michael." "Huh-uh," he said calmly, "Say it's the greatest!" He knew the response he needed and was able to ask for it.

A few months later, towering his blocks into a tall column that repeatedly tumbled just as he was achieving the height he wanted, Michael kicked his blocks in all directions. Putting an arm around him, his mother said, "Michael, patience does it, every time!" His rage subsided, and he began again to tower his blocks; they fell again, but he once more set to work, this time successfully adding the pinnacle. Turning to his mother, he said, "Mom! patience does it every *other* time!" Several days later, working alone, he managed a very impressive building. As he completed it, he was heard to comment to himself, "I'm really a very remarkable fellow!"

From these interchanges we have a view of the evolution of monitoring the signal of anxiety, the use of selfobject to comfort but also to admire and guide. These episodes are minute printouts of the manner in which selfobject functions are transmuted into self-functions and become the capacity for reestablishing cohesion, what M. Tolpin describes as "self-righting" (1982).

That Michael, now five years old, can reliably employ this capacity was illuminated by an exchange with his smaller brother who, in a similar episode with blocks, burst into tears. His mother started forward, but Michael rushed to his side first, saying, with a broad grin, arms akimbo, "It's okay, Mom, I can handle this."

A center of his own perception and initiative, he can give expression to his ambition, and through natural talents and developing skills, achieve realizable goals. The signals of cueing and response from a caretaker with interest and pleasure in his performance, reflected in these fragments of a small boy's life, do not begin to do justice to the myriad self/selfobject functions that preceded these events. They have now uniquely become his own self-functions, and go into making Michael Michael.

The infant lets us know his needs first by his stirrings and mewings, later by more sophisticated symbols. But parents as empathic selfobjects also use their mature psychic structure to anticipate the needs of the child of which, with his immature structure, he is unaware. If, during the period when the self of the child is in formation, these developmental requirements are unfulfilled to a traumatic degree, deficits result and the child's experience of a whole self, with a past, a future, and a place, crumbles. When legitimate demands or needs are not fulfilled, then symptom formation results.

The absence of soothing in caretakers who are empathically dull or impatient, or who intrude a frightened, anxious self into the child's new experiences, leaves the child with a deficit in his forming self. The absence of the capacity for self-soothing allows the spread of anxiety. Anxiety mounts to panic and results in states of uncontrollable fear or unmanageable excitement (Kohut, 1977). But when the mother-infant pair are mutually and reliably informative, prolonged states of minimal anxiety prompt a rescue signal—the child shows his need by facial expression, by calling or crying, or by running off to find the mother. Such a rescue signal in its earliest form allows her to perform caretaking functions. Later, the child's anxiety will alert his own internal regulation. It is this basic structure which accounts for a child's capacity to respond to new challenges, to accept the anxiety of such a challenge, to meet new tasks in learning, and to make new associations in friendship (M. Tolpin, 1980). These earliest memories, traces of maternal function, are laid down as lasting psychic structure forming a cohesive, vigorous, harmonious self.

Thus, if self/selfobject responses are reasonably attuned, the child's inherent vitality is preserved. "He automatically continues to exercise to the hilt all of his progressively growing and unfolding capacities and all of the expanding signals and signs at his disposal in order to continue to assert himself and to announce his legitimate developmental needs. . . . He grows into an older child who can respond to frustration with normal tendency to take over for himself where his selfobject functions leave off" (M. Tolpin, 1980, p. 55). His own capacities are heir to selfobject functions. He grows into adulthood with psychological capacities". . . which enable him to preserve a vital remnant of the original feeling of his own perfection and a vital remnant of the original feeling of his own and others' power and effectiveness" (M. Tolpin, 1980, p. 56). Through countless inphase optimal frustrations and injuries, he begins to modulate and transform his illusions of grandiosity and to accept when he cannot alter those frustrations and injuries that teach us the limits of our own and others' powers (M. Tolpin, 1980).

The development of self-esteem and ideals is a slow process, subject to many detours; it is not a steady state. The child acquires the ability to be aware of anxiety as a signal, to monitor it, and to take the necessary steps to regulate his self-esteem by continuing his efforts to manage with the functions he has transmuted, by seeking help from his selfobjects, or by the further development and expansion of skills with which to pursue life's tasks.

Selfobjects which the child seeks reflect his maturing and changing needs (Wolf, 1980a). His widening world offers a range of selfobjects which serve the function of strengthening and deepening cohesive self structure. From family to playmates, to school, to heroes of fact and fiction, the variety of his choices now reflects his capacity to discriminate his needs and, increasingly, to temper those needs in accordance with the growth of empathy in recognizing the needs of others.

RESTRUCTURING THE SELF IN ADOLESCENCE

Through adolescence and young adulthood, selfobjects continue to play an intense role in strengthening self-esteem and ideals. Indeed, the capacity to find and enjoy selfobjects, who either perform a confirming role or permit idealization, is evidence of health. It is cardinal to Kohut's theories that separation and individuation leading to an end result in autonomy fail to define the essence of the human condition: *we never outgrow the need for selfobjects though we do out grow their exploitation by achieving mature empathy as a self-function* (Basch, 1983a). Piaget's formulation (1940) of the development of cognitive processes from sensorimotor to concrete operational and then to formal operation centers the capacity for abstraction, logic, the use of symbols and reasoning in early adolescence.

The struggle to achieve mature empathy is most graphically engaged in adolescence when, in tandem, exploitation of selfobjects and exceptional generosity to selfobjects attest to the process by which empathy becomes transmuted as a reliable function of the cohesive self. The adolescent struggles to relinquish the centrality of parents as selfobjects and undertakes the necessary thrust toward a widening array of selfobjects. This threatens the sense of continuity in both generations.

It is helpful to examine the vicissitudes of cohesion which both generations, parents and adolescents, experience. That children are selfobjects to parents must be understood in the context of the sense of pleasure and competence the parental generation derives in facilitating the offspring's developmental progress, in providing the necessary milieu in which children may define their talents in expanding skills, and in setting and achieving goals. For the adolescent, sustenance for the continuing task of defining and pursuing realizable goals is found not in relinquishing parents as incestuous objects because of maturing sexuality, but in the engagement of expanding the selfobject world. Let us examine the twin process in which the self-esteem of both adolescents and parents is engaged.

Benedek (1959) originally described parenthood as a developmental phase (later she would substitute developmental process) (1975) in which parents repeat with each child in a different way steps in their own development. In fortuitous circumstances, they achieve further resolution of conflict. Embedded as it is in drive psychology, this description does not allow the broader experience of parenthood to be adequately understood.

Self psychology permits us to understand that parents may indeed experience with each child a reactivation of deficits or distortion in any phase of their development. But an increased empathy with childhood needs, increased wisdom, and creativity—specifically the ability to respond to the child and adolescent as a center of his own perception and initiative—now permit parents to perform their caretaking functions without unempathic intrusion of their own conflicts. Just as the adolescent now turns to a widening circle of selfobjects, parents confront the need to continue to function as selfobjects in the spirit of availability and acceptance of a less central position in their children's lives.

Anna Freud pointed out that "there are few situations in life more difficult to cope with than an adolescent son or daughter during the attempt to liberate themselves" (Freud, A., 1958, p. 276). But from the viewpoint of self psychology, it is less an issue of liberation than the necessary process of deepening and firming the self as a center of perception and initiative. The parents' support during this process is both vitally needed and rejected by the adolescent, who now reaches out to peers and other selfobject mentors as more in tune with the world he or she confronts. In the face of a broad sweep and quickening tempo of change within society, parents who have been accustomed to anticipating and adjusting to new behaviors in their children experience an even greater challenge to their values and beliefs. To relinquish their central position to a widening array of selfobjects, beliefs, standards different from their own, and vocational choices not within their own expectations, taxes the parental self. The response must not be abandonment of the adolescent but the continuation of such support and protection as the circumstances indicate and they may be able to provide. Some parents in their middle years, with a sense of stalemate in their relationship with each other, may be tempted to (and some do) experiment radically with new choices, new partners, preempting for themselves the developmental tasks that their children face (Elson, 1964). It is here that self psychology offers new understanding of the struggle, arising as it does less out of drive and earlier compromise formation than out of fragmentation and loss of vigor within the nuclear self of the parent.

THE SELF IN PARENTHOOD

It is at the point of their children's adolescence that parents have the greatest need for flexibility and strength in reviewing and expanding those enduring goals and values that are basic to a sense of their own continuity. In the light of newer societal norms, they must now examine within themselves the validity and importance of values, beliefs, and behavior as intrinsic to their own cohesive functioning. There can be a refreshing and vigorous increase in the stream of ideas between the generations. In a vital phase-appropriate thrust toward new selfobjects—peers, cult heroes, ideologies (Wolf, 1980b; Wolf, Gedo, and Terman, 1972)—adolescents now confront cognitively and affectively, as if for the first time, those values, ideals, and goals that have been laid down as psychic structure. Just as their adolescent children may jettison some, modify others, and include these standards more firmly and enduringly now as *their* values, *their* ideals, *their* goals, so, too, must parents examine and review what they will retain at all costs.

We may view this self experience in parents and adolescents as in the nature of a double helix, both mutually enhancing and supportive. But adolescence may also become a period when the self experience of parents and adolescent may be most vulnerable to enmeshment and distortion.

Adolescents may linger in a merger which does not permit that quickening opportunity for differentiation and congruence that is the necessary task of these years. Parents, lulled by this continuity, postpone tasks that lie ahead for themselves as well. They must endure the sadness their child's growing up entails, but they may also find creative outlets for the energy formerly absorbed in the task of childrearing. Even parents who have balanced both a full-time profession and parenthood face this change.

The leavening of humor may help parents accept a less central position in the lives of their children. It is not infrequent that in this context there now emerges and deepens an empathic awareness of similar critical periods which their parents traversed. They find sustenance in the companionship of other parents with children of similar age. They attend parents' meetings, read the comments of experts. In other words, they seek sustenance from selfobjects, both human and institutional, as they seek to repair cohesion, to restore vigor and harmony.

Thus, with each critical period in the lives of their children, the process of maturing narcissism within the parents, so intensely engaged in the adolescence of their children, continues. Each critical period may intensify the thrust toward maturer forms of narcissism or may precipitate fragmentation, enfeeblement, or disharmony within the parental self. The selfobject functions which the parents perform include the capacity to remain empathically in tune with the needs and tasks of their maturing children. When parents observe that their presence and their interest enable an adolescent to contend with disappointments, to weather ambiguities when he or she strives for new goals and the outcome is still uncertain, the performance of these selfobject functions may also enhance parental self-esteem. Without unempathic intrusion of their own goals, the parents provide that leavening which age and experience offer. Life is not free of struggles; in these struggles we sometimes fail; then what can this particular failure teach us?

As their children face complex changes in vocational opportunities, newer forms of courtship, and delayed marriage and parenthood, parental self-esteem and goals come under a powerful searchlight. An enlarged understanding of the young adult years may emerge and, from that enlarged vision, an informed and responsive capacity to accept the initiative and perception of their children as peers. This is especially tested by social norms of the current generation because of the tendency to delay marriage and family building. The transience of the parental generation, and now even the transience of their children's lives, add stress and must be mastered by accepting this reality more directly (Elson, 1984). Perhaps at this time parents intensify their search for sustenance by turning to new selfobjects themselves, such as new pursuits and skills.

SELFOBJECTS AS SUSTENANCE IN ADULTHOOD

We have seen how selfobjects join in the creation of the self in infancy, its consolidation in early childhood, its restructuring in adolescence, and its sustenance in adulthood. Each new phase of development provides the opportunity for further deepening and firming of self structure, for improving its resiliency. At times, certain experiences may expose deficits in either pole. As the individual grows to mature years, there are many transitions which severely test the cohesiveness of the self, resulting in periods of lessened vigor, loss of purpose, discontinuity. Selfobjects play a role both in sustaining an individual during a period of such reverses and in tempering the excitement of success. The capacity of the individual to seek and find appropriate selfobjects is the hallmark of health. As we mature, the selfobjects we seek for sustenance will include not only individuals, but also one's profession or vocation, particular skills or attributes, cultural and civic activities which reverberate to the standards, values, and beliefs of our core nuclear self.

As we learn the limits of our own grandiosity, as we learn to temper our disappointments and redirect our efforts, we find pleasure in strengthening enduring ideals or in forging new ideals. However modest our role, serving as leaders to newer generations, younger colleagues, is in itself invigorating and intensifies a sense of cohesion. As Kohut pointed out (1966), every major changeover or transition in life shakes up an image of the self and is usually accompanied by the loss of a selfobject. One important factor in the familiar depressions of older people is the loss of selfobjects, including such selfobjects as work, ideals, and goals, which the ascending generations may jettison (Elson, 1984). It is the hallmark of a cohesive, vigorous, harmonious nuclear self to experience wide swings in emotion in response to these changes but to respond with maturing ability to regulate self-esteem, that is, healthy narcissism.

Kohut has traced a line of development which is not a continuum from primitive narcissism to object love, as Freud described (1914), but a separate line of development in which narcissism achieves mature forms, as in empathy, creativity, humor, wisdom, and ultimately an acceptance of our own transience (Kohut, 1966). In other words, the bipolar self, the cohesive nuclear self, will find expression of its ambitions and aspirations in a manner and towards goals which spring from a central core of perception, with the accompanying ability to assert one's own initiative in realizing these goals. We may experience reverses, grief in losing cherished friends and longed-for goals. However, the set of functions that Kohut describes as mature forms of narcissism stand us in good stead as we ultimately accept our limitations and our transience as part of the human condition.

Kohut does not argue that self psychology overlooks the typical storms, rivalries, and envies of everyday life, or the excitement of joy and success. Instead, he allows us to see how throughout life, through its varied phases and vicissitudes, the nuclear self is restored to cohesion and renewed vigor by the soothing and calming availability of selfobjects. Indeed, the guiding ideals initially absorbed from the selfobject functions of early and later selfobjects become reliable self-functions that exert a profoundly calming and soothing force in restoring cohesion and harmony in the face of disappointment or loss. Freud's description of the ego as a respository of abandoned object choices and a history of these choices (Freud, 1917) takes on dynamic meaning in the context of self psychology. It provides us with an understanding of the manner in which functions performed for us by early selfobjects are transmuted into self-functions. In response to being hurt, wounded, neglected, out of favor, or disappointed, the capacity to restore and regulate self-esteem has been laid down through the experience of being allowed to merge in the strength and wisdom of earlier idealized selfobjects. Within the self there is now the power to calm and soothe oneself, to reach out to others, or to find solace in redirecting aspirations based on values that have become central to the self. One can absorb hurts and disappointments without losing oneself in destructive criticism. These are the experiences of everyday life.

BASIC CONCEPTS OF SELF PSYCHOLOGY

Let us now review the concept of human development embodied in the theories of self psychology. Kohut described a *nuclear self*, a central sector of the personality that was cohesive and enduring. He believed that this structure was the basis for the sense of self as an independent center of initiative and perception, that it was integrated with central ambitions and ideals, and with the experience of body and mind as a unit in space and a continuum in time.

He described that self as *bipolar*, one pole from which emanates basic strivings for power and success, and a second which harbors basic idealized goals. Between these two poles there is an intermediate area of basic talents and skills which are activated by a *tension arc*. He described this tension arc as an abiding flow of actual psychological activity through which skills and talents further the basic pursuits toward which one is driven by ambitions and led by ideals. He defined the relationship in which the constituents of the self (ambitions, goals, skills, and talents) stand to each other as the *tension gradient*. This tension gradient represents the potential for thought and action and is specific and unique for the individual, even in the absence of activity between the two poles. The availability for action (thought and behavior) arises by reason of the unique patterns and tensions existing between ambitions and goals.

The creation of the self is made possible by the responsiveness of an empathic *selfobject* milieu. At birth, the infant is preadapted and ideally equipped to cue and respond to others selectively. Kohut described three types of selfobjects: the *mirroring selfobject*, responding and confirming the child's sense of vigor, greatness, and perfection; the *idealized selfobject*, with whose calmness and omnipotence the child can merge; and the *alter-ego* or *twinship selfobject*, through whom the child is confirmed as a human being among other human beings, with a sense of likeness and of the capacity to partner, to work along with others.

These selfobjects perform functions for the child which, through *transmuting internalization*, are taken in and become uniquely his own. Kohut describes the process through which this occurs as *optimal frustration*. The selfobject performs a function up to a point, gradually withdrawing in just sufficient amounts to allow the child to perform a given function, or part of that function, in his own unique manner. Although Kohut described this as optimal *frustration*, it is clear that he meant it was based on *optimal response* to the child's level of capacity and tolerance. Thus, selfobjects and their functions are gradually replaced by a self and its functions. A healthy functioning self is not a replica of selfobjects and their functions. It is a unique self, making use of its own functions, its own talents and skills, and its own ambitions to reach its own goals.

Selfobjects are required for the creation and consolidation of the self and for the sustenance of the self *throughout life*. The world of selfobjects widens beyond those of infancy and childhood. Selfobject needs change and mature throughtout life. They include not only individuals, but vocation, profession, civic, religious, and cultural preferences, as in art and music, and with the end of life, cosmic values. In Kohut's own words, '' . . . (W)e must speak of selfobjects not only with respect to early childhood and the regressive states of later life, but in the context of the normal experiences of support, indeed the continuous stream of supportive experiences that we need to maintain as adults, in old age, and ultimately in death" (Kohut, 1984, p. 199).

Thus, in self psychology the concept of autonomy is replaced by the vital role which selfobjects perform throughout life. But it is not a concept that contemplates the use of selfobjects as a one-way process. Rather, there is a mutuality between self and selfobject. As we have seen from the earlier discussion of the self in parenthood, the parental selfobject is enhanced by the functions performed for the child, and, as the child matures, the capacity for responsiveness to others becomes a reliable self-function of the child. Selfobject needs are pathological only when a mature person demands that his selfobject needs be gratified in an infantile and childlike manner. And yet, mutually responsive selfobjects in a mature relationship can indeed allow and respond to such temporary needs of a partner in order to help that partner reestablish cohesion during periods of stress.

In this description of self psychology as a theory of human development, I have not singled out gender formation for special discussion. I propose to do this in the following chapter since Kohut viewed the oedipal *phase* as a potentially joyous period of integration and consolidation, in contrast to the concept that oedipal *conflict* is ubiquitous and an oedipal *complex* inevitable. He did not find it surprising that " . . . traces of an Oedipal complex can be found in every person. . . . The oedipal selfobjects are imperfect, just as they were imperfect before the oedipal period. And our selfobjects will remain imperfect throughout the whole span of our lives. . . . But the confrontations with such limited failures are part of the essence of life . . . since we are in fact equipped to deal with the limited shortcomings of the matrix that sustains our humanness . . . we are equipped to respond to these shortcomings with the most valuable possession of human beings, the capacity to respond to optimal frustrations via transmuting internalizations and creative change" (Kohut, 1984, p. 27).

In the next chapter, we shall examine the manner in which the subjective experience of the oedipal phase enters into gender formation.

3

Gender Formation From the Viewpoint of Self Psychology

G ENDER FORMATION CANNOT be viewed outside the context of the form-ing self of the child. It permeates psychic structure building from the moment of the child's birth and reception into a surrounding matrix of selfobjects. This matrix of selfobjects is unique to the child's place in his family and that family's place in society and historical period.

Gender is defined not only by acceptance of and pleasure in one's body. Gender defines the flow and direction of ambitions; it variously colors these ambitions and selectively determines the shaping of skills, depending on how sharply differentiated the male or female agenda is in the family of origin and in its historical period.

Even before the child's discovery of anatomical differences, parental response shapes the child's pleasure in discovering, claiming, and displaying body parts. From the time that the sex of the child is known, characteristically parents respond by touch, voice, and play differently to male or female infants. Although this will vary from sharply to mildly differentiated behavior, such differences are echoed in the extended kinship and friendship groups of the family. In addition, when the child evokes attention, even in resting state, casual encounters with strangers will further define the child's maleness or femaleness. It is true that the particular ethnic, social, and cultural milieu of the family will shape these responses, but it is initially and predominantly the manner in which parents accept their own gender, their responsive interplay with each other and with their child, that will determine the sturdiness of the child's self-esteem in consolidating core gender identity.

Long before the child's awareness of sexual differences that can be contrasted and valued, the child's announced sex at birth sets in motion parental attitudes and responses which form the basis for the little boy's feelings of masculinity and the little girl's feelings of femininity. Studies have shown that core gender identity is established between 15 and 18 months (Galenson and Roiphe, 1976; Jacobson, 1964; Person and Ovesey, 1983; Silverman, 1981; Stoller, 1968). Self psychology illuminates the process through which this is achieved. From the mirroring, confirming, and guiding responses of the parents, the child acquires a sense of bodyself. But it is not only the direct response to the child's feeling states and behaviors that contributes to the firming of a bodyself in which the child takes pleasure: silent communication in manner, posture, and attitudes also stimulates the process of gender formation. There are specific ways in which it unfolds and becomes a part of a prideful, cohesive self.

As the child grows into the oedipal phase, characteristic behaviors of femininity or masculinity emerge as integral responses of a cohesive and harmonious self. Anyone who has been in intimate contact with two or three year olds knows how much of their play focuses on activities imitative of the parent of the same sex. They also try out and repeat easily assimilated behaviors of the parent of the opposite sex. And this behavior is shaped by the responsive pleasure of parents in facilitating play by providing toys and fostering activities through which the child merges with the parents' strength and competence, defining skills and competence in the process.

The response of each parent, singly and jointly, will determine how the child uniquely experiences gender-linked activities. For it is the parents' own attitudes about gender that support or noxiously intrude upon the forming self of the child. The depth and sturdiness of the cohesive self depend on responses from both parents. Their responses will determine whether the psychic structure for integration of gender identify and ultimate choice of a sexual partner is attained.

Kohut pointed out that "for the little boy no less than for the little girl . . . disturbed self esteem is a pathological state with genetic roots in the flawed mirroring responses of the selfobjects of childhood" (1984, p. 214, n. 11) The little girl's anxiety about being female and becoming feminine is well-matched by the little boy's anxiety about becoming masculine and being male (Schafer, 1974). Castration anxiety, penis envy, and the behaviors which coalesce around these states are sequelae of failures of the selfobjects in early childhood. They are reactive to gross failures, rather than optimal failures of the parental milieu, in providing adequate response to the child's emerging and developing sense of masculinity or femininity.

For example, a student with a constant sense of impending doom whenever he was required to undertake new steps recalled an early experience in which he had been joyously splashing in his bath. His mother was called away, and after a time, chilled and ready to be dried and dressed, he ran to find her. He dashed naked through the house, his little penis erect, embarrassing his mother, who was talking to a neighbor. She covered him quickly, scolding him sharply for not waiting for her and running around naked. It was clearly not this one instance which resulted in castration anxiety, but rather numerous instances in which she curtailed his exuberant display rather than responding pleasurably and with appropriate control and guidance. She often exhibited embarrassment in tending to his needs. With his father, a reserved and distant man, she was quite solicitous, often placing her small son on hold while she took care of his father's requests. Although his father took an interest in him, particularly in his intellectual pursuits, he expected a very high level of performance and could be quite sarcastic when the child exhibited expectable immaturity. Such remarks as, "You'll never be a scientist at this rate!" were an undercurrent at every step requiring the child's mastering new material. Although as he grew to manhood he was able to pursue a graduate program with reasonable success, he often was fatigued, experienced doubt and shame, and lacked that joyousness in fulfilling his work that is the hallmark of a cohesive self. The details of this case would offer evidence that this was clearly not castration anxiety stemming from murderous rivalry with his father and punishment for his incestuous longing for his mother. His psychological impasse was not the result of conflict; rather, there was clear evidence of deficit. Both parents were unable to mirror his pleasure in his body and his mind while helping him to shape these gently toward acceptable display and expression.

To illustrate further, a young woman with a reputation for abrasiveness toward male instructors and classmates recognized that this interfered with her progress and robbed her of companionship for which she desperately longed. She could not withhold cutting remarks, a characteristic which had already earned her the reputation among her classmates of a "typical castrating female." In the course of treatment she recalled an episode in which she had been playing with a little boy. When they came in to urinate, she discovered how much more dramatic the little boy's way of urinating was than hers. Calling to her mother to come and see, she was greeted with her mother's sarcastic amusement. "Can't you see he's a little boy?" Somewhat later her mother gave birth to a baby girl. In watching her mother diaper the infant for the first time, she tugged at her mother's arm, crying, "Look, she's broken!!" Her mother responded impatiently, "Don't be silly. Can't you see she's a little girl?" But to the child then, being a girl and being broken were synonymous. The child's anxiety escalated to panic as she screamed, "She's broken, she's broken!" Her mother angrily called to her father to take the child away since she was interfering with the care of the baby.

Here, too, rather than responding to the child's anxiety with reassuring explanation that little girls were made in that special way and affirming his love for his little girl, this shy father took her to her room and began to read a favorite story. Although his response was comforting for a time, it did not really meet her needs of direct explanation and reassurance. There were innumerable instances of the child's experiencing her mother's sense of being overburdened, her discontent with her role, her longing to free herself from family care. With the birth of a son two years later, her mother seemed to take a new lease on life, or so it seemed to the child. Irritability and joylessness became the little girl's steady state. Her general abrasiveness could be viewed as penis envy but it was secondary; it represented the defensive solution to feelings of lack of worth and wholeness and the resulting feelings of depression and joylessness.

Kohut (1975) has pointed out that penis envy and castration anxiety are universal experiences but they are not universally distorting and damaging. Actually, they aid in differentiation. It is the response of the selfobjects of childhood that determines whether the little girl or little boy observes, understands, and values anatomical differences, accepting given bodily structure with pleasure and a sense of wholeness, or whether, on the other hand, these become the crystallization point for disturbance and vulnerability. Isolated body parts and drives may become the means through which the individual seeks to overcome depressive feelings of emptiness and lack of stimulation.

In the period since Freud (1905) formulated his views of psychosexual development, direct observation of infants and children, as well as research in child development by psychoanalytically informed men and women, has broadened and deepened our understanding of gender formation. The broad sweep of cultural change has provided greater opportunity for such observation and has at the same time accelerated that change.

We can now recognize the needs of the child for the confirming, mirroring selfobject and for merging with the omnipotent idealized selfobject as primary psychological needs of childhood. It is, thus, not the drives that structure personality but the vitally nourishing selfobject functions which can then mature into self-functions.

However, when the forming self of the child is not supported by these selfobject functions at specific phases, maladaptive behaviors and feeling states coalesce, giving rise to characteristic futile attempts to fill in deficits in order to reestablish a sense of wholeness. The preoedipal child, racked by storms of envy of the parent of the same sex and striving for the exclusive attention of the parent of the opposite sex, is, in effect, already exhibiting deficits in self-esteem. For the little girl, instead of a process through which she comes to recognize differences and value her own structural wholeness, penis envy is perpetuated and achieves driven intensity when there is no reliably reassuring response to her unique qualities and characteristics. Perhaps even more insidiously, the intrusion of maternal or paternal pathology confirms what the child's immature understanding of anatomical differences seems to demonstrate: *different and inferior* rather than *healthy and whole* organs which differ in function and program of action.

To say that the "Oedipus complex acts as a psychic organizer . . . consolidating libidinal and aggressive impulses, object relationships, gender identity and the superego" (Tyson, 1985, p. 6) is to obscure the whole process of transmuting internalization of selfobject functions through which the preschool child (and later the adolescent) establishes a cohesive harmonious self.

The oedipal myth has been a procrustean bed into which our understanding of developmental psychology has been forced to explain the passions and rivalries of early childhood, their subsidence in latency, and their recrudescence for a new resolution in adolescence. Moreover, there can be few more tortured phrases to describe the flowing and evolving experiences of a son with his father or a daughter with her mother than that of "the negative Oedipus complex." The superego ideal was said to be the heir to the negative Oedipus conflict (Blos, 1972), yet its formation consists of positive idealizations of specific attributes of the parent of the same sex. Self psychology offers a clear and direct understanding of the process of transmuting internalization through which the characteristics and qualities of selfobjects become the unique attributes of the offspring. The daughter is not a carbon copy of her mother; the son is not the spitting image of his father. A combination of optimal frustration on the part of the parent of the same sex allows the offspring to take into the forming self of early childhood and later the reforming self of adolescence those aspects which form the unique self structure of the individual.

The adolescent, capable now of reasoning and logic, may look to the parent of the same sex with vigorous renewal of early longing for merging. Yet, while savoring the experience of being like the parent of the same sex in selected attributes, the adolescent is absorbed in fantasies and feeling states that are in the service of further firming the psychic structure of gender identity and role; thus, the goal is to be like the parent of the same sex, and yet to be *one's own* person.

Newer views on evolving femininity and masculinity, then, do not place penis envy or castration anxiety as the central point in gender formation. Rather, they are viewed as disintegration products, failures of the mirroring and idealized selfobjects of childhood and adolescence to respond to the maturing child's sexuality, as the child traverses the oedipal phase, in a manner which permits the growth of healthy sexuality. Instead of pleasure and pride in their developing bodies and in defining gender role, such individuals experience anxiety, doubt, shame, and guilt, and the sequelae of oedipal conflict.

Thus, it was not, as Freud theorized, that feelings of inferiority, masochistic acceptance of passivity, and the ultimate wish to have a baby are the identifying character traits of mature womanhood. Where they are found, they are characterological distortions arising from failure of the primary selfobjects to provide responsive pleasure to the child's forming and reforming self.

The larger world of selfobjects, peers, and mentors enhances the process through which affirmation of a specific bodyself and strengthening of congruent values and ideals lead the adolescent toward ultimate sexual object choice. The healthy wish to conceive a child and become a mother proceeds from the very center of the self, flowing from a clear sense of gender identity and gender role, and follows upon the capacity to select a sexual partner. It is an act of joyful assertion of a cohesive nuclear self rather than a defensive maneuver to cover over injured narcissism and to compensate for organ inferiority (Kohut, 1975). Similarly, the wish to father a child represents a joyous assertion, proceeding from pleasure in perpetuating the species and in the capacity to function as propagator, protector, and facilitator for a new generation.

The issue becomes one of choice and whether the wish for parenthood springs from a joyous wish for a child, centrally perceived and initiated. For women who by choice elect motherhood and a professional goal that entails many years of devotion, the most unyielding reality they confront is that of the biological timetable. The problems they experience are not neurotic but an expression of understandable tension in response to balancing the realistic demands of motherhood and vocational goals (Ritvo, 1976).

Fathering a child does not entail bodily changes and only minimally impinges on a professional career. Indeed, in this historical time, the opportunity to share in the direct care of a child and to express tenderness more openly may stimulate deepening and firming of self structure. The sense of strength and competence in fostering the child's growth and the mother's well-being enhances self-esteem. Specific tasks assigned to specific gender roles are not as clearly marked as in the recent past. Inevitably there will be idiosyncratic solutions to given problems, but these solutions are what gives rise to the richness of diversity in personality and in relationships.

The question of whether there are other routes to maturity than parenthood for men and for women may be answered affirmatively. Kohut

(1984) suggests that if the cultural milieu and hormonal stimulation are lacking, the individual may still find fulfillment of the central core of the self through pursuit and attainment of other goals. Although his reference was to women, men who do not experience parenthood either by choice or by circumstance may also achieve maturity through vocation, profession, personal relationships, and community activities as the expression of a vigorous, harmonious, cohesive self.

The historical past still exerts a powerful force in its constraints upon young women as they seek to achieve professional or vocational goals. Passivity as a valued and expected attribute of femininity may, as a character trait, inhibit the joyful realization of a program of action which otherwise springs from the central core of the self.

We need to go back only 40 years or so to an article on adolescence published in the Encyclopedia Brittanica (1941) in which the advice was "to let girls run and leap with their brothers until age twelve . . . but that instead of pressure being put on a girl's intellectual education . . . time devoted to school and books should be diminished." The advice was antiquated even then, but it is within that same period that for women the largest single cause of leaving school was marriage. Large numbers were forsaking careers out of fear that their pleasure and success in shaping intellectual competence into vocational goals would interfere with forming close and lasting ties to men.

Young women today have experienced one set of ideals and assigned roles in their earliest formative years and must now respond to newly emerging ideals and roles. There is thus an added intensity to the typical struggles of late adolescent and young adult years in relinquishing dependent ties to adults, learning to know what standards and values are internally consonant with their own aspirations and ideals. Even when parents genuinely strive to foster the aspirations and goals of sons and daughters, in the context of recognizing their unique strengths, talents, and skills, a great deal depends on the sociocultural patterns and how we choose to organize these. As Lang points out, "The maturational sequence is 'programmed' to unfold sequentially so our best course as parents or therapists would ideally be one of facilitation rather than interference. But the same is not true for sociocultural patterns. We *create* these, and a great deal can depend on just how we choose to organize them" (Lang, 1984, p. 64).

Applying the concepts of self psychology to her analytic understanding of women she has treated, Lang emphasized the difficulty some women experience in overcoming an internalized standard of passivity. Inherited from an earlier historical period, these women experienced and described as "not me" activities which involved too assertive a role, despite the high level of professional competence they had achieved. Yet we must note that the social and cultural trends of the historical times in which these women have grown to maturity did not universally result in the experience of assertiveness as "not me." We do not question that problems with assertiveness have been broadly experienced by women. But we must study the exceptions and seek to understand the formation of a cohesive nuclear self capable of joyous self-expression in both motherhood and in vocation, or in one exclusively, as a fully realized program of action made possible by the responses of an early, continuing, and expanding selfobject milieu.

Still, the choices and options we have been describing are available to a relatively small percentage of the population. For most women, to have a family and to work is not an option. They must work; they do not have the luxury of choosing to remain at home devoting themselves to child-rearing. Moreover, for many young women parenthood is an early accidental aftermath of a search for wholeness, for mirroring response, for merging with the strength and competence of an idealized selfobject. Unmarried parenthood among adolescent girls has achieved epidemic proportions. This may reflect the aftermath of a period during which sexual freedom has become a way of life for young people before judgment, reflection, and delay, which are a part of gender role, have become structured in values and standards. Self disorders in the parental generation have interfered with, intruded upon, or failed to sustain the nurturant attitudes through which the restructuring of the self in adolescence may be accomplished.

The multiproblem adolescents seen in social agencies and clinics, and by social workers in private practice, show a broad range of self disorders, of which the issue of gender is but a part. Prone to fragmentation, unable to maintain self-esteem regulation, highly vulnerable to narcissistic injury or slight, these adolescents for the most part do not seek treatment themselves but are referred by concerned, exasperated, or despairing parents, or by court or educational systems. The range of symptomatic behavior extends from suicidal states through all the permutations of acting-out behavior. The emotional difficulties of adolescents—hypochondriacal concerns, depressive reactions, dissociative states, substance abuse, promiscuity or perversion, rebellious, destructive or delinquent behavior—cannot be genuinely understood from the viewpoint of oedipal conflict, fixation or regression to preoedipal functioning. Rather, these adolescents suffer from deficits in self-esteem, from inability to establish and pursue goals, as reflected in the fact that one of the commonest complaints in this area is school failure or dropout.

Emotional malnutrition—moderate to gross failures of the parenting milieu occasioned by the unavailability of parents or severe deficits in self structure of the parents themselves—has deprived these adolescents of appropriate mirroring, confirmation, guidance, and the opportunity to merge with the strength and competence of idealized selfobjects through which the psychic structure of esteem regulation, formulation of goals, and the ability to pursue them are acquired. Desperate measures to secure adequate response to their mirroring and idealizing needs and to their needs for partnering as they strive toward adulthood lead them towards enactment of behaviors which temporarily calm and soothe them, temporarily stimulate or vitalize them in ways which do not lead to the formation of reliable self structure.

Susan

An example may serve to illuminate this derailed process. Susan, 15, was a lonely, isolated adolescent, the youngest in a family of three, the two older siblings being boys. Though not unattractive, her appearance was marred by her shuffling gait and generally poor attention to dress. Blue jeans and shirt are typical of teenage dress for both boys and girls, but Susan wore her brother's ill-fitting castoffs. Her father was employed as a carpenter and her mother as a checker at a nearby supermarket. Both parents were hardworking, with little time for relaxation. The older boys worked at odd jobs and were often out of the home. When Susan was not at school, she spent most of her time at home; a good bit of the day-to-day running of the house fell upon her shoulders. There was little recognition of her work but complaints and criticism were frequent. When, occasionally, a matter of general family interest arose and Susan ventured an opinion, her father would silence her with, "Wait till you're asked." Her brothers would ridicule her comments, and her weary mother would intercede only feebly. In time, the defensive silence into which she lapsed became itself the subject of ridicule. At school, although she was a good student, and usually well-prepared, she seldom entered class discussion.

In her loneliness, casual encounters with the janitor of their building became an important source of stimulation. She looked forward to his teasing friendliness, and, in time, responded to his sexual overtures. Although she found intercourse distasteful, body closeness was preferable to her loneliness and isolation. When inevitably she became pregnant and reported her condition to the janitor, he took the position that she "had asked for it" and would have to get herself out of the predicament. Unable to confide in anyone else, she cut her wrists but was discovered in time by her mother. Brought to emergency medical care, she confessed her pregnancy. The family, shocked and angry, refused to be burdened with her needs at the same time that they adamantly opposed abortion.

In the maternity home to which she was sent, Susan continued her isolated behavior, distancing herself from her roommate and the other pregnant teenagers. She viewed with suspicion the friendly overtures of the social worker assigned to her. Her attitude was one of, ''What's in it for you?'' Her expectation was that she would soon be asked to undertake additional chores. When this did not occur, she began to respond to the social worker's interest in her views and suggestions. She was increasingly drawn into planning and organizing activities. When she was praised for her ideas, she would often flush and withdraw, but she formed an intense bond with the social worker. To her she confided her sense of estrangement from her body, her revulsion over its distortion in pregnancy. In her mind, the fetus was like a tumor to be excised. Her future was bleak, for she felt she could never overcome her shame and ostracism from her family. At least when she was home, she had a place to be, but now she had nowhere.

The experience of being listened to, of being valued, overcame her defensive isolation. She could expose her grief over her predicament. Instead of being subjected to recrimination, the experience of being enfolded in understanding stimulated her own understanding and acceptance of herself and her behavior. As pregnancy advanced and the fetus quickened within her, she began to compare the process with her roommate and the other girls in the home. She felt less estranged from her body and readier to join in activities. She took more interest in her appearance; when she was complimented, although she could still flush and appear uncomfortable, she did not withdraw. One of the girls commented to her, ''You know, even though you look like a house, you're really pretty.'' She laughed and glowed.

Susan was now engaged in thoughtful planning for her future. She had decided upon adoption as the best solution for the child and for herself. At this point, her family remained unforgiving of her behavior, but reluctantly offered her permission to return home. When her roommate's family, more compassionate and understanding of their daughter and Susan, offered the option of living with them after delivery, Susan placed her child in adoption and went to live with them as a foster family. In a new community she completed highschool with honors. The estrangement from her family lessened, but with the completion of high school she did not return home to live. Instead she entered nurse's training and moved into a dormitory attached to the school. She continued in therapy for three years, and at termination had begun to date a student from a neighboring campus.

The details of casework with this teenager are far more complex than this brief summary suggests. My purpose, however, is to illustrate that although we can observe the streams of experience which take form in gender identity, gender role, and sexual object choice, they can only be effectively understood as part of the formation of the whole self. Susan had no confusion about gender identity. The depressed drudge she had become was a gender role into which she had grown by reason of the selective response of the parental milieu to her capacity to fulfill the housekeeping needs of the family. Her depressed and weary mother worked long hours outside the home. But such mothers are still able to respond with pleasure to their growing daughter's developing femininity. Out of her own limitations, Susan's mother could not. Her father demeaned her and valued his sons. They, too, belittled her. In her depression she turned to someone older and available whose interest at least stimulated her. Reflecting later on this period of her life, Susan confided to her social worker, "Even to him I was a nobody; he, too, used me."

Informed by the theory of self psychology, the social worker's intervention with Susan provided initially a response to her mirroring needs, for confirmation that she was valued and worthwhile. A period of empathic merger permitted Susan to absorb the experience of response to her specific needs, a response that viewed these needs as genuine. Her self-esteem, her capacity to accept and assert her needs and to value herself, increased. She began to take pride in her appearance and to enhance it, although initially any response to her appearance or praise for her ideas stimulated flushing and withdrawal. She experienced praise as overstimulating of her untransformed grandiosity and expected to be cut down by ridicule. As she grew to understand her defensive withdrawal in isolation, she came to value approving response and to manage the stimulation it provided. Her estrangement from her body subsided, allowing her to express her grief and shame over her pregnancy to a selfobject who absorbed this painful state and to seek out her peers for experience of likeness and difference. She could respond to the interest of other administrative personnel. Her social worker's understanding of why and how her pregnancy had occurred now became the psychic structure of her own self-understanding and with this she experienced a freeing of vitality and purpose.

In earlier social work practice, it was common to describe casework intervention with such teenagers as modeling or role-playing. Unquestionably, identificatory processes were set in motion, but it is altogether a different view of psychic structure building which self psychology offers. The social worker as new selfobject, responding to the emerging transference needs of the individual, reactivates the point at which earlier attempts to secure appropriate response from selfobjects failed. The individual thus comes to understand the nature of the striving in the present to secure a belated response. These selfobject functions, transmuted into self-functions, now become the psychic structure of increased alertness to the signal of anxiety leading to contemplation, planning, and performance, steps through which calming, soothing, and competence or mastery may ensue. Susan was able to value herself, to shape her skills toward a vocation which arose from her own centrally perceived and formulated goals. One might question whether her choice of nursing had in it a certain drudgelike familiarity in serving the needs of others. But this was not Susan's view of her competence in responding to those in need of nursing care. She felt she had a gift and, indeed, her later course in nursing led to a supervisory and teaching position.

It was to Susan's whole self that the social worker responded. And it was in the matrix of that self/selfobject unit that Susan could reengage her need for affirmation. Her ambitions and display did not expose her to ridicule but were valued and worthwhile. Given a responsive selfobject, Susan could respond to the limited (optimal) failures on the part of the social worker, interventions which, for example, slightly missed the mark, requiring Susan's correction or filling in, with renewed structure building and creative change. Gender role and sexual object choice became a joyous expression of centrally perceived and initiated expression of her cohesively functioning, harmonious self.

As we said at the outset, gender formation cannot be viewed outside the forming self of the child. It permeates psychic structure building from the moment of the child's announced sex at birth and reception into a surrounding matrix of selfobjects. The self will take form and achieve biopsychic harmony from the interplay of endowment and nurture. That self will have processed—transmuted—and uniquely structuralized aspects of either parent. A feminine self or a masculine self will not be characterized by rigid, cliché-ridden notions of femininity or masculinity. In harmony with its human design, in biopsychic harmony, the self will emerge functionally capable of achieving a productive and creative life. The elaboration of skills and talents will be fuelled by pleasure in body and mind and, directed and shaped by ideals, will strive toward internally perceived and initiated goals.

The multiproblem families who are seen in child and family agencies and in outpatient clinics struggle less with the problem of gender than with distortions, deficits, and disorders of the whole self that have arisen from failure to secure a meaningful response to their developmental needs within the early parental milieu. Belatedly, with the therapist as a new selfobject, their reactivated developmental needs may be understood and the process of structure building renewed. Self psychology enables us to understand the specific ways in which gender unfolds to become an integral part of the cohesive self.

4

Self Pathology:
Disorders of the Self

I N SEEKING TO classify disorders of the self, their etiology and their form, Kohut emphasized that he was not engaging in parent blame. He was not laying an individual's characterological shortcomings and psychopathology on the shoulders of the parent. In his own words:

> . . . (I am not the) credulous victim of those who do not want to shoulder responsibility for their symptoms, actions and attitudes but waste their time accusing others, including and par excellence their parents. I am not simply falling in with the accusations my analysands may level against their parents even though I may listen to them respectfully for a long time without contradicting them. First, and foremost, the self psychologically informed psychoanalyst *blames no one, neither the patient nor his parents*. He identifies causal sequences, he shows the patient that his feelings and reactions are explained by his experiences in early life, and he points out that, ultimately, *his parents are not to blame since they were what they were because of the backgrounds that determined their own personalities*. (Added emphasis, Kohut, 1984, p. 25).

Self disorders arise not by reason of single events, though these may be, as Kohut points out, crystallization points for later disorders. Rather, the impact of the personalities of the parents on the forming self of a particular child—that child's *subjective* experience of his parents—accounts for the specific self disorder Kohut seeks to classify.

The capacity of a parent to respond empathically to the unusually great or highly specific selfobject need of a child is, in the last analysis, a function of the firmness of the cohesion of the parent's self. Certainly . . . in the case of any selfobject failure (we do not) judge the selfobject's shortcomings from a moral point of view. Such an attitude would be foolish since the parental disability is an outgrowth of the deepest early experiences that influenced the development of the parent's responsibility and is thus beyond control; it would also be completely out of keeping with the approach of the scientist whose aim is neither to blame nor exculpate but to establish causal-motivation chains that explain the empathically gathered, psychological data. (Kohut, 1984, p. 33).

What, then, do we mean by disorders of the self?

An individual may be troubled by feelings of worthlessness, of ineffectiveness, of loneliness ranging from a state as mild as feeling at sixes and sevens to that of total confusion and irrationality. How unyielding are these feelings? How long do they last? What effort does the individual make to ease his suffering? To comfort himself does he abuse substances? In vindictive rage does he engage in delinquent or destructive acts? Is his isolation and disorder so profound and so extensive that no meaningful contact with others can be established?

Kohut, in a paper co-authored with a colleague, Ernest S. Wolf (1978), offered a nosology of self disorders, a classification to illustrate type, severity, and etiology. It was not their intention that these classifications be rigidly applied. One finds embedded in all Kohut's writing a deep-seated respect for individual variance. His conviction that even maladaptive behavior can be viewed as a way station on the path to health permeated his work with his own patients and with individuals whose treatment he supervised. And this has always been a deeply held belief in social work practice, stemming from a respect for the individual and his strivings. In defining the various disorders of the self, Kohut would have us recognize that they do not exist in pure state. The self is not monolithic. Even within the psychotic individual, there may be healthy structure.

Before reviewing Kohut and Wolf's system of classification, it is necessary to understand the position Kohut assigned to drive and conflict theory—libido theory. Kohut initially viewed self psychology as a theory of human development complementary to libido theory, drive and conflict theory. But increasingly, from his immersion in the psychic life of his patients, and from the experience of analysts whose work he supervised, he came at first reluctantly and then firmly to the conclusion that the drives become notable, stormy, with a variety of behaviors coalescing around them, when the forming self, or the self in the process of consolidation, is phase-appropriately unsupported. Ultimately, he viewed self psychology as encompassing the drives.

For Kohut, it is not the drives, but the parents' appropriate response to the child's emerging, sequential needs as each drive in turn achieves ascendancy, that will determine whether deficits in the self of the child will result. In the creation of the self, parents as prestructural selfobjects perform appropriate selfobject functions, and their selfobject functions are transmuted into self-functions as optimal frustration allows this to occur. Empathic failure on the part of selfobjects results in deficits: the energy of the drive remains outside of the forming self, giving rise to driven thought or behavior.

Let us examine the concept of oral greed, presumably arising because of the strength of the oral drive and the failure to achieve its sublimation. In the past, oral greed, devouring hunger for individuals or for food, was viewed as an untamed drive. Yet, if we examine such behavior in the light of self psychology, we can understand that the child's cues were grossly unresponded to at that particular phase, and that the driven quality of the behavior resulted from the failure of earlier selfobjects to respond to the child's phase-appropriate need. Instead of the experience of child and mother in synchrony, the individual has split off a part of the experience in an effort to recover a state of harmony, of being whole. It is not the food the individual craves; it is *the experience of the foodgiving, empathic mother, in tune with the child's needs* (Kohut, 1977) (emphasis supplied).

Let me offer an example from the case of Jennie, a depressed, 26-year-old woman. Her relationships with others had a driven quality which resulted in her being rejected, after which she would retire into haughty, aloof behavior and a compulsive need to fill herself with food. She felt herself to be different from others; looking about at her carefree peers enjoying themselves, she commented bitterly,

JENNIE: They're just putting on an act.
THERAPIST: What makes you say that?
JENNIE: I know, I was *always* putting on an act. How could I tell them Mom would go off her nut every now and then and had to go to the hospital?
THERAPIST: What happened then?
JENNIE: I'd come home and clean up that messy old house. I'd have to take care of Jimmy while those kids were off doing things. I had to pretend to everyone!
THERAPIST: But here you don't. I can understand.
JENNIE: Dad was never around and Jimmy was too little.
THERAPIST: But here, together, we can understand how it was.
JENNIE: (Beginning to cry) I'd look around at all those kids. I'd think, "They've got something I don't have!"
THERAPIST: What did they have, Jennie?
JENNIE: (Bursting into sobs) They had mothers. (Her sobbing subsides, and after a time she looks up with a puzzled smile.) I smell chocolate chip cookies baking. I love them. I can eat a pound all by myself! When Mom was well and I'd come home from school, she'd have

cookies baking. I'd go on about everything at school and she'd listen. I knew she was proud of me. We had a lot of fun, me eating
those cookies and her smiling and being herself. (Crying again) Why
couldn't it always be that way?

In this fragment from Jennie, a case which will be described in detail
later, it was not the cookies she craved but the experience of the foodgiving empathic mother, in tune with her needs, as the caseworker, a new
selfobject in the present, was now in tune with her needs. The drivenness of her expectations of others, which might have been described as
stemming from oral greed, could be seen, rather, as unresponded-to affect, which intensified in the face of repeated and prolonged failure to
secure a response to her needs from early selfobjects. And it was the intensity of her need that, disavowed, led to cold, aloof behavior with her
friends when they did not immediately respond to her wish for their
presence.

Similarly, during the years when attention is focused on the anal drama
of producing and withholding , the child seeks a response to these activities. The child whose products are accepted with approval and guidance transmutes into self-functions appropriate producing, withholding,
timing—forerunners of productive efforts in a variety of areas. Caretakers
who intrude their own anxiety or demands for perfection, for performance
in accordance with their needs, do not permit the child to develop confidence in his *own* perceptions, in *himself* as a center of initiative. He may
split off a fragment of the longed-for whole experience, as poignantly illustrated in the comment of an isolated, lonely child to his therapist, ''I
like my B.M.'s. They make me happy. I don't feel alone when there are
B.M.'s in my room.''

Such problems as fecal retention, smearing, messiness, and procrasti-
nation may invade the whole process of learning—not because of an untamed drive, but because of the failure of selfobjects to respond to the
child's affective needs and wishes in a manner that permits him to transmute into self-functions monitoring his perceptions, regulating his produc-
tion, and achieving a sense of his own effectiveness. When the selfobject
is able to admire his productive efforts and encourage his own perception of readiness to produce or ability to withhold, these functions ''go
inside''; they are transmuted into self-functions.

As to the oedipal conflict, Kohut's immersion in depth psychology over
many years increasingly led him to question whether the familiar storms
and difficulties of the oedipal period were indeed based on the child's
rivalrous and murderous feelings toward the parent of the opposite sex.
An example will serve to illustrate the different viewpoint which self

psychology offers. A 15-year-old youth, standing in front of a mirror brushing his hair, first with a part and then straight back, was startled and frightened when his father spied him and said, sneeringly, "Aw come on, quit shoving that mop of yours around and start pushing the lawn mower." The boy's fear and anger had nothing to do with murderous rivalry toward his father. Rather, it signaled his fear of fragmentation in the face of his father's harsh ridicule. He was flooded with shame and embarrassment at a time when his longing for admiration and confirmation of his manly attractiveness was at its height. (This is a fragment of a case reported in greater detail in Chapter 11.)

In a family in which the parents admire without intrusiveness a son's or daughter's developing sexual maturity, in which they can, by their responsiveness, facilitate gender definition, affective needs on the part of their children do not intensify to the point of drivenness. Such children do not turn to the stimulation and regulation of a depressed self in addiction or perversion, as in the behavior disorders, or in hypochondria, sadistic or masochistic fantasy, as in the personality disorders (Kohut, 1971, 1977).

What of the concept of aggression as a basic drive? In what way does this fit into our understanding of the psychology of the self? It was Kohut's belief that aggression is not a basic drive. As research has demonstrated (Stern, 1983), a child is naturally assertive and requires such assertiveness to explore the many wonders of his world. When assertiveness is traumatically and repeatedly thwarted, demanding, explosive, irritating behavior takes over. The child who is grossly unmirrored, grossly prevented from merging with a powerful, idealized other in whose strength he may revel, in whose wisdom he can bask, drives others away when he most needs help. Such behavior in children, later adults, often covers over legitimate demands that were not responded to earlier in a manner permitting inner regulation to form and thrive. As a consequence, abrasive behavior or driven thought arises. Such individuals are not infrequently seen in social agencies, their very manner threatening to repel those from whom they seek help.

In short, it is not "unruly drives" around which certain self-defeating and dangerous behaviors coalesce to make individuals demanding and unlearning. Rather, it is unresponded-to affect, which then intensifies to become driven. Behavior becomes driven in an effort to replace the missing selfobject functions of self-esteem regulation, soothing and calming, which permit self-regulation and mastery. Thus, self psychology as a theory of human development encompasses the drives and permits us a clearer understanding of disorders of the self that result from repeated failures of the necessary responses from selfobjects. Driven behavior is an attempt, repetitiously and belatedly sought, to shore up faltering self-esteem. When in a new self/selfobject relationship such behavior is understood and interpreted, the individual is able to transmute as a self-function the capacity to regulate anxiety, to calm and soothe himself. Being understood in the present provides the conditions under which the nuclear self establishes or restores cohesion.

SECONDARY DISORDERS

Disorders of the self are classified as primary and secondary (Kohut and Wolf, 1978). Let us first examine secondary disorders of the self. When an individual feels good about his physical and mental attributes and his ability to pursue goals, and is reasonably content with the manner in which he has been able to develop his skills and talents for the particular goal he has chosen in life—that is, when the self is firmly cohesive, vigorous, and harmonious—then he can tolerate disappointment without feeling destroyed and can rejoice in accomplishments without manic overvaluation. Secondary disturbances of the self arise through the unavoidable vicissitudes of life.

Injury, illness, loss, separation, failure to achieve an anticipated goal, being passed over for another—in short, life's vicissitudes—may for a period of time bring about a sense of emptiness, of depletion, of grief or rage. Although the individual may experience severe fragmentation and loss of vigor, he may still be able to recover through his own capacity to draw on inner resources and to turn to selfobjects that have always had restorative power—husband or wife, parents, colleagues, good friends, or symbolic selfobjects such as work, study, and cultural activities. But when such a state is prolonged the individual may need to seek treatment in order to recover. The traumatic experience may have exposed deficits in the self structure that prevent the individual from undertaking restorative steps on his own. The therapeutic task requires a process through which restoration of psychic structure or new structure building can be initiated. The example of the aviatrix in Kopit's play, *Wings* (1978), illustrates the rage that a formerly able-bodied individual experiences when rendered helpless by a stroke. He vibrantly portrays her struggles to make her way back to some form of mobility and to reestablish continuity with her formerly cohesive, vigorous, and harmonious self.

PRIMARY DISORDERS

Primary disorders of the self include psychoses, borderline states, and narcissistic personality and behavior disorders. In *psychosis*, self disorder results from pervasive, prolonged failure on the part of the parenting milieu to respond to the child's presence. The parents offer little dependable, consistent joy, interest, or excitement in the child's development, nor do they make adequate provision for available, dependable selfobjects who can respond to the child's cues. And this may occur in the period of the forming self of the child or in the period of consolidation of the self. By reason either of their own faulty structure or of unavoidable vagaries of fate—absence because of illness, separation, or death—parents are not available as reliable selfobjects confirming the child's worth, allowing the child to merge sufficiently with their idealized strength and benevolence. The self of the child emerges as chaotic, without the capacity to enlist the help or interest of selfobjects. If the child has a particular talent or skill, this may be responded to, but in isolation, accounting for healthy structure within a self otherwise poorly held together. But the self of the child in general does not achieve cohesion or direction.

There may also be a physiological component, so that the child's cues to his needs may be minimal or so poorly exhibited as to be nonexistent. Parents become confused and self-blaming, further limiting their responsiveness. Stern (1977) and his associates have indicated that parents of such children can be helped to recognize minimal cues and, by parental response, to invigorate their children's capacity for more readily recognizable cue-giving. But a combination of empathically unresponsive parents and physiological deficit results in a psychotic core, leaving the individual prone to repeated fragmentation.

In *borderline states*, the self of the individual can be likened to an *ad hoc* committee. It is as if each problem must be tackled afresh; there is little sense of continuity, of cause and effect. The failure of selfobjects is less severe than the absence of confirming, idealized selfobjects in the childhood of the psychotic individual; nevertheless, inconsistency on the part of early selfobjects in responding to the child's forming self or self in the process of consolidation accounts for missing functions in the borderline individual.

It is important to stress once again that in the borderline states the self is not monolithic. The very term suggests the range from the border of psychosis to healthier functioning, as in the narcissistic disorders. Gunderson and Singer (1975) have described certain consensus features of borderline states, such as 1) vacillating relationships that are shallow, intense, transient, manipulative, and devaluing; 2) impulsive behavior, including drug abuse, mutilation, and suicidal attempts; 3) intense hostility; and 4) psychotic episodes. Paul Tolpin (1980) has pointed out that these are the desperate efforts of individuals struggling to cover over numerous deficits in self-esteem regulation, monitoring anxiety, calming and soothing themselves as they struggle toward mastery of numerous life tasks. Although such individuals have been considered not analyzable, Tolpin suggests that the skill of the therapist and exceptional talent in remaining empathically sensitive to such individuals may allow the use of analysis (P. Tolpin, 1980). In a volume published after his death, Kohut suggested that the concept of 'borderline' pathology '' . . . is a relative one, depending, at least in a substantial number of cases on (a) the analyst's 'empathic intention' despite the serious narcissistic injuries to which he is exposed and (b) ultimately [on the ability] to enable the patient . . . to reassemble his or her self sufficiently with the aid of the selfobject transference to make possible the gradual exploration of the dynamic and genetic causes of the underlying vulnerability" (Kohut, 1984, p. 184).

In the *narcissistic behavior disorders*, the self has greater capacity for cohesion, for self-righting, even though the symptoms of perverse, delinquent, or addictive behavior expose the individual to grave physical and social danger (Kohut and Wolf, 1978). Such behavior may erupt in response to even slight narcissistic injury to self-esteem.

In the *narcissistic personality disorder*, it is not destructive behavior that erupts, but, rather, a psychological state expressed in hypochondriacal concerns, depression, sadomasochistic fantasies, and diminished energy. Kohut (1977) has postulated that the failure of empathic response from the parenting milieu has occurred earlier or may have been more prolonged in behavior disorders than in personality disorders. In any case, in narcissistic disorders of the self, whether personality or behavior disorder, the breakup or distortion of the self is temporary. It is through the empathic bridge established by the therapist as new selfobject that the individual can understand the genetic origin of his vulnerability and gradually transmute the psychic structure of soothing and mastery.

TYPICAL SELF STATES

In further classifying self disorders, Kohut and Wolf describe typical syndromes—clusters of experience. These are: the understimulated self, the fragmenting self, the overstimulated self, and the overburdened self. They do not exist singly or in pure culture; there may be a predominance of one such syndrome at a given time, or there may be admixtures. But it is helpful to examine these clusters of experience singly.

The Understimulated Self

In the understimulated self the individual feels boring and dull and is often so viewed by others. A quality of apathy pervades as a result of a lack of joy or interest on the part of the parenting milieu. It may be a chronic or recurrent state—but it is one in which early efforts to elicit affirming interest have been thwarted. Rather than being able to regulate self-esteem through reaching out to others in a buoyant manner that may then elicit interest, the understimulated individual falls back on stimulating himself—through headbanging in early childhood, compulsive masturbation in later childhood, daredevil activities in adolescence and adulthood, retreat into fantasy and hypochondriacal concerns, various perversions, substance abuse, even hypersociability.

Illustrative of the understimulated self, a 25-year-old young woman recalled her desperate efforts to get her mother to respond to her by all sorts of conforming behavior; failing this she would engage in playful tricks. She would perform endless household tasks varied with all sorts of acrobatic exploits to gain her mother's notice, but this very depressed woman would turn away, absorbed in her own thoughts. The child would long desperately for her father's return at night, striving in every way for his attention, but after the most perfunctory of greetings, he would be off to his evening courses. By means of sadistic fantasies, she would seek to overcome her sense of deadness. Always the silent member in groups or in classes, she could respond briefly to overtures of friendliness, but would soon fall silent. Later in therapy she described her emptiness, the feeling that others must have of her. "Why wouldn't they be bored with me? I bore myself."

The Overstimulated Self

In constrast to the understimulated self, the overstimulated self is one in which the experience has been that of selfobjects who respond with exaggerated attention to a particular aspect or part of the child rather than to the whole child. In response to a child's emerging, embryonic interest and skill in a particular field, the parents whose own grandiosity is poorly contained or shaped use the child's skills for the purpose of their own display to friends, neighbors, and colleagues. Although the child may go on to develop proficiency, he experiences no zest or joy in performance. Zest and joy are the hallmarks of a cohesive, vigorous nuclear self harmoniously responding to its own perceptions and initiative in directing its own talents and skills to its own goals.

The child does need the affirming and guiding response (mirroring) of the selfobject initially, but the continued intrusion of that selfobject, not only in shaping the child's performance but in displaying himself, robs the child of the sense that his skill or talent is his own. He may lose interest. He may remain unable to fulfill his very real potential because of the anxiety which the overstimulation of his grandiosity arouses. And this anxiety may be present whenever the display of his bodyself is necessary.

We do not know enough of the background of the composer Stephen Sondheim, for example, to explain his intense inability to stand before an audience and hear acclaim for his work. But we do know from his own published statements that he must stand at the back of the hall or leave the theatre in order to contain his anxiety over the response to his work (*New York Times*, 4/1/84). For such individuals, creativity may be unimpaired so long as no exhibition of the bodyself is involved. For many, however, "the creative-productive potential will be diminished because their intense ambitions . . . remained tied to unmodified grandiose fantasies [which frighten them]"(Kohut and Wolf, 1978, p. 419). The grandiose exhibitionistic pole of the self will be weaker than that formulating idealized goals and standards.

But the pole harboring idealized values and goals may also be subject to overstimulation. Longing to merge with the strength and wisdom of the idealized selfobject on the way to transmuting goals and standards of his own, the child may instead be forced into remaining an admiring audience by a selfobject still in need of response to his own exhibitionism. Instead of healthy enthusiasm for admired mentors, the longing for contact with such an ideal will pose a threat. Contact with the idealized selfobject is experienced as a danger to be avoided. A healthy capacity for enthusiasm will be lost, an enthusiasm for goals or ideals that people with a firm self can experience in response to those whose greatness they admire.

This was poignantly illustrated by a talented young man whose skills lay in a number of directions, but who would repeatedly work up to the point of virtual completion of a dissertation and then fail to offer it for review and defense of the thesis. Repeatedly, the first flush of enthusiasm and hard work in shaping his ideas would gradually evaporate as the time came closer to submitting his work to his idealized chairman. How could he presume to command the attention of his mentor, whose own work was of such vast distinction? Numerous memories of his father, idealized because of his prominence in a particular field, surfaced in the process of therapy. He recalled his father's criticism of various projects he had shown him, and he cringed as he repeated biting comments for some minor failure in execution. His father would then display his own meticulous craftsmanship, totally losing sight of the age of his son and the level of performance that might be expected of him. Deeply as this student needed and longed for appropriate guidance in the present, he persistently avoided seeking contact out of fear of once more exposing himself to the possibility of wounding evaluations of his work.

The Fragmenting Self

In contrast to the overstimulated self, the fragmenting self is a chronic or recurrent condition which results from the lack of integrating responses by earlier selfobjects to the forming self of the child. Individual behaviors, rather than the whole self of the child, are responded to. For example, a child rushing in to tell his mother about some important school exploit is interrupted with the mother's focus on his dirty face, disheveled clothes, or some item he has forgotten. The response of her needed admiration is not to the child's whole pleasure and excitement in describing the event but to a minor flaw which could have been dealt with later. Such individuals develop a sensitivity to the slightest rebuff; they quickly lose a sense of continuity and purpose. They may develop a propensity to brooding about bodily concerns or aspects of work in response to narcissistic slights. They fragment readily instead of experiencing a healthy flow of self-esteem and the capacity for self-righting.

The Overburdened Self

The overburdened self repeatedly has suffered the trauma of unshared emotion because selfobjects have been unable to offer, or to allow, the use of their mature psychic structure for calming and soothing. As only one example from her childhood, a young woman reported that, as a six-year-old, distraught because she had broken a favored toy, she rushed to her mother for comfort. Her mother, a survivor of the holocaust, brushed her aside, asking, "How would *you* feel if *your* little brother had been sent to the ovens?" On another occasion, trying to open a door from which a broken window pane had not been removed, she cut her wrist very severely. Her mother, exasperated at this additional burden, scolded her roundly for her carelessness. The experience of unshared emotion, the absence of enfolding warmth and comforting through which an individual transmutes self-soothing and calming, results in an overburdened self. The individual feels the world to be hostile and uncaring and, additionally, feels guilty because of his needs.

CHARACTER TYPES

The self disorders described above lead the suffering individual to undertake characteristic protective behaviors, resulting in certain character types. These character types are not to be applied rigidly but are to be understood as a means of clarifying certain behaviors and feeling states, thereby enabling the empathic therapist as new selfobject to make his understanding and intervention effective.

"The mirror-hungry individual thirsts for selfobjects whose confirming and admiring responses will nourish their famished self" (Kohut and Wolf, 1978, p. 421). Even when they are genuinely responded to, deficits in self-esteem regulation lead *mirror-hungry individuals* always to thirst for more. Still, they establish more such relationships, and even though they are anxious and uncomfortable about their need for admiration, they continue to seek attention and recognition from new selfobjects (Kohut and Wolf, 1978).

The need of the individual is beyond that for a selfobject in the usual sense. Here there is a bit of missing structure which the individual seeks to fill in by sequential mergers with individuals who initially satisfy the need for affirmation and mirroring. Sooner or later, the familiar response no longer satisfies and the mirror-hungry individual seeks another attachment. Many such people continue through life in this fashion. Others may seek amelioration of this state. Mrs. D., for example, sought help because she felt she was a pest to her growing children and to her husband. She constantly sought their approval and admiration, but, even when this was forthcoming, the effect did not last. Her physician's suggestion that she get a part-time job, which she was able to do, did not relieve her but only added another arena to her need for mirroring. Her discontent and sadness ultimately led her to a social agency as she realized that, despite the fact that her children and husband were doing well, that indeed she was doing well in her job, she was unhappy. Initially responding to the focused empathic attention of the caseworker to her problems, she warned the caseworker that she, too, would find her a pest and turn away. Engaging and holding such an individual in treatment can be wearing, but the unfolding mirror transference provides numerous opportunities for the individual to understand the mirroring need arising in the present and its childhood origins. Knowing that one hurts and why is a step in uniting affect and cognition. Being understood in the present provides the conditions under which the individual can recognize the source of anxiety, monitor it, and transmute as a self-function the ability both to modulate grandiosity and to enjoy inner approval and the added pleasure which unsolicited approval from others may bring.

The *ideal-hungry individual* feels worthy only so long as there is a selfobject who can be venerated. The persistence of a structural deficit in the pole harboring ideals leads him to attach himself to others whose greatness he can admire and in whose glory he can bask. Such relationships may persist and be sustaining, but sooner or later the ideal fails in some crucial way. His stature is diminished and the search begins again. The ideal-hungry individual is often a name dropper whose self-esteem is thus bolstered by the recognized importance of the name he utters. Such individuals may demean the help they need and seek if the helper is not well-known and at the top of his profession. And social workers, given the hierarchical nature of the mental health profession, not infrequently find themselves initially being deprecated by ideal-hungry individuals, as illustrated in Chapter 11. Here the self-esteem of the social worker, her pleasure in her work, and her own sense of professional competence stand her in good stead. Indeed, her self-esteem provides diagnostic insight into deficits in the idealizing pole of the ideal-hungry individual and becomes an element in structure building.

The *alter-ego-hungry individual* seeks a selfobject who gives reality to the self by similar interests, appearance, taste, and values. Such relationships may persist for some time, but since there are inevitable failures and disappointments, a restless search for a new alter-ego begins. This is not unlike the search of the mirror-hungry and the ideal-hungry. When we discuss transference, we shall see that the need for twinship, alter-ego or partnering selfobjects, is part of the process of consolidation of a cohesive nuclear self that takes place in early childhood. The need for sustenance from partnering selfobjects continues throughout life; it is the persistent intensity of the need that signifies a deficit. We shall see how this transference need emerges in the transference in Chapter 5 and how it can be responded to as it arises in the new self/self-object unit so that structure building may ensue.

There are elements of such personality directions—mirror-hunger, ideal-hunger, alter-ego-hunger—in relatively cohesive, strong individuals. But even when more pronounced, the hunger states described above are viewed less as psychopathology than as reflections of variations in normal human personality, with its range of strengths and weaknesses. It is the location of the self-deficit that produces the characteristic stance of these individuals, not the extent of the defect in the self. The next two types are notable more "for the intensity and depth of the deficit than by its particular location within the self" (Kohut and Wolf, 1978, p. 422).

The *merger-hunger individual* seeks the selfobject out of an intense need to complete psychic structure. The selfobject is not perceived as separate. The merger-hungry individual has difficulty in distinguishing his wishes and needs from those of the selfobject, a selfobject who exists only to complete the psychic structure of the merger-hungry individual. Thus, anything less than a perfect response is felt as an injurious affront. The expectation is almost that of a preverbal child that the selfobject will know without being told what is needed and will supply it.

An example comes to mind of a young husband, married only two years and immersed in medical studies, who sought help for ungovernable rage following his wife's leaving him. In his distraught state, he reiterated endlessly, "We had a perfect marriage and she broke it up."

The perfect marriage consisted in his wife's managing everything about the house, having his meals ready on time, his clothes in good order, being available to respond to his sexual needs, and repeatedly abandoning her own studies because of the demands of his schedule. He was totally unaware of her disappointment and mounting rage in the relationship, of the importance to her of her own studies, to which he gave only a bemused ear. Thus, the merger-hungry individual experiences the selfobject as part of himself and is enraged at failure to respond to his needs.

In contrast, the *contact-shunning individual* yearns so intensely for the selfobject of his choice that he cannot risk rejection of the closeness for which he longs. This is not only the fear of rejection, but also the fear that closeness itself will overwhelm and engulf him. The loneliness and isolation of such individuals are striking. An example of contact-shunning in its mildest form is the individual who suffers what is commonly called a crush, who must worship his choice afar, but who, rather than risk an ordinary encounter, will cross the street to avoid this. Yet such an example does not begin to describe the intense suffering and restricted lifestyle of those with the self pathology of contact shunning.

Such lonely, isolated individuals are not infrequently encountered in the populations of social agencies and of outpatient clinics. The tentative, tremulous groping for human sustenance that characterizes the treatment relationship and the hasty withdrawals that even slight variation in empathic intuneness may precipitate tax the ingenuity of the practitioner. Perhaps there is in the practice of social work a special intuneness with those who are emotionally, physically, and developmentally handicapped, those who are the victims of racial and economic discrimination. This may be so in part by reason of preadaptedness of those who go into social work to extend empathic understanding to such individuals, as well as by reason of professional training, since from the outset of their training students are placed in fieldwork settings in which these poulations predominate.

Although the clusters of symptoms and personality features described as disorders of the self were derived from psychoanalysis of individuals with narcissistic behavior and personality disorders, they are applicable generally to broader populations. They are useful in helping us to understand the selfobject functions that must be provided to enable the troubled individual to renew the thrust to complete development, to fill in missing functions with the psychic structure of self-esteem regulation, soothing, and mastery. Through the experience of the therapist as new selfobject in the present, the thwarted striving for growth can be revitalized in the capacity to establish at least a less restricted matrix of selfobjects.

5

The Treatment Process
in Clinical Social Work

Ow CAN AN UNDERSTANDING of self psychology be applied to problems in social casework? How can it help us in our work with troubled individuals who lead tormented lives? Regardless of social or economic conditions, such individuals experience little fulfillment; they
do not find meaningful employment, or, being employed, they encounter
difficulty in pursuing their tasks. In family life they are unable to respond
to their mates and children in a protective and supportive manner. Some
plod on under intolerable conditions; others fragment readily. They appear unable to establish relationships or, having established them, unable
to maintain them. Their troubles encompass all the permutations of human discontent or illness expressed in behavior or feeling states.

In our work with these individuals or families an understanding of self
psychology permits us to recognize the healing function to be played in
the present by the therapist as a new selfobject. The type of transference,
whether mirroring, idealizing, twinship (partnering), or elements of each
alternately, helps us to understand deficits in self structure and the nature
of needs and wishes to which the individual seeks response.

As we have seen, Kohut conceived of the self as having three major constituents: the pole of ambitions, the pole of ideals, and the intermediate
area of skills and talents. Individuals with deficits in these areas are highly
vulnerable to narcissistic injury. They lack the capacity for self-righting
or are limited in their ability to seek out appropriate selfobjects for this
purpose. Kohut describes the need for the experience of selfobjects in the
creation and sustenance of the self as undergoing a lifelong maturation,
development and change: " . . . we must not confuse 1) the archaic [early]
selfobjects that (a) are the *normal requirements* of early life and (b) are required later on, either chronically, in disorders of the self, or passingly,
in periods of special stress in those who are free from self pathology with

2) the mature selfobjects that all of us need for our own psychological survival from *birth to death*'' (emphasis added, Kohut, 1984, p. 193).

Thus, three major selfobject needs may, alone, serially, or in tandem, emerge in the process of treatment, the attempt to assuage pain and rekindle will and purpose. These needs are to experience mirroring and acceptance; to experience merger with greatness, strength, and calmness; and to experience essential likeness, a sense of being a human being among human beings. Unfolded in a transference to the therapist as new selfobject, the unfulfilled need exposes self deficits which then may become the focus of understanding and interpretation in a working-through process which the individual then transmutes into self-understanding.

In his earlier work (1977), Kohut stressed his belief that weakness in one pole of the self could be compensated for by strength in the second; the child has "two chances as he moves toward consolidation of the self— self disturbances of pathological degree result only from the failure of both of these developmental opportunities" (1977, p. 185). If the expectation of mirroring is repeatedly thwarted so that the child cannot reliably find pleasure and pride in his physical and mental attributes, then he will turn to an idealized selfobject with whose strength and competence he can merge. The pole imbued with values, standards, and ideals will emerge strong and will compensate for weakness in the pole of grandiosity. The experience may also occur in reverse.

But from his introspective and empathic immersion in the life of his patients, as well as those whose treatment he supervised, Kohut added another transference need to those of mirroring and idealizing: that of alter-ego, twinship, partnering. He believed that "disabling disorders of the self come about only when at least two of the three constituents of the self have serious defects because of flawed or insufficient selfobject responses in childhood. . . . The selfobject's inability to respond appropriately to the developmental needs of one of the constituents of the self will bring about an intensified attempt to obtain adequate responses to the developmental needs of the two others" (1984, p. 205).

It was his belief that serious disorder of the self, i.e., failure in the process of consolidating a vigorous, harmonious cohesive self, will occur only if two of these three basic needs are unmet. It was also his experience that the pivotal transference which emerges will "frequently be organized around the less traumatic aspects of the two selfobject parents" (1984, p. 206).

If it is primarily a mirror transference which unfolds, it is to the therapist as a new selfobject that a long buried yearning to be admired, with fantasies of greatness and derring-do, can now be exposed. The failure of earlier selfobjects to perform this function at appropriate phases has left

deficits that the individual strives to fill in by driven behavior or thought. And it is not that the therapist now takes over the role of earlier selfobjects, gratifying infantile needs and wishes (Goldberg, 1978). It is that the therapist provides healing understanding in the present of the pain of unfulfilled longing for that earlier wish for admiration and guidance, and, cognitively, knowledge of what the individual was seeking. It is in the context of an empathic merger (the self/selfobject unit in tune) that the conditions for healing deficits in self-esteem are provided. Such a mirror transference frees the previously thwarted need to grow. In place of grandiose ambitions, short-circuited in daydreams or in destructive or fruitless behavior, the legitimacy of the need and wish for affirmation and guidance (mirroring) is now confirmed. The therapist as new selfobject enables the individual to confide his dreams of greatness and his wish to be admired, and in so doing allows him to reinstate cohesiveness and expansion of the self. The individual may now acquire as psychic structure the self-function of monitoring anxiety, patience in enduring the slow process of shaping grandiose schemes into the mastery of manageable goals.

In like manner, the emergence of an idealizing transference signals an unfulfilled need to be permitted to merge with the calmness and wisdom of earlier selfobjects. Whether through pathology or unavoidable vicissitudes of life, earlier selfobjects were unable to provide that enfolding power and generosity through which ideals, values, and standards are transmuted and become reliable self structure. In the healing merger with a new selfobject an individual can be helped to absorb the pain of frustration and disappointment, even failure, as he sets about redirecting his aspirations (Goldberg, 1975). He can accept modificaton of grandiose ambitions without being lost in abject humiliation or surrender (Basch, 1983c).

The conviction that a twinship transference expressing alter-ego needs deserves separate status and has a separate line of development came to Kohut long after he had substantially documented mirroring and idealizing needs. Earlier, he had included the experience of twinship needs under mirroring needs. His work with specific patients stimulated his awareness that from the earliest beginnings in the child's nestling in the mother's arms, sniffing her odor, experiencing the warmth and softness of her body, the need to be affirmed as a human being among other human beings changes and matures. Closeness to the father's body, savoring his strength, provides another dimension of the experience of being human. Through the experience of being and working side by side, the child shapes his talents into skills, which are initially primitive and awkward. Bodily care, care of toys and tools, social and work behaviors have as their genetic origin the myriad elements of partnering. When twinship or alter-ego needs have been partially frustrated or inadequately responded to by the early selfobjects of childhood, such needs will emerge in a transference different from the idealizing or mirroring transference. It is not a cliché to say that hope springs enternal in the human breast: it is available to be rekindled—that hope is to be accepted as a worthwhile member of society.

By separating out the specifics of a particular transference, the intention is not to assign scientific simplicity to the complexity of the human psyche. Kohut recognized that the various genetically preformed patterns of childhood needs and wishes that are called transferences are always artifacts. But he believed that his classification of transferences, genetic clusters of developmental needs, could be useful in allowing us to understand the origin of specific deficits in the formation of the self and the response that the individual seeks to elicit in the present.

The manner in which transferences emerge and intermingle is illustrated by the following vignette. A 19-year-old university student, formally dressed in suit and tie, with the demeanor and bearing of an adult in his forties, described feelings of distance from his peers; nor was he able to respond to his instructors, even when his high performance in his studies aroused their interest. He admired his instructors but remained aloof from them, although it was in his interest to respond to their overtures.

He could remember a time when he felt easier with people, but it was hard to recall much about that earlier time. He was the older of two children, his sister being three years younger than he. His father was away a good deal of the time, and he was aware of loneliness and sadness as a steady state. He referred with some irony to the closeness of women: "My mother and my sister . . . jabber, jabber all the time. You couldn't get a word in edgewise. Not that I wanted to; all that stuff about clothes and parties." They did make some effort to include him but he "preferred" to stay alone when they went out. He recalled that his loneliness would lift on the weekend when his father was due home but soon returned as his father was caught up in household or social activities. His own tasks at home were mowing the lawn, vacuuming, performing errands, and later, chauffeuring his sister to her activities. Although a well-built young man, he felt himself to be clumsy. His manner of entering and leaving the office, and sitting in his chair was formal and stiff.

Over the course of several months, the therapist's warm interest in his day-to-day activities gradually produced a thaw in his manner, occasionally a genuine burst of laughter in response to a particular interchange. His formal attire was gradually replaced with typical campus dress, T-shirt and slacks. There emerged memories of his early interest in building model boats, and, quite by the way, his father's work as a manufacturer of marine supplies. He could recall his father taking him to the factory and letting him work on his models alongside his own much more complex scale model-building. "I felt like a man among men." At home his father built him a special shelf to display his models. His mother's interest seemed passing, but he did not recall a sense of being closed out from the tight relationship between mother and daughter as he later did.

He recalled that, when he was about 12, the nature of his father's work changed following a promotion. His new job required that he travel about the country. He was gone for long periods of time. The son looked forward eagerly to his father's return and their continued work, but such times seemed never again to arise. Occasionally, his father would give him a hand with his models but it was obvious that his father was no longer as keenly interested. In retrospect, he realized that there were many problems relating to his father's new work, and that, though the promotion brought added income and prestige, the demands on his father left little time for leisure.

The family moved to a larger home and to a new school district. Away from peers with whom he had grown up and neighbors who knew him, he pursued a lonely course of school work and duties at home. His mother, struggling with her own reactions to his father's absence and her new surroundings, tried to interest him in other activities but soon became impatient and turned to his sister's activities and friends. He did well academically, but when it came to making friends he backed away. He felt different from everyone, a stranger among people who seemed to know each other and enjoy being together. He expressed a sense of puzzlement and bewilderment. Maybe he was just different; "maybe something was left out when they packed the parts for a model" of himself.

The therapist recognized his loneliness and his sadness with the loss of his father's companionship. She pointed out his understandable pain at losing this close relationship, a pain others had been unaware of, struggling as they were with their own problems. In response, he described long hours with his model boats until his mother, impatient with his "mooning about" in his room and certain that his model-building was the cause of his isolation, swept the models off the shelf, damaging a few. As he told about this experience, he leaned forward, shielding his face with his hands, finally bursting into tears.

Absorbing his grief and allowing him to feel by her silent presence the legitimacy of his pain, the therapist shared with him her speculation that these models were important to him; in his father's absence they had comforted him. Particularly at that time, they had represented the long hours of joyous companionship he had shared with his father. They represented, too, his own skills and productivity. He confided somewhat shamefacedly that he had always thought it was a "damn fool kiddish thing" to do and that he himself had finally shoved the models into a closet. But he was surprised at how often, particularly at night, he would be thinking about those models and the special way he and his father had solved certain problems.

When he returned for his next appointment, he had a great deal of difficulty in beginning. Finally, his face flushed, he confided that the night after the last session, unable to sleep and feeling excited and alive in a way he had not felt "for years," he had gotten out of bed. He had posed in front of his mirror, arms akimbo, fantasizing himself at the controls of a spaceship. He felt there was nothing he could not do. Still flushing, he asked if the therapist didn't think he was really some kind of a nut. She assured him that, far from indicating that he was some kind of a nut, his fantasy showed that he was again in touch with the wonderful feelings children have about all that the future holds out in terms of what they can accomplish. For him the process of gradually shaping and modifying such fantasies had been sidetracked by the interruption in his companionship with his idealized father. Added to this loss was the family's simultaneous move to new surroundings and the interruption of familiar sustaining friendships.

An essentially mirroring transference, in which the therapist responded with understanding to his painful sense of the loss of affirmation and confirmation, allowed him now to understand the origin of his sense of being a stranger among people who knew each other. The capacity to recognize in himself his *likeness* to others was released. He began to seek out classmates whose interests and capacities were similar to his own. Although most tenuously, with much caution and retreat at the slightest rebuff, a thrust toward growth in the area of friendships was reinstated. He would enthusiastically report long conversations with classmates and shared activities.

Much slower in emerging was his capacity to respond to overtures from faculty members and a particular professor in whose class his work was apparently exceptional. His reserve gave way as, with the understanding gained in therapy of his fear of opening himself to the risk of the trauma, rebuff by or loss of an idealized figure, he was gradually able to respond to his friendly instructor's seeking him out and explaining his own bewilderment at the student's standoffishness.

It is of no small interest that the course involved a branch of physics in which the forces and tides of large bodies of water were being examined. As therapy terminated, this young man had developed a strong idealizing transference to his instructor and had undertaken a research project with him. Prominent in their relationship was the partnership between the two, the older man's ability to work along with him, their solving knotty problems together and moving on to the next phase of their work. Moreover, in prolonged absences of his instructor, the student was now able to proceed with zest on his own in his research.

The transference needs which emerge in therapy shift and change, representing not so much the chaotic bits of a kaleidoscope settling into a clear and well-formed design as a spectrum when white light passes through a prism. The therapist functions as that prism, permitting an exploration and examination of the broad range of feelings and behavior and enabling that wide range of feelings and behavior to then reintegrate as white light—a cohesive, vital, harmonious self, with the zest to shape talents into skills. That capacity permits an individual to feel in charge of himself and his purpose in life.

Kohut believed that self psychology must pursue an understanding of the changing, maturing course of mirroring, idealizing, and twinship needs *from birth to the end of life*, in normal development and in pathology. And it is these changing needs emerging in transferences that the therapist as new selfobject seeks to understand.

These transferences expose deficits in self structure and elicit the response of the therapist, who can now help the individual to *understand* earlier unfulfilled longings to be comforted, admired, stimulated, preferred, and forgiven (Basch, 1980). This growing awareness of how things were, this union of affect and cognition, can now free him for taking even hesitant steps toward seeing how things can be. He can, in partnership with the therapist, contemplate a changing and expanded vision of himself. The feeling states which the individual arouses in the therapist, described as countertransference, also play a diagnostic role. When freed from the therapist's own personal agenda, countertransference becomes available for understanding the help the individual is seeking in order to transmute missing functions into self-functions.

The selfobject functions which the therapist performs have been described by Gedo and Goldberg (1973) as pacification, unification, optimal frustration, interpretation—all potentially culminating in self-awareness (Basch, 1980). By this we understand that a process is set in motion through which the therapist is able to provide his calm understanding, absorbing stress that has proved overwhelming, in much the same way that an adult picks up a frightened, hurt, or angry child. But it is the therapist's *understanding* which now provides the equivalent. A further step is in helping the individual to bring order out of what happened. "Let's see what happened; tell me again how it came about." And it is this process which helps the individual order his universe. The therapist's calm, enfolding *understanding* provides the conditions for an empathic merger through which the individual can now bear to confront his own part in the events that came to be. This optimal frustration, with the therapist as understanding selfobject, allows the individual to examine his behavior without destructive self-blame but with recognition of what his contribution may have been. This can open the way to interpretation and to the ability to understand the childhood roots of the present dilemma. With this understanding the individual can dare to initiate new behavior.

It is also optimal frustration when the therapist misunderstands, and the individual is able to set things right in a continuing dialogue. Such dialogue has been foreclosed to him by earlier selfobjects, who may have been unable to brook contradiction or who were not adequately available. His thoughts and behavior take on clarity and enlarged meaning, opening the way for the development of reliable self-awareness.

It is with the therapist as a new selfobject in the present that the process of healing and filling in of earlier deficits takes place. Through myriad bits of interplay, the missing functions of monitoring stress, self-soothing, and mastery are realized (transmuted) in self-functions of a cohesive, expanding self. It is in the employment of self-functions that the individual now finds the vigor and courage to undertake new paths or to redirect himself along older paths. Feeling valued, he can now value himself, value others, and respond to them. The world of selfobjects now becomes one which is not exploitive; nor is he exploited in it. A vigorous, harmonious, cohesive self can now seek goals and relationships that are fulfilling and enriching, with tensile strength—the ability to recover from trauma—to endure inevitable adversity and to enjoy achievement.

In the cases that follow, we shall illustrate the process described above from the initial phase of treatment, through its intermediate stage, and finally to termination. They are drawn from specific periods in the life cycle and represent typical problems. We shall illustrate the manner in which the therapist absorbs intense emotional states that threaten the integrity of the self, allowing the individual to understand and, by her interpretation, helping him to bring order to chaotic events. There is healing power contained in the therapist's remembering the events in the individual's life, the words used to describe it, the feelings disavowed at the time but identified in the present (Basch, 1983b). Cognitive awareness is added so that the individual now knows that he hurts, what has hurt him, and why. Instead of struggling with bits and pieces held together haphazardly and prone to fragmentation, the individual comes under the healing power of being heard and responded to, allowing the bits and pieces to come together in a sense of continuity and history. The therapist as a new selfobject in the present, a selfobject who remembers and reacts, thus allows the individual to identify a wider array of feelings and to use these in monitoring anxiety, regulating self-esteem, and seeking mentors, companions, and activities to assist in the establishment or restoration of a cohesive self for whom life can become meaningful and purposeful.

There is a natural congruence between the social work treatment process and the insights provided by the theory of self psychology. Using their mature psychic structure to provide initially for missing structure in those they treat—performing selfobject functions—is an old and familiar experience for social work practitioners. Self psychology now supplies an understanding of why this is so and how selfobject functions may be understood and directed.

Our discussion thus far has centered on the reawakening of transference needs thwarted in the past and expressed with driven intensity in current life problems. Renewed and given legitimacy, these needs are understood not only in their childhood antecedents but as cues of expected behavior from the therapist. As new selfobject, the therapist serves as releaser of maturational development (Lachmann, 1984). Since empathy is the means by which the therapist gains access to an understanding of the individual who seeks help for emotional or behavioral difficulties, we must examine the manner in which empathy and introspection become the tools of clinical social work and of psychotherapy.

Kohut continually developed and deepened his understanding of these terms, from the time of the first formal presentation of his views, "Introspection, Empathy and Psychoanalysis: An Examination of the Relationship between Mode of Observation and Theory," presented in 1957 (published in 1959), through to the posthumous publication (1984) of *How Does Analysis Cure?* Kohut did not claim that self psychology provided psychoanalysis with a new kind of empathy; he claimed only that it had supplied analysis with new theories that *broaden and deepen* the field of empathic perception.

Kohut defined empathy as "vicarious introspection," an attempt to experience the inner life of another while simultaneously retaining the stance of an objective observer. It is employed, therefore, to define the area under exploration and to gather data for understanding and then explaining to the individual the nature of his pathology, its childhood origins, and its reverberation to the present.

In the analysis of the psychoneuroses, frequency of sessions, use of the couch, and free association—that is, the obligation to say whatever comes to mind—foster the development of a transference neurosis. "The individual transfers to the person of the analyst incestuous oedipal wishes which had previously been dealt with by neurotic symptom formation" (Basch, 1980, p. 39). Oedipal conflict arises by reason of the "too close, too distant, or too unreliable response" of earlier selfobjects to the developing needs of the individual in the oedipal phase; resolution of the oedipal conflict is central to the treatment of structural neurosis by analysis. But, as we have seen, it was by his use of empathy and introspection that Kohut gradually recognized earlier transference needs. In the unfolding of these transference needs, he was not an incestuous object to be loved or a hated rival to be overcome. Instead he was "the direct continuation of external reality [the archaic parental selfobject milieu] that [had been] too distant, too rejecting or too unreliable to be transformed into solid psychic structure" (Kohut, 1984, p. 219).

Kohut ultimately described these transferences as mirroring, idealizing, and alter-ego or twinship needs. The analyst's empathic intuneness provides the conditions under which these needs are reawakened, accepted, understood, and given recognition as legitimate. Through inevitable disruption, interruption, and reinstitution of the analyst's empathic selfobject functions, earlier deficits are filled in. The individual becomes more reliably capable of modifying and meeting his needs through shaping his abilities and widening his circle of selfobjects. Newly acquired or restored psychic structure leads, then, to a renewal of oedipal longings and strivings, which can now be relived with the analyst, who provides nurturant responses allowing the integration of sexuality and the relinquishment of symptomatic neurotic behavior or thought.

In clinical social work, as in analysis, empathy defines the field of observation and also serves as a means of gathering data. It is the controlled immersion in the psychic life of another for the purpose of the treatment and amelioration of states of imbalance or self-defeating behavior. But the goal of intervention is more narrowly focused and delimited.

Much of social work practice is with seriously disadvantaged populations whose difficulties reflect generations of untreated psychical and emotional illness and the economic deprivation and family disruption which flow from these difficulties. Many individuals who seek agency help or who are mandated for treatment are highly vulnerable to narcissistic injury and fragment readily. They are described as "multiproblem" individuals and families, "hard to reach," "early dropouts." And yet we can observe in our work how in the initial phase of treatment there is exposed the earliest need for mirroring, for affirmation, for guidance, as well as the earliest wish for merging with idealized wisdom and strength. The theory of self psychology does not propose simple mirroring or an unguided opportunity to use the practitioner as the target of idealization. The therapist continuously absorbs data from the individual's spoken words and unspoken behavior. Her empathic absorption allows her to formulate assumptions about the individual's inner state as he attempts to function within a complex environment. Empathically in tune with that individual's readiness and ability to consider her tentative formulations, she shares these; they can then be affirmed, elaborated, or contradicted. Failures in her understanding can be set to right by the individual and may lead to an enhancement of his own capacity for self-righting. Occasionally, the simple act of absorbed, empathically focused listening can provide a source of limited healing.

The following example is used only to illustrate how the experience of being heard can enable an individual to feel strengthened and, with that renewed strength, to draw on inner resources and undertake behavior which a weakened self could not contemplate.

Mrs. K.

A neophyte social worker was in tears because she could think of nothing to say or do with Mrs. K., a single mother of six children who had been seeing her on a once-a-week basis without missing a single appointment in eight weeks. The burdens of this mother were enormous. She had been referred to the agency for help in managing two of her children, who were in school difficulty for persistent tardiness and school absence. The problems of coping unaided with the needs of six children under the age of 14 would have taxed a highly organized, well-functioning individual. Yet this mother never missed an appointment and was always on time. In fact, the social worker reported to her supervisor that Mrs. K. would often just plop down in her chair and say nothing for several minutes while her rapid breathing, testimony to the energy she had expended in getting there on time, subsided. As the social worker was encouraged to extend her empathic introspection to consider what might make this time and place so important to this mother that she never missed her appointment, she gradually recalled several of the mother's comments: "It feels so good to be here. . . . You don't scold or tell me what to do. . . . You're so young but you seem to understand. . . . You remember what I say even though you see a lot of people. . . . I just can't get myself together. . . . I feel more together—like when I leave here, then I know what to do next."

We shall see that the pacifying and unifying selfobject functions which this neophyte practitioner provided constitute only an element in the process of working with Mrs. K. An experienced worker might have been able to move the process ahead with more purpose as she explored with the mother various community resources for the younger children, worked with her toward unifying clinic services for medical problems, and considered with her whether additional treatment services were needed for the children who were in difficulty at school. But this mother could respond to being the focus of attention to her needs. Without competing demands for this interval of time, for this space in her week, she had the experience of being heard, of being appropriately preferred, and this was comforting. In other instances the caseworker's youth might have been resented, but in this case it was not; to talk to and with a young worker stimulated her. Subsequent interviews indicated that this contact had reestablished a continuity for Mrs. K. with her own past in which her earlier hopes and aspirations had been formulated. She responded to this worker's genuine admiration for her courage and determination in staying with her children, in trying against great odds to meet their needs. In a new self/selfobject unit, even with a neophyte practitioner, the earliest need to be admired was rekindled, there was a response to her earliest longing to be enfolded in the strength of an idealized selfobject.

The experience of being idealized can evoke anxiety in experienced as well as inexperienced social workers. But self psychology teaches us that if the practitioner can understand the need of the individual with whom she is working to use her as a target of idealization in the process of structure building, then she can modulate the anxiety arising from the stimulation of her own grandiosity or from the recognition that there are areas in her professional training that are as yet unfulfilled. In her subsequent work with Mrs. K., this young worker was able to provide the conditions under which a degree of healing, of structure building or restoration, could take place. The twin experience of being mirrored, confirmed, and guided, and of being provided an opportunity to merge with an individual who functioned well, allowed Mrs. K. to feel in charge of herself. This enabled her to work with her children in establishing more regular bedtimes and mealtimes; the problem with school absence and tardiness dropped away.

This brief example is only a fragment of a treatment process that extended over several years beyond the worker's placement with the agency. Indeed, one of the therapist's concerns was that, when she left the agency, Mrs. K. would lose what she had gained from the relationship. The genuine conviction that the work they had done together would not go away must be based on realistic assessment of the degree to which there is evidence of repair or restoration in cohesiveness and vigor of the nuclear self. Mrs. K. expressed sorrow at her therapist's leaving; her therapist also experienced sorrow at having to transfer Mrs. K. to another worker.

The reaction to loss and separation may be profound and give rise to secondary disorders of the self. But it may also provide an opportunity for firming and deepening the capacity to accept life's vicissitudes and to seek and accept new selfobjects. Mrs K. did so not out of shallowness, but out of the structure-building and life-enhancing recognition that the world was a friendlier, more responsive place in which to rear her children and to pursue a rewarding life for herself. The practitioner also experienced a deepening and firming of her professional self. A vital element of that professional self was the continuous refining and improving of empathic awareness of the unfolding and changing needs and strengths of the individuals she treated.

THE PROFESSIONAL SELF OF THE SOCIAL WORKER

The professional self of the social worker, no less than the self of the individuals with whom she works, undergoes transformation. Self psychology offers an understanding of how this comes about. Just as there is a great variety of selfobject relations that support the cohesion, vigor, and harmony of the adult self, so too is there a great variety of selfobject relations through which the social worker acquires the cohesive, vigorous, harmonious structure of a professional self. Mentors in coursework and fieldwork, as well as writers and practitioners in related fields, become the idealized prestructural selfobjects. Their selfobject functions mature, then, into the self-functions of a professional social worker.

A glimpse into the childhood roots of this process may be illustrative. Several years ago, in a class on the "Self of the Social Worker," I asked a group of students to describe the earliest roots of their interest in social work. In surprising numbers they cited episodes reaching back to preschool years. Their earliest recollections were of trying to assuage the sorrows of family members or to assist them in surmounting difficult problems. Long before empathy as a mature use of self could have been achieved, these students came to fulfill the role of helper throughout childhood. One example will illustrate this.

A young woman wrote that when, as a small child, for the first time she saw her mother burst into tears, her whole world shook as if by earthquake. She was so young she had to reach up to take her mother's hand in hers, and, from her own sense of desolation, clung to her mother's knees. She wrote, "My mother's tears flowed from my eyes, my body trembled with her sobs." Her mother mistook this for an act of sympathetic understanding on the part of the child, and from that point on the child was perceived as someone who could be counted on to understand and to help. Her self-esteem was rooted in this capacity, for she seemed able to allow a calming and soothing use of herself to family members at times of acute stress. As she matured, her sense of pleasure in her effectiveness and the response of others to this led her into fields of learning and knowledge focused on human needs. She eagerly sought ways of understanding behavior and the manner in which individuals realized their aspirations or were thwarted in such aspirations by problems arising within them or by reason of external problems rooted in family or society. In time she turned to social work as a profession.

From this vignette I do not mean to suggest, in simplistic manner, a direct line of cause and effect, or that all social workers find their profession through such early experience, although it is likely that they and other members of the mental health profession have analogous background experiences in their choice of a profession.

Acquiring a professional self entails graduate training in a school of social work leading to the master's degree. It encompasses study of the person in a social context brewed of the interaction of psychological, familial, economic, and cultural factors. Training in modes of intervention with individuals, families, and groups—clinical social work—constitutes a field of specialization within social work. Other areas of specialization include community work; management and leadership of social organizations; design and implementation of public policies at federal, state, and local levels; and research arising from issues in clinical social work practice and social policy. The ability to recognize, define, and institute measures of prevention for vulnerable populations focuses attention on such varied groups as the mentally and physically disabled; children and families with impaired capacities for successful growth and development; elderly people whose capacities for independent living are similarly impaired; young people with problems at home, school, or in their communities; individuals whose behavior is self-destructive or harmful to others; those who lack skills for any but the most rudimentary jobs; victims of crime, discrimination, violence and serious illness; and residents of deteriorating, poorly serviced communities and neighborhoods.*

The student who selects clinical social work as an area of specialization continues the study of interpersonal and intrapsychic theory following graduation and continues the practice of clinical social work under supervision. Currently, the doctoral level of clinical social work is offered by some schools.

Of the many theories of human development to which social workers have turned, self psychology uniquely describes the living experience of social work practice. Kohut's theories provide us with an understanding of how, with the practitioner as new selfobject in the present, the thrust to continue growth may be reawakened and specific deficits may be healed. Even though the deficits may be deepseated and extensive, the process of structure building may be rekindled. We shall see in our later discussion how small gains become absorbed and provide a micro enhancement of the capacity to delay, to reflect on, and to plan behavior.

---

* "Statement of Purpose," *School of Social Service Administration, University of Chicago*, 1984.

The self of the practitioner becomes a diagnostic tool through whom such transference needs as the wish to be comforted, admired, stimulated, preferred, and forgiven can be understood. As a new selfobject, the practitioner does not function as a better mother or father, but, rather, provides a new opportunity for structure building as she performs those functions which the individual lacks, or possesses in immature or impoverished state. It is not that she takes over and does for him what he cannot do for himself. Her function is to help him understand his needs and wishes in the present, as well as their childhood roots.

Within this new self/selfobject unit the individual experiences an empathic response. The healing function which social workers perform is contained in that empathic response to the needs of troubled individuals and families. Such individuals struggle not to be overlooked or discarded but to be recognized as worthwhile. They seek renewal and purpose in their lives and in this search they borrow the strength, the mature psychic structure of the social worker as an intermediary process in acquiring or restoring their own. Self psychology with its concept of the selfobject enables us to understand why and how such a process is restorative. The social worker is that selfobject through whom their ambitions, however modest, can be recognized. It is with the calmness and competence of the social worker as idealized selfobject that the individual can merge as he strives to formulate and reach his goals. Through her response to specific and unique mirroring and idealizing needs, he takes inside, as self-functions, the capacity to calm and to soothe himself, to regulate his self-esteem as he meets obstacles and strives to work toward goals he has formulated. The tools which the social worker employs in this process are empathy and introspection, an integral part of the professional self.

THE TREATMENT PROCESS

Although in subsequent chapters we will be considering the treatment process in a variety of cases across the life cycle, the following outline is an attempt to structure the process. It should not be regarded as a rigid formula; it is suggestive only and offers an opportunity to reflect on what transpires in treatment. Although treatment has a beginning and an end, there will be many setbacks along the way, providing for reworking and strengthening the individual's ability to understand himself and to respond to others, to initiate activities in response to his own needs and wishes and to those of others.

From the outset and throughout treatment, the therapist is alert to the diagnostic implications revealed by the vicissitudes of the relationship.

The individual will test the therapist both verbally and behaviorally. There is a delicate balance between hope aroused when needs are understood and the fear engendered by the intensification of these needs, which the therapist in the present, like selfobjects in the past, may fail to recognize (Wolf, 1981). The very intensity of reactivated needs may bring about a degree of withdrawal on the part of the therapist, triggering narcissistic rage in the individual. Kohut (1971) likens the explosion of rage when a selfobject fails to respond to a vulnerable individual as equivalent to the explosion occasioned by the fission of an atom. It is difficult to recognize that at such times the individual self is in pain and need and attempts to marshall whatever resources are available, even negative behavior or withdrawal, in order to convince the carrier of selfobject functions to supply these functions (Wolf, 1981). When this occurs, and when the therapist can by introspection begin to understand what may have caused her own withdrawal, she then may bring to the attention of the individual his understandable reaction to that lessened attention. The therapeutic dialogue is reestablished and the treatment process, once again, continues. There may, however, follow a regressive period of lessened cohesion in the individual, of acting-out, which has the defensive purpose of maintaining the old self structure and holding the disappointing selfobject at a safer distance (Wolf, 1981). Despite the fact that such behavior is counterproductive and has been the very reason an individual has sought treatment in the first place, the individual may cling to these archaic modes until he can once more endure, permit, and seek the selfobject functions provided by the therapist. Ultimately, because of the acquisition of reliable self structure, he will be able to establish and experience empathic resonance beyond therapy in his own social world.

Termination is determined both by the nature of the difficulty for which the individual has sought help initially and by mutually agreed upon goals. It is typical of the termination period that earlier states of fragmentation may reappear, as the individual once again tests the process of growth and change with the firmer structure of a cohesive self and with the requisite strength to withstand and overcome temporary setbacks.

In outline form, the treatment process may, then be rendered as follows:

1) A sustaining matrix, self/selfobject unit, is established.
2) The therapist is a new selfobject.
3) Emergence of transference needs and wishes are monitored and recognized as mirroring, idealizing, or twinship (partnering).
4) The therapist seeks to understand the emergence of the transference in the contemporary self/selfobject unit and its childhood roots.
5) Countertransference manifestations are explored for their diagnostic

significance: how do these self states reflect needs and wishes of the individual being treated?

6) Manifestations of defense are recognized as basic to the protecton of a weakened self (an intrapsychic phenomenon) or as response to a failure in empathy on the part of the therapist.

7) Manifestations of resistance are explored as an individual's effort to protect himself against reexperiencing the trauma of failure of empathy, its sequelae in shame, and fear of punishment reverberating from past selfobjects.

8) Such reverberations are understood and interpreted to bring about the lessening of defense and resistance. This allows a degree of controlled regression by focused empathic understanding, which provides a healing and soothing function.

9) The individual's reactivated developmental need is tentatively exposed and structure building is reinstated through transmuting internalization of the therapist's selfobject functions into micro selffunctions.

10) Optimal frustration becomes the facilitating force in transmuting internalization: micro failures in selfobject function set the stage for structure building and acquisition of self-functions.

11) As the hermeneutic cycle of understanding and interpretation offer the individual an opportunity for confirmation, elaboration, or contradiction, structure building is fostered.

12) A renewed cycle of defense and resistance may be anticipated as the individual seeks once more to avoid reexposure to the intensity of feeling.

13) The individual acquires an ever increasing ability to recognize and integrate what was once disavowed, leading to the repair of deficits in self-esteem regulation, and to increasing firmness and resilience of the cohesive nuclear self.

14) As the individual can now trust his perceptions and initiate activities from the center of his own being, a functional continuum is established from grandiose ambitions shaped by skills and talents to be directed toward realizable goals.

The process of treatment is replete with cycles of disruption and restoration of the therapeutic dialogue from beginning to end. As long as these are not too severe or too prolonged, they serve "to increase the trust that one can be understood and that one can learn to understand others" (Wolf, 1984b, p. 155). Self psychology allows us to understand that the phenomena of defense and resistance following these disruptions are not directed against the drives. Instead they are desperate attempts

to protect a fragmentation-prone self from the pain of new selfobject failures.

The treatment process outlined above has been adapted from discussions and publications of Kohut (1971, 1977, 1984) and of Wolf (1979, 1981, 1984b). Addressed to analysis for the purpose of analysis, its relevance for psychotherapy is determined by more limited goals (Goldberg, 1977; Basch, 1980, 1984). Its applicability is also determined by the manner in which transference and countertransference manifestations are responded to. In the following chapter we shall examine and explore those differences, historically and in current practice.

6

Transference and Countertransference

TRANSFERENCE IS UBIQUITOUS, existing wherever there is relationship. It is an expectational set derived from earliest experiences of the infant with his caretakers. It may be continuously enriched and strengthened so that the individual responds to new relationships with hope and the capacity for productive interchange, or it may be based in deprivation and inconsistency, resulting in despair and distorted expectations leading to conflict and disruption. The expectation that another individual will respond in specific ways leads to behavior which evokes such a response and thus confirms and entrenches behavior patterns. In treatment, both insight and new experience allow an individual to contemplate and then institute changes.

The patient's transference of expectations to the therapist exerts pressure on the latter to behave in ways conforming to these prior expectations. These expectations arouse countertransference reactions. In analysis, interpretation of the transference is the central focus of the treatment process. In psychotherapy and clinical social work, such interpretation is limited and controlled.

It is not my purpose here to summarize the vast literature on transference and countertransference. Rather, I will examine the history of these concepts in social work practice and consider how they are employed.

Social work from its inception was engaged with individuals who struggled to find meaning and worth in their lives. Overburdened, understimulated, and fragmenting, such individuals searched for connectedness, for an opportunity to achieve attachment to others, to find a way into the mainstream of society. Their needs, expectations, and wishes, transferred to the social workers who sought to help them, by their very intensity aroused disturbing feelings in these helpers. Individuals with severe deficits need to attach those who help them in order to feel whole. Individuals in dire need, whether of food, housing, employment and medical care, or of support and intervention to ameliorate emotional disturbance, tax the resourcefulness and reserves of those who seek to help them. Social workers, thus, may feel helplessly drawn into the vortex of these chaotic lives.

It is not accidental that the professionalization of social work took place in the climate of new insights into human behavior infused by the concepts of psychoanalysis. Early theorists in social work were not only wide readers in psychoanalytic literature, but also frequently in analysis themselves. Their understanding of the centrality of relationship in the casework process and their concern with working with this relationship productively prompted these theorists to surround the concepts of transference and countertransference with cautionary instructions, which were at times confusing and contradictory. Perhaps Towle most clearly recognized that transference was ubiquitous. She viewed the urge to be at one with others as a fundamental human urge rooted in the child's experience of being mothered. She sought to teach social workers that in the unfolding casework process, the individual may need to go through a process of identification with the caseworker, taking in her ways and attitudes and striving to meet situations as she would meet them. In this period of emotional dependency, if the social worker fears dependency and flees from the client's needs as a "bugaboo" never to be aroused, she will lose the opportunity to respond appropriately in a growth-enhancing manner. Towle differentiated the nature of the transference in analysis—its development, its interpretation, and its resolution—from its appearance in casework. "To be sure, in many instances the feelings of the client may be more diluted and the projections less distorted—but they are there in *shadow form* and consequently may be less clear and less comprehensive. In order to understand how the client is using or responding to him, the worker must be able to examine his own feelings and behavior in order to examine the client's reactions" (emphasis supplied, Towle, 1935, p. 35).

Thus, transference and countertransference manifestations were part of the relationship; they were to be understood and responded to as they emerged in the present, illuminating, as well, their childhood origins.

As social workers began to understand the transferential aspects of their relationships with their clients, there was a growing emphasis on helping the client to bring his feelings for the worker to a conscious level through verbalization. Although Burling (1934) stressed the value of explicit acknowledgment of the transference in social casework, stemming from his own training as a psychiatrist, Bibring, from her work as a psychiatric consultant in social agencies, recognized the "environmental approach" as the unique contribution of social work (1947). Seeking to differentiate the treatment process of social casework from that of psycho-analytic and psychiatric practice, theorists of the developing and expanding field of social work struggled with definition of the unique manifestations of transference in casework practice.

Garrett (1950) pointed out that, in varying degrees, transference and countertransference existed in all aspects of casework and required the caseworker's understanding, but casework was part of the client's reality: giving relief, placing children, suggesting resources of various kinds, medical opportunities, etc. In casework practice transference was not supported to foster infantile dependence.

Hamilton (1951) emphasized that, although transference is a major component in all forms of psychotherapy, in casework reactivation of past feelings is a less dominant focus than expression of current emotions mobilized around specific situations. Although the treatment situation is used to release feeling, to support ego, to increase self-awareness by bringing to the client's attention attitudes and behavior, both in life experience and in the interviewing situation, emphasis tended to be more on the current experience. The caseworker's tendency was to use transference to redirect the client's psychological energies into reality channels (p. 210).

Yet Hamilton also stressed that it was not possible to "restrict the casework function to the modification of 'outer conditions' since the problem is usually intrapsychic as well as social. . . . Not only can one not successfully separate environment and emotional factors, but the client's psychological insights are put to use in meeting 'real situations'" (p. 4). "The essential nature of basic conflict must however be understood in any truly therapeutic endeavor, even though that conflict may not be touched directly in limited forms of therapy" (p. 84).

These were early imprints on the developing field of social work. Throughout the 1940s and '50s, psychoanalytic concepts attracted social workers as a means of understanding human development and behavior. Just as previous concentration had been on the environment and economic forces, now concentration focused on the worker's own psychological functioning. Knowing and accepting oneself was critical to knowing and accepting others; the essential nature of the basic conflict must be understood in any truly therapeutic endeavor. Transference and countertransference were to be recognized as important elements in the process, although social workers were urged to modulate and control the type and depth of transference reactions so that the forces of the unconscious—of which transference was only one manifestation—would not be unleashed to overwhelm client and worker.

In her problem-solving approach, Perlman (1957) urged that, by maintaining the relationship on a realistic basis, the transference, when manifest, need not be excited. Although transference must be recognized, identified, and dealt with, the caseworker must manage the relationship and problem-solving work so that "excitation of the transference would be minimal"—managed rather than used in a search for patterns of behavior and for insight into origins and meanings.

Austin (1956) stressed that transference and countertransference should be regulated and selectively interpreted as they emerged, in order to allow the development of insight. Garrett (1958) elaborated the difference between the transference neurosis, which is the focus of treatment in analysis, and other forms of transference, while emphasizing that "transference reactions can no more be avoided in a helping relationship than can reality manifestation." Transference could be managed by cautious interpretation recognizing the client's current feelings. Interpretation would remove the distortion of transference reactions and permit reality to hold sway.

Along with enthusiastic adoption of psychoanalytic concepts, however, concern began to center on the fear "that casework had become so preoccupied with the inner life as almost to lose touch with outer reality and the social factors with which social workers were most familiar" (Hamilton, 1958, p. 23). It was necessary to recognize that there were broad areas of service and specialization for which the concepts of transference and countertransference had less relevance.

Hollis (1964), describing casework as a psychosocial therapy, pointed out that, for example, transference reactions might have little bearing when a worker was seen as an expert in treating certain problems. Yet she recognized that there were periods within therapy when attention must be given to dynamic and developmental issues in order to release temporarily blocked functioning. Once this was accomplished, the way would be cleared for better perception and handling of current affairs (p. 158). She differentiated these from tranference cures, in which a positive transference might enable a client temporarily to find support in the relationship, thereby lessening the effect of factors contributing to his maladaptive behavior and easing his distress by allowing him time to reflect and marshall his inner resources.

In some detail, Hollis (1964; Hollis and Woods, 1981) emphasized that the fear of going too deeply in interpreting transference reactions was based on misunderstanding. Such fear arose from a lack of clarity about the elements of transference as they appeared in clinical social work. Hollis and Woods recognized irrational elements in the relationship affected by childhood experiences, even those based in infancy and early childhood. They believed there was no more danger in touching upon these elements as they appear in the transference than in other elements of communication. Like others before them, they stressed the marked difference between casework and psychoanalysis. The client might reexperience a phenomenon from early childhood in a fragmentary way but he was not encouraged to regress. Reality elements of the relationship controlled the degree of transference: face-to-face interviews once or twice a week as against more frequent interviews and the use of the couch. The individual was encouraged to speak freely, but this was vastly different from the obligation in analysis to say whatever came to mind. The latter obligation fostered regression; it repeated earlier experiences of feeling like a disobedient child if one failed to, or, if one did reveal one's thoughts, coerced to confess to wrongdoing and to expose oneself to punishment. Free association fostered reliving with the analyst such early childhood experiences—thus, the development of a transference neurosis. The social worker did not seek to establish such a transference.

Social work theorists continued to examine the thrust of transference, its implications, and its management in various fields of social work, particularly in clinical social work (Blanck and Blanck, 1974; Goldstein, 1984). Perlman (1979) noted, ''the rise of associations between past and present needs, frustrations or sought-for gratification, is almost inevitable. Sometimes, then, evidences of transference must be dealt with directly . . . (showing) acceptance of the naturalness and understandability of the client's association at the same time he places before the client some correction of vision. . . . (T)hus—gently, firmly—drawing the person back into this time and this place and *this* transaction'' (p. 77). In sum, these leading theorists struggled to define transference manifestations and to offer guidelines for their control.

It is precisely here that self psychology so clearly illuminates the concept of transference. For it is not that the individual mistakenly views the practitioner in a parental capacity, not that he mistakenly attributes to the practitioner past associations, frustrations, or sought for gratifications. What he is seeking from the practitioner as new selfobject in the present is a response to legitimate needs for structure building. And as these needs are exposed in mirroring, idealizing, or partnering transferences, the individual seeks the wherewithal from the practitioner—the selfobject functions—that he may then transform into his own self-functions. It is the wish to be understood in the present for which he seeks gratification. These are not irrational elements in the therapeutic relationship, as Hollis suggests, but legitimate needs. Indeed, Hollis appropriately recognizes that there is no more danger in touching upon these elements as they appear in the transference than upon other elements of communication. Social work theorists cautioned practitioners to avoid fostering or exciting the transference neurosis, yet this is a transference phenomenon which arises primarily in the context of analysis.

As Basch has pointed out,

[This is] a pseudo problem that often prevents a student from learning how to deal effectively with transference feelings. The fear is that, by encouraging the emergence of transference feelings, the therapist may open a Pandora's box of sexual and aggressive feelings that cannot be controlled. This fear, however, is based on a confusion between transference, a ubiquitous phenomenon, and transference neurosis, a rare variant form, iatrogenically promoted for the specific purpose of carrying out a psychoanalysis. The transference neurosis is exactly what its name says it is. It is the transfer to the person of the analyst of incestuous oedipal wishes which had previously been dealt with by neurotic symptom formation. The fear that the psychotherapist will inadvertently precipitate a transference neurosis and put himself and the patient in an untenable posture has led to the idea that transference in psychotherapy should be avoided if possible, and, if it does manifest itself, should be minimized by avoidance or generalization. (Basch, 1984, p. 39)

Few individuals who appear in social agencies exhibit the sequelae of neurotic conflict. More frequently, *neurotic-like behavior* covers over *self deficits* in the bipolar self.

It is precisely our expanded understanding of transference as it is described in self psychology that makes it possible for social work practitioners to respond with improved understanding to the strivings of those who come for help. "Hope, wish and fear are names for patterns of expectations that either develop directly through experience or are taught by example. Once established, these anticipatory configurations are mobilized in response to situations that resemble, or seem to resemble, the original conditions that gave rise to the pattern. This process is called *transference*" (Basch, 1984, p. 35). "It is the basis of all meaningful relationships, including the therapeutic relationship" (Basch, 1980, p. 36).

Self psychology has enabled us to differentiate transferential phenomena in psychotherapy and analysis more effectively. Such transference needs as the wish to be comforted, stimulated, admired, preferred, and forgiven (Basch, 1980, 1984) are expressed in mirroring, partnering, or idealizing transferences. The practitioner responds to such needs not by gratifying them but by enabling the individual to understand his longings, the situation in which they arose, and their legitimacy. Such needs are not dismissed; they are understood in the present. Although the therapist cannot change an unfortunate childhood, her focused empathic understanding in the present can aid the individual in resuming his interrupted development with new understanding. With the therapist as the new carrier of selfobject functions in the present, the developmental process is freed. Optimal frustration, rather than frustration of traumatic proportions, now permits selfobject functions to become the unique self-functions, the psychic structure of the individual. Cohesive, harmonious balance is achieved, and when inevitable disturbances in this balance occur, the individual now is capable of "self-righting" or newly acquired reliable regulation of self-esteem and the capacity to find and use selfobjects within his environment (M. Tolpin, 1982).

It is precisely the individual's experience of the therapist in the present transference that creates the conditions for healing, for resuming the interrupted developmental process. The question we must address is how and when transference is made manifest to the individual in psychotherapy.

In the cases presented in subsequent chapters, transference and countertransference manifestations are never out of the therapist's empathic focus, though they are at times obscure and confused. The therapist seeks to overcome the confusion, to illuminate what is obscure. To do so, she uses herself as a diagnostic tool, alert to the individual's striving to achieve closeness or maintain distance, as well as to her own behavior which may have triggered the response. In addition to verbal communication, affect—its absence, distortion, displacement, or exaggeration—is an "alphabet of communication" (Basch, 1983a) to which the therapist remains sensitively alert. When inevitable failures occur and the dialogue is derailed, the therapist seeks to understand the cause of the interruption—not by a confrontation but by allying herself with the individual's fear of humiliation, injury, or exposure once more to a repetition of past trauma echoed by something in the present.

Self psychology offers casework practitioners an alternative understanding of defense and resistance as these arise in the transference. Individuals cling to self-defeating or self-destructive thought and behavior even though they are engaged in treatment for these difficulties. Over the course of the therapeutic endeavor, there are innumerable intervals of defense and resistance. Kohut points out that fear of rejection or humiliation, which is the basis of defense and resistance, gradually subsides when it is recognized and accepted as understandably self-protective. The therapist's empathic intuneness dissipates the need for defense and resistance. In the working-through process, the repeated experiences of defense and resistance, if met with acceptance, understanding, and explanation (Kohut, 1984), will enable the individual to endure his sensitivity to seeming slight, to the preference of others. Each cycle of disruption and restoration of cohesiveness is accompanied by increased insight, as the therapist strives to remain empathically in tune. When empathic failures occur, the work of therapy is to offer plausible reasons, to which the individual responds with his own description of the experience. As we have already

discussed, Wolf (1979) describes this as an hermeneutic cycle of speculation, confirmation, or correction. The individual experiences a failure of
empathy as a loss of a necessary selfobject function. As Kohut has described it (1984), each loss of a selfobject function is replaced by a self-
function, as long as the loss is within that degree of frustration that the
individual can tolerate. It is this loss of a selfobject function and its replacement by a self-function that leads to restored structure building.

It is one thing for an individual to achieve increased awareness of his
transference needs and wishes. It is another to be able to communicate
these needs and wishes in place of responding to hurts and slights with
feeling states and behaviors which distance him from others. In innumerable repetitions of misunderstanding, silent withdrawal, or narcissistic
rage, the individual comes to distinguish his own contribution from that
of others. In minute bits he acquires the resilience to withstand the vicissitudes of social and work relationships, of all relationships. From the
crucible of the therapeutic relationship, he draws understanding, explanation, the capacity to reflect, to verbalize, to act when indicated, and to take
pleasure in his ability to control his life rather than to be its helpless victim. These restored or newly won capacities allow him now to turn to the
world outside the treatment setting with renewed or newly acquired
strength.

In clinical and social work practice, response to and interpretation of
the transference will focus more directly on the specifics of the relationship between individual and therapist, as these intrude and obstruct with
their childhood antecedents, than would be the case in the broad range
of casework in agency settings.

Clinical social work at its most advanced level is not distinguishable from
psychotherapy conducted by psychiatrists or psychologists. Attempts to
differentiate it reflect a social phenomenon deriving from separate histories
of different professions, rather than factual differences (Watson, 1966).
Psychotherapy and clinical social work alike focus on intrapsychic disturbance and its impact on interpersonal objectives. The playing out of intrapsychic conflicts in the therapeutic relationship constitutes the transference; the therapist's reactions to being the target of expectations, wishes,
and fantasies derived from past experiences constitute the countertransference. The past leads an individual to respond to events and relationships by way of realistic and transferential reactions in 1) current events;
2) current relations in the treatment situation; 3) events of the patient's
past.

It is this interpretation of the specific transference manifestation within
the self/selfobject unit that frees the individual from his tendency to evalu-
ate and create situations in response to driven needs originating in the
past.

Insight into one's patterns of interpersonal interaction at the same time one is being exposed to a new pattern of interpersonal relationship is the most mutative of all [interventions]. . . . Especially is this true if the insight is into the comparison between the old and the new at the very moment that the inclination to behave according to the old pattern is being met by an opportunity to relate in a new way. (Gill, 1982, p. 232)

Implicit in the above statement is the increase of cognitive awareness, bringing the unconscious to consciousness, increasing the sphere of the ego. However, self psychology recognizes missing functions, deficits which through structure building—transmuting internalization—can be filled in by self-functions. The formulations of self psychology allow us to understand how such structure building proceeds, how in the transference the therapist as new selfobject performs functions which through transmuting internalization become self-functions, the psychic structure of a cohesive self. Cognitive awareness is surely one of these self-functions, but is better explained by the increase in an individual's ability to become more reliably a recipient of his own impressions, a center of his own initiative.

In Chapter 2 we have seen how the cohesive bipolar self is created, consolidated, and sustained. In normal development this is accomplished through the selfobject milieu. Where significant empathic failure has occurred, transference needs for being mirrored or for the use of the therapist as an idealized selfobject reemerge in the treatment of self disorders and can be understood and interpreted in the new self/selfobject matrix. It is in this specific interplay that early transference needs may arise in an almost preverbal state. The individual "expects" the therapist "to know" his inner state, just as in earliest times the caretaking selfobject "knew" when he was hungry, cold, wet, tired, or lonely, even though that selfobject failed to respond. In the arousal of such an early merger state, even moderate empathic failure on the part of the therapist may bring about the eruption of narcissistic rage threatening to engulf both individual and therapist. Such behavior arouses countertransference reactions of anger, hurt, and the wish to withdraw from the pain of having one's efforts misunderstood. It is here, in the redirection of empathic focus, that the therapist recognizes with the individual the legitimacy of his needs in the past and their reverberation to the present, and helps him through interpretation to understand the injury and his reaction to it. By this two-step intervention, understanding and interpretation, the individual "metabolizes" the experience (M. Tolpin, 1983b). The needed selfobject functions of the therapist become the self-function of understanding and cognitive awareness.

There is no question but that exploration and interpretation under the lens of the transference provides the most opportune insight into an individual's characteristic behaviors or feeling states that obstruct adequate functioning. The response to the therapist, transference, may be unbearable because of feared, unmanageable warm or angry feelings. The experience of being understood in the present sets the healing process in motion or maintains the momentum (Kohut, 1984). In the cases that follow, drawn from a variety of settings across the life cycle, we will have an opportunity to examine the manner in which self psychology enlarges the understanding of transference and countertransference for social work practice and permits us to remain more in tune with the needs of the individual as he strives for a meaningful life and the capacity to enjoy it.

There are large numbers of individuals for whom it is not interpretation of the transference but the experience in the present that in effect provides the wherewithal for healing through a "corrective emotional experience." This can be a pejorative term if we fail to understand the need of certain individuals to borrow the structure of the therapist in order to enact what earlier had been frustrated, that is, acquiring those abilities which will "stand him in good stead, in good times and bad, when alone and with others, when successful and when disappointed. [They] require(s) an atmosphere in which [they] can learn to develop, mobilize, identify and work on fulfilling age appropriate ambitions, gaining in this way a sense of mastery over their fate. In addition they can have the opportunity to relate to models that will serve as ideals, permitting (him) the experience of a nondestructive union with admired others . . . " (Basch, 1983c, p. 235).

As we examine specific cases—a harried mother cited for child abuse, a young woman mandated for treatment as a requirement for a probationary sentence for shoplifting, a defeated unemployed father—we shall see that transference manifestations are dealt with in some instances in less direct fashion. In other cases, transference reactions to the therapist's failure in resonance to the individual's needs, her seeming emotional dullness or absence, are brought into the treatment situation through direct interpretation. But in all instances the directional force of the therapeutic experience is the combination of insight and new experience which brings about the achievement of psychological balance between the metaphorical poles of the self, ambitions, and ideals, in the pursuit of goals, however modest, which give meaning and purpose to life.

SECTION II

Treatment in Childhood and Adolescence

7

Self Disorders in Childhood

CHILDREN WHO ARE brought to social agencies, clinics, and hospitals reveal a broad range of deficits in their ability to regulate behavior and mood and to engage in play, learning, and mastery. It is not the unruly drives around which self-defeating and dangerous behaviors or feeling states coalesce, making these children demanding, unlearning, and hyperactive; rather, their crucial selfobject needs have been grossly unmet. Although single events of traumatic proportion are often cited as precipitants or causes of a condition, it is more often the total personality of the parent or caretaker that determines the child's failure to achieve cohesion (Kohut, 1977).

The history of such caretakers is often chaotic. Inadequacies in their caretaking functions simply reflect the inadequacies of the selfobjects of their childhood. How can adults, unable to monitor the symptom of anxiety within themselves, enable their children to lay down such structure within themselves? Children have an imperative need to have functions performed by others so that they can transmute primary self structure. Their immature psychic equipment cannot yet perform these functions reliably but must transmute selfobject functions into self-functions, the essence of psychic structure.

Social workers confront and are constantly assailed by the complex needs of these parent-child pairs. Such individuals establish fluctuating selfobject transferences which are difficult to decipher and to maintain. They do so because of persisting needs for multiple psychological functions which the social worker initially performs, but which ultimately they must be able to perform for themselves. Their own capacities must become heir to the functions which are performed for them.

Whether to work with parent and child together or in individual treatment must be determined by the nature and depth of the parental deficit, by the degree of cohesiveness in the self of the parent and in the self of the child. In this chapter, however, we are concerned with examining the manner in which self psychology illuminates disorders of the self and structure building in children.

Many of the children seen in agencies and clinics bear the diagnostic label of borderline personality disorder. Kohut describes this disorder as the permanent or protracted breakup or weakening of the nuclear self, with a variety of defenses covering over a vulnerable, readily fragmenting self (1971, 1977).

As we have seen, parents reasonably in tune with their children take pleasure in their being, respond joyously to their presence, define their feeling states, encourage and help them to shape their assertive behavior. As prestructural selfobjects, they are vital to the formation and consolidation of the child's self. It is from gross, unrelieved failures in phase-specific responses to the child's appropriate needs and wishes that the well-known childhood disorders follow. As M. Tolpin points out (1971), relating Kohut's work to analytic work with children, disturbances of cohesion are reflected in free-floating anxiety, states of depletion, empty depression.

These states are expressed in rage, clinging, demanding behavior, in functional impairment or inhibition in the capacity for new steps in learning, motor skills, socialization. Injured cohesion or failure to achieve cohesion is also expressed symbolically in fears of the dark, witches, goblins, abandonment, and annihilation, and in more structuralized phobias. The self, repeatedly in a state of fragmentation, may sexualize needs and deficits in such well-known behaviors as fecal retention, wetting, soiling, lonely masturbation, precocious sexual behavior. The child attempts to put together "fragments of normally developing sexuality and assertive behavior" in driven fashion. These proceed from compulsive efforts to fill in missing psychological self-regulatory functions (M. Tolpin, 1982, p. 18).

The psychological functions and capacities that are normally heir to the multiple functions of childhood selfobjects have failed "to go inside." And such children suffer deficits in the "normal workings" of the mind: perception, delay, reflection, planning, the capacity to fantasy action and its consequences.

Josie

From the history of parent-child pairs grossly out of tune, we can better understand the diagnostic label of borderline personality disorder. Consider the first four years of Josie's life. During her pregnancy with Josie, her mother developed many illnesses but followed medical advice inconsistently, reflecting her own chaotic self structure. The child's birth was nevertheless uneventful and her mother initially welcomed the child as someone to nurture, in effect soothing herself. At a little over seven months, Josie was walking, holding onto her mother's hand, but her mother described her as clumsy, bumping into objects. She evidenced little understanding of the needs of an infant for control and guiding. The child developed food poisoning and was ill for several weeks because she was "dumb, always putting things in her mouth"; this again revealed how little the mother understood the need of an infant to explore her world in this way and to be protected in her exploration. Within the next three years, in addition to many severe colds and high fevers, the child suffered burns from a fall onto an electric heater, a fall from her high chair requiring hospitalization, and a severe throw from a bicycle seat. These were only the physical trauma she suffered.

The child enjoyed having her mother read to her, but her mother stopped this because Josie was "too destructive." "Too destructive" in this instance referred to the child's turning pages "too clumsily" and tearing several.

Placed briefly in a day nursery, she was abruptly removed by her mother because, "They spoil children there; they hold them and let them have their own way." She was unable to accept this as appropriate behavior in focusing on a child's wishes, affirming her ability to perceive and to function as a center of her own initiative.

Thus, Josie was a child who had only the most evanescent and insubstantial images of herself reflected, often with a negative connotation: as early as seven months she was described as clumsy. Her indiscriminate intrusiveness with others attested to her need to have selfobjects perform functions for her on a catch-as-catch-can basis. For this child there were only the most fleeting moments of merging in the strength and power of an idealized selfobject. The nuclei of the self were fragmented, chaotic, feeble.

Self psychology enables us to recognize driven, repetitive behavior as a desperate attempt to achieve belated recognition and response to vital needs for affirmation of a mirroring selfobject and to merge with the strength and wisdom of an idealized selfobject. A child with massive deficits, such as Josie, taxes the ingenuity of the therapist who undertakes to help her achieve a more cohesive, less chaotic involvement with available selfobjects. When we can understand her, not as a child of untamed drives which must now be brought under civilizing influence, but as a child who desperately seeks confirmation and response by any means at hand, we have a clearer understanding of the therapeutic task and goal.

Extending her empathic understanding, the therapist observes, responds, and remembers, offering her mature structure to provide the child a sense of continuity and history. The therapist provides that confirmation and guidance which assist Josie in transmuting in minute bits the capacity for self-regulation. With Josie, for example, finally referred to a children's agency at age eight, it was helpful to provide firm structure, short-term goals within each session, and immediate gratification when modest goals were achieved. Her mirroring needs expressed in the transference were not only for affirmation but for guidance. Quick to pout, sulk, or cry when she felt deprived, she could be comforted and even calmed by firm restrictions when she could understand their purpose, a purpose which flowed from reality and not the inconsistent whimsy of her fragmentation-prone mother.

There was a commingling of mirroring, idealizing, and partnering needs and the transferences which flow from them. Since she had severe deficits in the ability to cue others, Josie and her therapist, in a new edition of self/selfobject unit, worked toward broadening the range of affective signals, modulating their intensity, and building in (transmuting) the spirit of reflection and delay before acting.

The ability to assess internal and external reality is an ongoing maturing process and, indeed, never ceases. For Josie, the process of therapy was directed toward enabling her, to the current level of her ability, to bring external and internal reality into concordance. When this could not be accomplished, the therapist affirmed and helped her to shape her grandiosity and to modify her need for immediate gratification. Memories of having been soothed and calmed could be rekindled by the therapist's smile, nod, or, in stormy times, reengaging her in the verbalization of her feelings and identifying their precipitant. This process of structure building—self/selfobject functions in minute bits "going inside," transmuted into self-functions—permitted Josie to work toward bringing external reality and internal reality (expectations, wishes) into concordance. There followed the growing capacity to accept limitations. Increasing strength in regulating self-esteem allowed Josie to recognize alternative opportunities and solutions. She could then tolerate that ambiguous period of undertaking work in defining her particular talents, increasing those skills through which these talents could be expressed in undertaking new activities. In place of a chaotic, readily fragmenting self, prone to seeking others on a catch-as-catch-can basis, Josie was on the way to firming and consolidating a cohesive nuclear self through which she could purposefully seek out selfobjects for comfort, for play, and for instruction.

Thus, viewing the emotional problems of children through the lens of self psychology offers a more direct glimpse into their struggles to acquire primary self structure and to achieve consolidation of a cohesive nuclear self. Let us examine how this comes about in treating both mother and child.

Susie

Susie was five and a half at the time of referral. Although she was of average intelligence, she lagged considerably behind her classmates in knowing alphabet, colors, or numbers. She was unable to sit still, easily distracted from her own activities and into everyone else's, intolerant of being left out. Her intrusive behavior alienated teachers and children alike. The list of her parents' complaints, particularly those of her mother, were endless. Susie was afraid to be alone; she was a restless sleeper and wet her bed. She spoke baby-talk and was hard to understand. She needed constant praise and was hard to please. She lied, had few friends, and was bossy with other children. These behaviors had been present for a prolonged time and showed no indication of abating.

The caseworker to whom she was assigned found her to be a very feminine child who liked pretty clothes and hairdos and was very well-groomed. She had a humorous, dramatic quality in acting out her feelings and fantasies. Although she was not diagnosed as clinically hyperactive, her restlessness and hyperactivity made her an exhausting child to deal with. She flitted from game to fantasy to various toys to items of the caseworker's clothing or desk at such high speed that it was impossible to engage her or slow her down. She would fly literally out-of-control, sweeping things off the shelves, kicking and throwing objects about the room. The therapeutic response of holding the child firmly and soothingly seemed to have a reverse effect on Susie, whose screaming and kicking efforts to free herself intensified. Rather than soothing her, physical closeness seemed to terrify her. What came to be more helpful was to allow the tantrum to spend itself, protecting the child from harming herself by removing dangerous objects, and avoiding the child's flailing arms and legs. During such episodes, the caseworker at first would sit silently and then would comment in a quiet voice that she knew Susie was hurting inside. What could it be? Was it something the caseworker had done or had not done?

Although such episodes could be exhausting for Susie and her caseworker, and at home or school would result in rejection and isolation, the caseworker maintained firm contact by her attention and concern. At the height of the storm the caseworker's silence enfolded the child with her interest and concern; then she would attempt to identify in words the angry, hurt, longing feelings Susie was acting out in her rampages.

In quieter moments, Susie would flit from game to game in a manner which would "drive others crazy" and, indeed, was very draining to the caseworker. During one such period the caseworker playfully called her "my little jumping bird because you're so like the warblers outside the window flitting from one branch to another." This opportunity to have

a meaningful image of herself reflected by a selfobject struggling to identify and remain in tune with her needs proved comforting to Susie, who
fell into playing with the concept in a manner that gave some order to her
behavior. She was placed in a classroom for emotionally disturbed
children and, though not clinically hyperactive, was maintained on a small
dose of ritalin, which controlled her hyperactivity during classroom hours.

Her mother, in treatment with another caseworker, described the child
as a monster. Nothing she did pleased her. An attractive woman, dressed
with a fine sense of style, she had been a beautician but had given up
her work to make a home for her husband and child. When the worker
commented on how attractively the child was dressed, her mother replied
that the only time Susie would stand still was to have her hair brushed
and styled. Though out of tune with the child's developmental needs, in
this area she felt competent and took pleasure in her mothering, and the
child responded. Otherwise child and mother were in constant conflict,
Susie intruding on anything her mother was doing, unable to be alone.
Her list of complaints underlined Susie's struggle to elicit response to her
curiosity, her playful efforts to engage her mother's interest or to join her
mother's work about the house, and her driven intensity in seeking a
joyful response from her mother. Viewing Susie as another ornament to
be picked up or put down according to her schedule rather than her
child's, Susie's mother was empathically out of tune with her child. Her
impatience and anger left Susie with deficits in her forming self, resulting in an intensifying cycle of temper tantrums responded to by the mother's own angry outbursts. Her natural wish for closeness was repeatedly
thwarted as an intrusion on her mother's activities.

The caseworker encouraged the mother to accept the reality that some
children and some mothers have a difficult time in understanding and
working together and said that she was glad Susie and her mother had
come to the agency for help. An idealizing and partnering transference
developed as Susie's mother responded to the caseworker's ability to absorb her tension and anger in her relationship with her child. As a consequence, she became less punitive about herself and her own angry feelings. The therapeutic process (self and selfobject in tune) provided numerous experiences of being understood, as well as cognitive awareness
of what was being derailed in her dialogue with her child. She began to
transmute the ability to delay her response to her child and reflect on her
needs without falling into either extreme of rejection or explosiveness. As
her helplessness and despair began to lift, she could more readily monitor
what provoked tension, reflect, and delay before undertaking a response
to her child rather than meeting the child's temper tantrum with one of
her own. Paradoxically, although the child's therapeutic sessions con-

tinued for a prolonged period to be difficult and dramatic, Susie was getting better outside of therapy. Her mother was pleased and moved when the child began to seek her out, not in a demanding angry fashion, but to be read to, to be played with. She began to take pleasure in the child's responsiveness. What had been freed for growth was the double helix of the child's self-esteem and the mother's self-esteem (Elson, 1984). The child was able to express her needs and wishes in words and behavior which elicited from her mother responsive guiding and aiding functions. Engaged in an idealizing transference, the mother was able to relinquish the child as a narcissistic prop and to acquire self-functions geared to the child's developmental needs. In so doing, her pride and pleasure in facilitating the child's growth, confirmed and aided by the caseworker, infused her with dependable capacity to regulate her own self-esteem.

Susie and her mother remained in treatment for over three years. The child moved to a regular classroom and showed the ability to work toward mastery of typical reading and numbering skills although she was still somewhat behind her classmates. She was able to engage in a few mutually responsive friendships. Her speech problems disappeared and her relationship with her parents continued to be gratifying. She was still a vulnerable child who, under stress, would revert to bedwetting and to temper outbursts, but these episodes were becoming less frequent.

In Susie's presenting problems we may see the absence of reliable psychic structure, the missing functions of being able to calm and soothe herself, which remained outside her forming self. At a time when consolidation of the self should have been proceeding firmly, subject as a matter of course to disruptions in which selfobjects could respond appropriately to mirroring, idealizing, or partnering needs in shaping her talents through the acquisition of skills, Susie struggled with driven behavior. The observation that she was hard to please indicated the very early level of preverbal needs to which she had been unable to cue her empathically out-of-tune mother. Her restlessness in sleep and her bedwetting were further indications that she could neither monitor anxiety nor alert the caretaking selfobjects to her needs. Her desperate demands for praise and her inability to tolerate being alone signaled her anxiety, which intensified as she was unable to elicit appropriate responses, leaving her with deficits in self-esteem regulation. Lying represented not only defensive behavior to avoid punishment—mother's earlier view—but more typically an attempt to elicit the interest of an important selfobject by exaggeration or fantasy. Rampaging behavior, a desperate attempt to fight the sense of deadness within, at least let her feel alive. Her caseworker had noted that there were times when Susie's storms seemed to proceed from a wish to be confirmed as a bad child. To have needs, and particularly needs which were intensified by reason of her prolonged inability to signal her early selfobjects to the validity and legitimacy of such needs, confirmed her as "a monster" and, at some deeper level, maintained a merger with her mother. She both desperately longed for and intensely feared closeness.

These behaviors dramatically identified the many ways in which the forming self of the child at crucial periods had been unsupported. They could be understood as frantic signals proceeding from chaotic self structure. Through the efforts of her therapist to identify the feelings underlying the stormy behavior, provided in a soothing and calming manner, the child was able first by hindsight and then through foresight to recognize signal anxiety. As she transmuted these calming and soothing selfobject functions, she could more reliably seek out responses while her own resources (self-functions) were still in a primitive stage.

It is a common experience in treatment of children that sessions may continue stormy and difficult even though behavior outside of therapy improves. Things were better at home and in school but continued stormy in Susie's sessions with her therapist. Susie, at this phase merger hungry, required an almost perfect intuneness with her unspoken wishes and exploded into rage when the therapist failed.

The process of therapy in the new self/selfobject matrix assisted the child in understanding and verbalizing these needs and wishes. And since the therapist, unlike others in the child's environment, did not respond by rejection and isolation but rather by remaining concerned and in tune, the child ultimately transmuted mild failures on the therapist's part into psychic structure.

Rescue signals—rampaging, screaming, abrasive behaviors—initially alerted the therapist to undertake caretaking functions. Later, signal anxiety alerted internal regulation on Susie's part, which allowed her more calmly to seek appropriate selfobject response, to say what she needed and wanted.

The nuclear structure of a cohesive self, functioning more reliably, permits the further consolidation of the bipolar self in a manner that permits the grandiose exhibitionism of the child to flow more harmoniously and vigorously through the shaping and elaboration of skills and talents into rudimentary, and later more mature, ideals and goals. As we have said earlier, the development of self-esteem and ideals is a slow process subject to many detours; it is not a steady state. But Susie, at the point of termination, could more reliably perceive her needs and her wishes; she could initiate behavior toward accomplishing goals, whether in relationships or in activities; and she could both enlist and permit the widening world of selfobjects to assist her in shaping her interests; she could also brook disappointment as she continued to learn what her capacities and limitations were.

To be empathically in touch with a child's inner life at all times is not humanly possible. But it is out of small failures of short duration that structure building occurs. And it is in a milieu in which old needs are reactivated for specific responses from the therapist as a new selfobject that deepening and strengthening of psychic functions can ensue. For Susie, storms and raging behavior could be ticked off by preverbal needs which taxed the therapist's ingenuity to disentangle. Her own countertransference reactions helped her to understand the depth of those preverbal needs. Her focused empathic attention, her struggle to remain in tune even in the face of numerous ruptures, in the end allowed Susie to reinstate the process of structure building, to acquire as her own, and employ in her own way the empathic interventions of the therapist. Through myriad cycles of rupture and resolution, the therapist's enfolding and soothing understanding was transmuted into Susie's embryonic capacity to allow soothing interventions and then to calm herself. Engrams of memory, memory traces of having been soothed, now allowed Susie to engage in verbal descriptions of the affect of the moment, reinstating a process that had been derailed between child and mother.

In an ongoing process the therapist offered her understanding of the feelings which Susie's affective cues signaled. Gradually this selfobject function became the self function of cognitive awareness of what the feeling was, what precipitated it, what it signified, and the capacity to reflect and delay before acting. Rather than erupting in rage, she could ask for comforting when she was lonely, hurt, or angry, for companionship with some recognition of other children's or adult's wishes, and for help in acquiring or defining a skill.

Jim

In working with older children, their greater verbal capacity is an asset, but there is also a more entrenched structuralization of defenses to cover over deficits. Jim, for example, was 12 years of age before his despairing, angry mother brought him for treatment. In his behavior he presented a facade of social adequacy. He engaged peers and adults through clowning, wit, and a sense of the absurd. But he would use these behaviors to dilute the anger his uncontrolled, inappropriate behavior would arouse in his classmates and teachers. He would then become insulting and threatening, bringing on retaliation from those he most wished to engage in friendship.

In classes, he was withdrawn or fidgety, avoiding assigned tasks. He did not read for information or turn in assignments. He talked out loud, disruptively, and, when he was ignored, would suddenly jump to his feet, sounding a machine gun rat-a-tat as he mowed down his classmates. He would take on the menacing features and behavior of TV monsters. But in certain areas his interest and response could be aroused. When material was presented to him alone, orally, he showed better than average capacity for comprehension. In athletics he seemed purposeful and his skill led him to be readily chosen as a teammate. However, efforts to assist him in carrying over this behavior to classroom and studies, or to ordinary social relationships, were thwarted by the clowning, disruptive behavior discussed above.

It is not my purpose here to give a detailed history of Jim's early years and the parental milieu, except to point out that this child, bright and imaginative at the toddler and preschool level, was used by his feuding, depressed parents to distract them from their quarrels. Their laughter and egging-on, their amusement and challenge, served a faulty mirroring function for this boy, whose grandiosity and exhibitionism were overstimulated. The youngest of four sibs, he would be displayed whenever the family needed distraction. Mirroring under such circumstances becomes faulty mirroring. Behavior that in a young child can engage others becomes offensive in an older child. His parents would abruptly dismiss him and scold; his sibs would invite him "to get lost." He would redouble his efforts to engage them, for, as long as he was clowning, entertaining others, keeping attention focused on himself, he felt alive.

Mirroring affirms, confirms, and guides the child in modifying and shaping his grandiose exhibitionism into new skills, helping him to turn to new tasks. It assists the child in a bit-by-bit process to lay down self structure: knowing when behavior is appropriate, and, when it is not, having the ability to turn to other pursuits. Parents assist the child in turning to other activities, in finding pleasure in the more silent workings of the mind. But for Jim, it meant being plunged from the center of attention to being totally abandoned and ignored. This state, akin to the feeling of annihilation, aroused narcissistic rage, which precipitated his taking on the persona of TV monsters and mowing down his classmates.

The work of learning requires the capacity to tolerate aloneness, to work quietly to master the escalating intricacies of subjects. For Jim, such aloneness was filled with the terror of non-existence. Working on his own did not stem from something he wanted to accomplish or learn. In a classroom, witnessing everyone silently at work was to be isolated and abandoned. Even though such behavior was counterproductive, talking aloud, machine-gunning his classmates, and taking on the persona of TV monsters overcame the feeling of deadness.

That he could respond to individual oral instruction became a means of engaging his interest in working with a therapist assigned to him. The process of allowing Jim to establish an empathic, creative merger was

slow, with many derailings. It was useful for the therapist initially to read aloud sports stories, which Jim proceeded to dramatize. This gave way to Jim's reading aloud to his therapist. As his reading skills increased, he became engrossed in the story and would fall into silent reading, but with a sharp lookout for his therapist's attention to this behavior. As long as she was watching him he felt at ease and at one with her. As structure building proceeded in stepwise fashion, he could become absorbed in his reading, needing only her presence to feel whole. Later he was able to dispense with this and pursue his own activities.

It is not my intent to describe the lengthy process of treatment for Jim, but, rather, to examine deficits in structure building which exposed themselves for understanding and filling in. During therapy, through drawings that indicated a flair for caricature, he portrayed himself as a huge encompassing figure whose arms were concealed by clouds through which lightning bolts were directed at sleeping figures. At one point he included his therapist among these figures, following an episode in which she had focused too strongly on attempting to help Jim prolong a period of silent reading. This was brought to Jim's cognitive awareness and broadened to include the many ways in which silent work in class, school-work generally, exposed depression, associated as it still was with something to keep a mischievous, obstreperous child out of the way. Moreover, since his skills lagged behind those of his classmates, he could not strengthen self-esteem through pleasure in his skills and talents. Jim could now share with his therapist his terror when his parents quarrelled and his efforts to deflect those storms. His distress was absorbed and his needs for comforting given legitimacy, in contrast to his experience at the hands of a middle brother, who handled his own fears by belittling and shaming Jim's. There also appeared now the memory of a brother, 15 years older, whom Jim idealized as an athlete, one who had shown him the rudiments of various sports and who would sometimes comfort him by reading him to sleep. This brother had left home when Jim was about five. He had not been home for a number of years and was the subject of a good deal of resentment and anger on the part of his parents and sibs.

There now ensued many experiences of continuity between a past idealized selfobject and the new selfobject therapist. There emerged a reliable, vigorous flow from the pole harboring his ambitions to the pole imbued with idealized standards and values. He elaborated various skills, particularly his talent for drawing caricature. He was sought out to create genuinely admired illustrations for school activities.

In classroom sessions, in a very slow process which taxed everyone's ingenuity and time, he moved from acting out desperately to compel the attention of his teachers and classmates to being able to monitor his own

needs. Like the infant who could still his cries when he heard his mother's footsteps down the hall, Jim acquired in minute bits the structure for calming and soothing himself. A smile or a nod from his teacher could ease him. His reactivated needs for mirroring and merging with an idealized selfobject, through innumerable, infinitesimal experiences of optimal frustration between self and the therapist as a new selfobject, were transmuted into reliable psychic structure. The therapist's calming and reasoning response to him, as they worked together to identify underlying feelings, was transmuted into a self-function. Other self-functions included the ability to recognize signal anxiety within himself, to identify his needs and wishes, to monitor them, to contain them, and then to assert them legitimately for further confirming and guidance in ways to which others could respond. His cohesive, vigorous harmonious self was, of course, subject to disruption which would then alert him to the process of self-righting. He was open to the world of selfobjects in a manner which allowed him to be confirmed as a center of his own perceptions, the enactor of a program of action which he could initiate. No longer clown or monster, Jim had the power to initiate and to formulate goals, as well as an abiding trust that his own perceptions had value, which now fueled his ambitions. He moved into an adolescent world of friends and activities which were sustaining to him. He no longer needed the presence of the therapist to confirm his worth. This self-affirming capacity had become reliably his own.

8

Self Disorders
in Adolescence

EVERY MAJOR CHANGEOVER in life shakes up an image of the self and its world of self objects (Kohut, 1977). There is, of course, no static period. What appears static is an imperceptible process of change which at significant intervals intensifies in speed and becomes notable. Adolescence is one such period.

Prominent in adolescence is the rapid pace in physical growth. The bodyself matures slowly, yet its manifest stages are dramatic. The world of selfobjects responds to each phase with expectation. Parents look ahead with and for their offspring, musing nostalgically over what has been and what will not come again.

The adolescent's mind-body self responds to being enfolded in the larger vision of the world of selfobjects by transmuting their vision into a unique vision of that world. The stories woven by joyous parents in contemplating their daughter's or son's future become a self-function in facilitating the process of establishing idealized goals. Structure building occurs by reason of optimal frustration—the selfobjects are in tune with the individual's needs and wishes, but not quite. Hearing, listening, and taking in the vision offered by selfobjects, the adolescent will give that vision special emphasis and new direction.

In experience with extended family, neighbors, and playmates, the adolescent, through the process of optimal frustration, continues deepening, firming, and elaborating self structure. Response from the "widening world of selfobjects" (Wolf, 1980) provides sustenance for the enhancement of native endowment. Mirroring needs—affirmation, confirmation, guidance—blend with the need for merging with the idealized wisdom and competence of a broadening range of mentors. Twinship and partnering needs are more obviously prominent in the early school years than at any other time except adolescence, when they are asserted even more vigorously. One has only to observe the intense bond of doing things together: This is what we are . . . this is what we do . . . and this is the way we do it.

The way we do it is almost more important than who is the swiftest or the strongest. Key expressions, rituals, typical dress, and possessions are sought and defended with an intensity that can bewilder and irritate parents. For the adolescent they are confirmation of a special place in the world. Increasingly that unique self with its special place in the world will be enriched, defined, and confirmed as selfobject functions become the self-functions of more sophisticated monitoring of signal anxiety, greater strength in the capacity to self-soothe and thus to undertake the mastery of new tasks.

There is a vital, phase-appropriate thrust toward new selfobjects in peers, cult heroes, and ideologies (Kohut, 1974; Wolf, 1980; Wolf, Gedo and Terman, 1972). The world of thought and the strength which lies in the mind become increasingly the focus of mastery and growth for some adolescents; for others the focus is on body strength and prowess in athletics. For still others both worlds are available. There appears a simultaneous intensifying and loosening of the ties to primary selfobjects. Parents are put on hold, needed yet resisted. Their opinions and judgments are sought after, but their suggestions may be abjured even when they coincide with and confirm the adolescent's deeply cherished longings. They are tested against the values and standards of selfobject peers, or older selfobject mentors, which in turn must be vigorously argued with parents. The process attests to the intense scrutiny to which the adolescent subjects external and inner world in the struggle for confirmation of the self as a center of perception and initiative.

There can be a refreshing and vigorous increase in the stream of ideas between the generations as the adolescent confronts cognitively and affectively, as if for the first time, those values, ideals, and goals that had earlier been laid down as psychic structure. Some they will jettison, others they will modify, and still others they will now include more firmly and enduringly as *their* values, *their* ideals, *their* goals (Elson, 1984).

It is at the point of their children's adolescence that parents as selfobjects have the greatest need for flexibility and tensile strength in reviewing and expanding those enduring values and goals that are basic to a sense of continuity of the self in space and time. While much has been made of adolescent turmoil, the profound upheaval which parents experience in this transitional phase has been less noted. In the light of newer societal norms, parents must now examine within themselves the validity and importance of values, beliefs, and behaviors intrinsic to their own cohesive functioning.

Through each developmental phase, child and parents inform each other. Factors impinging upon the parent-child relationship are reciprocal and complex; they are not just unidirectional. The child influences the parent to nearly the same extent that the parent influences the child (Cohler, 1980). This is the unique significance of the simultaneous ongoing process of the experience of self and other in parents and children.

Throughout the course of family life, there are periods of vibrantly intense joy experienced by parents and children alike, when each enhances a sense of radiance and power in the other. There are equally intense periods of anger and despair. There may be times when the explosive force unleashed by the narcissistic needs and demands of one or both parents may be thoroughly distorting and destructive to the child, giving rise to severe breaks in empathy. Parental behavior may be excessively punitive and counterproductive to the adolescent's growth and development or unrealistic in relation to the adolescent's genuine interests and abilities. Anxiety, guilt, and depression may then hamper a necessary search for understanding and resolution of the impasse. Pathological forms of parental narcissism may perpetuate parental control long after the adolescent has signaled need for and capacity to forge a course and to use others in the expanding world of selfobjects for this purpose.

Out of their own needs, parents seek to halt development. History is strewn with the locked combat of parents and children in this arena when the immaturity and rigidity of the parents' narcissism exact behavior from the adolescent that will exactly mirror the parents' needs. Unable to be free of a noxious merger, the adolescent cannot elaborate skills and talents that will permit the expression of ambitions in realizable goals stemming from centrally perceived initiative.

Parents may also be threatened by their adolescents' maturing adult form and may enviously compete for their beauty, power and opportunity. In other instances they may misunderstand rebellious attitudes or behavior, which often cover regression and retreat. The battle is joined interpersonally rather than intrapsychically, as adolescents struggle against their archaic needs and the fear of engulfment and as parents cling more tenaciously to their former encompassing central position in the lives of their children. The selfobjects an adolescent seeks out to overcome this fear at times seem to represent in gross form the values exactly opposite to those which are central to parental self-esteem and have earlier seemed central to that of their preadolescent children. In other instances, fearing separation and the task of self-definition, adolescents may linger in a merger which does not permit that quickening opportunity for trusting and expanding their perceptions, for initiating a unique program of action which is the necessary task of these years (Elson, 1984).

Disorders of the self in adolescence become manifest in low self-esteem, lack of goals, immobilization, or in dangerous acting-out behavior, such as substance abuse, delinquency, or perversions. The following excerpt from a three-year period of treatment will illustrate the deficits which are exposed and the understanding offered by self psychology to the process of filling in these deficits.

Tom

Tom, almost 15, was brought to the clinic by his parents, who felt themselves helpless to move him from his entrenched taciturnity. At home his typical day was spent sleeping or sitting before the TV; at school he moved from class to class "like a zombie." He had few friends and those he did have were, like himself, "deadwood" in classes.

In a joint interview with his parents, he sat silently, appearing vaguely uncomfortable when his frustrated mother, bursting into tears, exclaimed, "If he goes on this way I don't know what's going to become of him." His father patted her shoulder, proclaiming gruffly, "Aw, he'll snap out of it; it's just a stage."

An argument erupted between the parents, during which Tom's face took on something of a sneer and he shifted uncomfortably in his chair. The burden of the argument was that Tom's behavior was worsening, not getting better. His sisters, 12 and 10, gave no trouble; they did their homework, were into a variety of activities, and were good company. Tom just kept to himself, sleeping long hours or watching TV. He never did anything he was asked to do unless "you just shout at him!" His grades were "abominable" and getting worse. It was clear that his mother was responding with narcissistic rage to her loss of Tom as a selfobject. His father's attitude was bland. "You just make a big case of it. Like I tell you, he'll snap out of it; give him time." Tom appeared bored when his father spoke, but his face flushed.

In the course of the interview the intensity of feeling between the parents subsided, but it was apparent that Tom's father had agreed to therapy in order to appease his wife. He firmly believed that Tom was just going through a phase and would "shape up" after he did "some more growing."

His mother presented Tom's industry throughout earlier grades and middle school in glowing terms and expressed her great disappointment that he had ground to a halt "just when grades were so important." Efforts to draw Tom into the discussion were met with uneasy shrugs. He did not, however, resist the therapist's suggestion that he stay a while after his parents left so that together they could come to an understanding of whether therapy was in order.

Tom volunteered little information, appeared sleepy and yawned several times in the silence which followed his noncommittal responses to questions. It was the therapist's belief that Tom not only was expecting the therapist to react to him as his parents did, but also was in his way attempting to diminish intense feelings of being the center of attention. His attitude induced an inner state of exasperation and bewilderment in the therapist who sought to engage this unwilling adolescent. Tentatively he suggested that it was possible Tom felt coerced and angry. Although he could not say whether he could help Tom, he would like to see if they couldn't work together to figure things out. Tom seemed to lose some of his sleepiness, but, with something of a sneer, asked, "Like those shrinks on TV?"

THERAPIST: I don't know what programs you've been watching. (As Tom did not respond, he continued.) What's really important is our working together; we help each other in puzzling things out.
TOM: Isn't anything to puzzle out. . . . I just don't get a kick out of anything.
THERAPIST: That's just it; what's happened to the kick?
Tom volunteered his first half-smile.
THERAPIST: I think it's worth trying to see what we come up with; I've worked with other kids who seem to have lost it.
TOM: (After a pause) Well, for a while.
THERAPIST: I don't think a while will help much, but it may give you a sense of how we work together and whether you want to go on.

Tom agreed to the proposed weekly interview. In the first few weeks the taciturn behavior of which his mother had complained was much in evidence. He was often late and lethargic. Comments volunteered by his therapist were met, for the most part, with a shrug. On one occasion, prompted by Tom's unusually disheveled appearance and the strong sweetish odor of marijuana which emanated from him, the therapist commented that sometimes things hurt so much that it just felt better to pile the covers on and just hope it would all go away. When Tom did not respond, the therapist asked how long Tom had been medicating himself.

TOM: (Startled and uneasy) What do you mean?
THERAPIST: The odor from your clothes is very strong.
TOM: (Flushing) So what?
THERAPIST: I think only you can say *what* is troubling you. I only know from my work with many young people your age that when things get to be too much, some of them turn to drugs to overcome those low times. They're really trying to treat a depression.

TOM: Are you going to tell my folks?
THERAPIST: What goes on is between us. The only time I change that agreement is when it seems clear that your behavior creates a danger for yourself or others. And I would take such a step only after telling you first why and when. Fair enough?
Tom reluctantly agrees.

The therapist seeks to establish how often and for how long a time Tom has been medicating himself. His replies are not so much evasive as confused, and the therapist considers whether there may be a beginning thought disorder. He points out that when Tom medicates himself it is not possible to understand what prompts the low states. Tom protests that it is nothing special, but the therapist points out that the effect of self-medication is to dissipate painful feelings and therefore it seems as if there is nothing especially upsetting. He asks Tom's cooperation in trying not to medicate himself but to come in for an extra hour when he feels he cannot hold out. Tom agrees, but volunteers that his parents are always arguing about whether therapy does any good and about the expense. The therapist comments that even coming in to see him, then, probably adds to the bad feelings, and Tom, with a thoughtful, direct look at the therapist, agrees. The therapist asks whether Tom would like to have him see the parents again and prepare the way for sessions twice a week.

Whether or not to arrange to see parents again or at regular intervals is a matter of therapeutic judgment. The therapist had observed Tom's sneering when his parents began to quarrel in the first consultation. He had also observed Tom's discomfort, particularly when his mother burst into tears. He believed that the crucial issue was that of extending an empathic understanding of Tom's obvious discomfort but that a consultation now might help Tom by removing therapy from the arena of parental disputes.

TOM: Are you going to tell them about the pot?
THERAPIST: (Firmly and without taking offense) You and I have a clear understanding about that.

The consultation goes well. There is despair at home over Tom's grades, which are failing in three out of four subjects. His father is no longer taking the position that Tom is just going through a phase. The parents' problems with each other are faced more directly—his mother's excessive orderliness, his father's tendency to let things slide around the house, in his work. His father's defensiveness is much in evidence as well as his mother's disappointment in his father's achievement. She is openly envious of a younger sister whose husband has achieved more in the world. His father reminds her that they aren't too badly off, precipitating a long discussion accompanied by tears over their lost youthful aspirations. This ushers in memories of earlier good times and feelings they had about themselves and their world.

The therapist uses this opportunity to point out that Tom seems to have ground to a halt because the future may look frightening to him, full of adult problems he is not as yet equipped to handle. The parents together talk over how much he used to consult them, what good company he used to be, but that now he won't let anyone talk to him or help him. They are concerned about the few friends he has and that they seem to be such slouches. The therapist suggests that perhaps when he is with these friends he doesn't feel so bad about himself. He enables them to see that Tom's having ground to a halt is not willful rebelliousness but immobilization proceeding from depression. When Tom's emotional and behavioral state is viewed in this light, the parents become less exasperated and more concerned. Twice weekly appointments are agreed to.

In the next few months, Tom misses appointments and reverts to bouts of self-medication. The therapist telephones and does not scold but firmly takes the position that Tom is doing all he can at present; it is hard to examine bad feelings and what precipitates them. Tom counters sneeringly, "You're the shrink, you ought to know." The therapist's response is that sometimes bad feelings are too deep for words and that at such times Tom must feel exasperated with the therapist's failure to provide answers. There is a long period in which Tom essentially comes in promptly and regularly but says very little.

> TOM: Well, my folks are paying for this so I guess I may as well come in and sit.

At one point, as he is leaving, he comments with a sigh that it feels good just to sit in the office with the therapist not hassling him. The therapist accepts this with a quiet comment, "I'm glad it helps."

In the next sessions, Tom begins to talk about his two friends and the fact that when he is with them, he doesn't feel so bad, or at least they all feel bad together. His mother objects to them, thinks they're a bad influence on him. He asks defiantly, "How does she know *I'm* not a bad influence on *them?*"

He comments rather sneeringly that Cynthia, his 12-year-old sister, came home with all A's. "Mom was dancing all over the place," and that's what she used to do with Tom. But getting good grades at that school is no big deal. After a pause he adds that, again, it just feels good to be with

someone who just accepts him as he is and doesn't hassle him about
school and grades and what's going to become of him. He sits silently for
some time, his eyes moisten and he brushes the tears away, flushing. With
sudden anger he bursts out, "I guess you think I'm just a kid." The
therapist comments that "memories of earlier years help us to understand
ourselves; they don't mean one is just a kid."

As Tom absorbs a sense of the therapist's interest and respect, he begins
to talk about his earlier school years and interests. "I used to get a kick
out of things then." Taciturnity, surliness, cynicism, much in evidence
earlier, have given way as Tom shares with his therapist his earlier enthusiasm in school activities. He offers himself and his activities to the
therapist for admiration, at first shyly, and then with zest, as he recalls
his excitement over each new project and the response of a particular
teacher to them. When he moved to eighth grade, this teacher continued
her interest, often stopping him in the hall to inquire about his progress.
"I felt she was really interested in what I was doing and what it meant
to me, not like my mom, as if I were a feather in her cap." Tom described
the experience of being used as a selfobject by his mother for her own
exhibitionistic needs, an intrusion which deprived him of a joyous sense
of growing strength in shaping his ideas and his skill in expressing them.
With some resentment and shame, he confided that his friends began to
tease him about his teacher's interest in him. He began to avoid her also,
ashamed of his earlier response and attachment to her.

It was difficult to determine from Tom's description whether his teacher
had been too intrusive in her interests. She used to put her arm around
him, something he didn't mind earlier: "Grownups were always doing
that to me." But what a prepubertal child can tolerate becomes uncomfortable for the pubertal adolescent. Perhaps more striking was that Tom
had been oblivious until teased by his friends. Somewhat slower than his
friends in pubertal changes, he began to avoid old friends as well as to
withdraw from a central position in his class. He was uncomfortable with
his mother, shying away from her and shrugging off her embraces. She
was always fussing with his sisters' hair and clothing. He remembered
with deep flushing and considerable difficulty in expressing himself that
she used to bathe him and then supervise his bathing for longer than most
mothers. She was always inspecting him, his ears, his fingernails. Even
his father would sometimes say, "Let the boy alone!"

Tom felt demeaned by his father's statement and withdrew from both
parents. His mother became more intrusive as Tom tried to shrug her off,
pursuing him with questions as to how thoroughly he had scrubbed
himself; as Tom persisted in avoiding her, she would add, "You know
what I mean?" He flushed very uncomfortably as he blurted out, after

some hesitation, that his mother always used to wash the area around his anus and penus very vigorously. When, as he grew older, he began to push her away, she would let him wash himself but under her supervision. Occasionally his young sisters would barge in until he rebelled and began to lock them all out.

After particularly trying times, he would run into his bedroom and lock the door. His mother would say, "I know what you're doing in there." Since at one point this coincided with his attempt to soothe himself in what became compulsive masturbation, he was frightened and confused. Interrupting himself, he commented, "Aw, this is all just a bunch of garbage; I'm just a mess." His therapist replied that he could understand Tom's confusion and the intensity of his feelings about these early experiences. Perhaps he was fearful that the therapist would, like his mother in earlier days, think of him as a smelly little boy, or that, like his father, he would not be able to help him get to the root of things.

THERAPIST: It's not garbage; you are not a mess. You and I together are trying to clear away your confusion about these experiences and your reaction to them.

Tom said that he was often the subject of arguments between his parents, his father taking his usual position that it was just a phase that all boys go through. His support did not work toward modulating the intensity of Tom's guilt and anxiety. After one particularly stormy session, his father agreed to talk to Tom in response to his mother's insistence that he would not listen to her.

His father's discomfort was obvious. Their discussion essentially terminated with his father's ruffling his hair and saying, soothingly, "That's my little guy." Since Tom was by now 13, he was enraged and his discomfort grew; his disappointment, resulting from further de-idealization of his father, intensified. At night he would have disturbing sensations in which it seemed to him that his body was too large for his bed, that his arms and legs were out of all proportion. He grew uncomfortable with his friends as their physical development became obviously more rapid than his own. His interest in schoolwork began to decline. He avoided activities he formerly enjoyed, finding some degree of companionship in three classmates with whom he began to turn on with pot. In the next few weeks Tom began to talk about these early experiences of turning on. "John could get the stuff any time. We used to go to his house and hang out. I didn't feel bad anymore; I just didn't care; it was great; just like floating. But when I came down, it was worse. I couldn't wait for the next time."

Pointing to his chest he said it felt "like a heavy weight in there." He would sit slouched in his chair confiding that at least, when he was taking pot, the heaviness seemed to go away. He asked poignantly of his therapist, "Have you ever been depressed? Does it ever go away?"

Empathically in tune with this distressed adolescent, his therapist answered that he knew the feeling he was describing, and that initially their work together probably added to his pain. He pointed out that it was a little like an infection in which things had to be drained away before healing could take place. He had a lot on his mind that he had been unable to talk over and clarify. His well-meaning parents were unaware that Tom was no longer the small boy he had once been. Some mothers found it hard to give up that earlier close contact, and when "things get tough, we, too, long for that earlier time." He could understand Tom's efforts to soothe himself through medication, but since it didn't really help him get to the bottom of things, all it did was to drive him to turn on again and again. When things aren't cleared up they grow more intense. As his therapist absorbed Tom's feelings of distress, his sense of being at sixes and sevens, he was able to help Tom understand the state of fragmentation reflected in the sensation of his arms and legs being out of proportion.

Questions beginning "Could it be . . . " or "Is it possible . . . " allowed Tom to merge with the calming and soothing strength of the therapist. As Tom examined the feelings states that followed sharp breaks in his relationship with his parents, particularly his mother, he could identify precipitants for and consequent states of fragmentation. His natural sexual curiosity, linked with his mother's vigorous scrubbing and her concern with cleanliness, both stimulated him physically and provoked unmanageable anxiety associated with feelings of filthiness. At the same time, his father's laissez-faire attitude, which under other circumstances might have been helpful, left him more at the mercy of his mother's intrusiveness. His father's attempt to offer help more directly had dissipated when he took the easier outlet of regarding Tom as "my little guy." Tom's rage and frustration were understandable, since his difficulties did not represent a phase that he would outgrow but a struggle to understand and make some order of his conflicting wishes to be understood and cared for and, at the same time, to go beyond such needs.

The relationship with his therapist grew very intense. If there were a small delay in the time of the interview, or if Tom's path crossed that of another patient, there would be recurrent states of feeling out of proportion. After occasional unavoidable cancellation of an appointment, he would become sullen and withdrawn. A petulant quality characterized his questions and responses; he was irritable and quarrelsome. He would attack his therapist, saying, for example, that he knew what his therapist was thinking about him but he was wrong. Tom confided with some shame and with difficulty that he found it hard to wait for his sessions; he felt whole when he was with his therapist. In the months that followed, Tom discussed with his therapist disturbing fantasies of sexual activities, intense absorption in his parents' relationship, curiosity about his sisters' development, concern about his own sexual equipment, and guilt about masturbation. He began to separate normal interest in exploring his body and testing his equipment from guilty, confused feelings of being dirty. Tom was increasingly able to monitor signal anxiety and to transmute the therapist's soothing by taking steps to soothe himself that did not include "turning on" or returning to driven sexual fantasy and masturbation. He expressed a good deal of curiosity about the therapist's life and outside interests; when appropriate, the therapist would respond factually, allowing himself to be used as a target of idealization as Tom sought and defined his own goals.

Tom was now well into his fifteenth year. He had grown several inches and broadened. There were longer periods of his seeming to be in charge and at ease with himself. At such times he would talk about his "kid sister," now 13, and the way she would come to him for advice. With his parents, there appeared to be an uneasy truce. But he quickly bridled when his mother sought to question him about his school work or activities. activities.

As she had occasionally over the past 18 months of Tom's therapy, his mother sought an interview with the therapist. She appeared depressed and confided that she thought she would like to undertake therapy for herself. Even though her relationship with Tom was still "like walking on eggs," she felt he had improved; his grades were at the top; she could see he felt better about himself. But she was beginning to have trouble with her middle daughter. She felt the problem was more with her own feelings about herself. She felt increasingly unsure and doubtful about her relations with her growing children. The therapist helped her to recognize that the process of gradually giving up the central position in their children's lives was difficult for most parents and, perhaps, for compelling reasons, particularly so for her. For this mother, individual therapy appeared to be an important step. The therapist was able to refer her to a woman therapist with whom she made a very effective therapeutic relationship. She smiled as she commented that Tom, in an unguarded moment, had once said to her, "Mr. T. never scolds; he just understands, but he also tells you where to get off."

Tom continued to work very intensively with his therapist. In his sixteenth year he became interested in an advanced course in constitutional history. He didn't think he would go into law as a profession, but "it wouldn't hurt to have that background," whatever he did. He was getting into heated arguments with his father about politics, challenging his passivity, stoutly defending his conviction that "there are things you can do to change what's going on in government." His father typically believed in letting things ride: "You can't change things overnight." Tom smiled ruefully as he shrugged his shoulders and commented, "When I was a kid, I used to think he had the answer to everything and I guess he did, for a kid." Tom began to quote, with admiration, an admired advisor to an advanced group of students, of which Tom was now a member. He was also increasingly attracted to a classmate who was "awesome" in her studies but "fun to talk to." What he liked about this girl and his advisor was that they didn't try to "shove their ideas" at him. They just "asked good questions that made you think about what you felt and what you were saying"; he added, with a flush, "like you."

In his seventeenth year, Tom was intensely caught up in school and related activities. He said that he would like to try cutting down on his hours. He needed the time, and, more important, he thought things were going okay. There had been a number of trying episodes which Tom had handled well. As an example, the girl to whom he had been attracted, and whose way of thinking had pleased him, did not respond to his moves toward a closer relationship. She was happier with just being part of a group, doing things together. Tom was deeply dejected, experiencing doubts about himself. He struggled uncomfortably with the feeling that perhaps she could see through his asking for a date as just an excuse to "make out." But he was also able to relate this to his earlier feelings about his mother's intrusiveness and his fear that she could see through the door into his room. As he struggled to regain his self-esteem, he was both amused by his fears and at the same time able to free himself from such distortion. After several weeks he observed with some surprise and relief that things didn't throw him as much as they used to or for as long a time. "It just feels good when you listen to me. You don't tell me what to do and you don't tell me what I should have done. You give me space to think for myself."

In therapy he began to check out with the therapist, as "one guy to another," what the guys were saying and doing—"or rather, *saying* that they're doing"—in their relationships with girls. He still felt uncomfortably behind in his own experimentation, worrying about the strength of his masculinity. There were times when the "whole thing" seemed to be too much and he wanted to turn on or to crawl into bed and sleep it all away. He described uncomfortable fantasies of crawling onto his therapist's lap and being closely held. He dwelt longingly on those earlier times when his father had seemed such a big man to him; he had enjoyed being his "little guy" and would often sit on his lap. He recalled that he enjoyed roughhousing with his father, how excited he would get and how he would struggle against being pinned down. These memories now triggered sensations of physical arousal, which both frightened and shamed him, though they were at the same time pleasurable. And these sensations could also be stimulated by the feeling of being affirmed by his therapist.

The therapist offered his understanding that it was natural for a little boy to enjoy the strength of his body, in all its parts, just as now he was learning to enjoy and understand his maturing body. Being understood in the present reverberated to those earlier times when it felt good to sit on his father's lap absorbing his strength. "When we work together and you feel understood, it's like being held."

It was hard for Tom to accept the frustrating slowness with which the process of defining his sexual tastes and proclivities proceeded; he was envious of his friends and their exploits. He felt comforted when his therapist commented, "But Tom, isn't it *your* own time schedule, *your* body, *your* tastes?" Tom's eyes moistened when he replied, after a struggle to regain his composure, "You just don't know how good it feels not to be pushed. To have some space."

There emerged more clearly periods of intense lusty feelings toward girls, which would arouse anxiety in his relationship with his younger sister. Since she was somewhat into "the same scene," he would become uncomfortable about the fantasies her nearness triggered. With a combination of pride and concern, he reported that she was very popular with his friends and that he kept warning her about guys, trying to slow her down.

His mother began to consult him about his sister. In the midst of reporting his reassuring comments to her—"It's just a phase; give her time; she'll snap out of it"—he appeared startled and burst into laughter. "Just like my Dad! I guess sometimes it *is* just a matter of waiting and maybe with her it'll straighten out, but with me, I know now I needed your help."

Tom's behavior with his parents was undergoing a change. In place of his earlier withdrawal and later brittle irritability and explosiveness with them, he reported pleasure, at times, in being with the family. He had observed his mother's attempts to give them all "more room." He said, rather shyly, that he thought she was getting a lot out of *her* therapy, too. She seemed more content. His parents were doing more things together. "She isn't after us so much."

As the school year drew to a close, Tom's vigor and zest in his studies and activities continued with only minor upsets. He enjoyed his friends, a different group from those of his earlier years and those of his depressed period. In class activities, he played an important role and was sought out by his peers. He used his therapy hours now mainly to work over and work through things that hadn't gone as well as he had hoped, looking for the reasons. He would be disappointed, even dejected, but he would recover and reengage himself in ongoing activities. He was also accepting of his own unique skills. When a close friend won an award in a science fair, he was genuinely glad for him while observing that he himself wasn't the kind of person who could work "all those long hours alone." He got his "kicks out of working with people . . . like you do." But he also differentiated his interests from those of his therapist by stressing that, for him, working with people would be in politics or in government. He wanted to change things; he wanted to make the world a better place—and it could be, he just knew it!

He blurted out that his girlfriend thought so, too, laughing in some excitement as he commented that he guessed he hadn't said anything about her. This was a beginning relationship, but one he felt hopeful about.

> TOM: I guess I wanted to keep it to myself until I was sure we'd hit it off.
> THERAPIST: You were concerned that I might pry, not let you handle your affairs on your own, as earlier you felt your mother intruded on you.
> TOM: I like the space you give me. You listen; you let me go until I'm ready to share if I want to share.

Tom was now actively engaged in the adolescent process with increasingly effective self-awareness. This awareness enabled him to use signal anxiety to alert internal regulation of self-soothing, of seeking and finding those selfobjects necessary to his sustenance, of enduring ambiguity and uncertainty as he sought to master those skills which would put him on the road to achieveable goals. The zest with which he approached his life differed markedly from the immobilization of the young adolescent who had initially been presented by his parents for therapy. Termination now seemed clearly in order and a date was set toward which he worked. As the time for this approached, Tom was aware of sadness along with a sense of excitement.

> TOM: It's not like I'm depressed the way I used to be. I guess I'll miss coming here, miss being able to talk things over with you. It used to be everything I did I was always hearing your voice or wondering how you'd look at it. Now, lots of the time I just lose myself in what I'm doing. Even when things don't turn out so great, I'm thinking about how I can work it out; . . . not "wait till I see Mr. T."

He became engrossed in plans for college and graduation from high school. With his father, he visited several campuses. He struggled with uncomfortable feelings about whether he might choose his father's college because he still wanted to be "his little guy" or because of its genuine appropriateness for his interests. He was accepted by several colleges and felt a heady excitement about the way in which the world was opening up for him. He said, with a grin, he and his girlfriend had turned handsprings, "just like kids," when they were accepted by the same colleges. They weren't sure what their decisions were going to be, but Tom did not feel threatened by the possibility of a separation. They would still get together on holidays.

What seemed firm in Tom was this ability to work independently on his problems, as well as the capacity to seek out and work with mentors, parents, and peers. He felt in charge of himself, and when things did not go well he did not shrink from looking within and determining what initiatives were available to him. In their last therapy hour, Tom thanked his therapist, saying he knew he would miss him, wondering if he could drop by at the Christmasbreak to talk things over. His therapist replied that he would miss him, too, that he felt they had worked well together, and that he would be glad to see him.

Reflecting on the experiences of this adolescent from the vantage point of self psychology, what may be striking is the absence of focus on oedipal conflict. The therapist did not approach the problem of treatment from the viewpoint of libidinal theory, a retreat from the demands of puberty. Tom's need to medicate himself appeared rather as a driven attempt to reinstate a feeling of wholeness, to calm and soothe himself. In the treatment literature of adolescents, consideration of the oedipal conflict seems to overshadow all else, and most pathology is diagnosed and interpreted from the viewpoint of regression from oedipal issues, fixation at preoedipal levels, or neurotic pathology arising from faulty resolutions of the oedipal conflict. Kohut's depth immersion in the psychic life of his patients, and those patients whose analysis he supervised, led him to the conviction that the storms of adolescence proceeded from the failures of the selfobject milieu to respond to the whole developing child. In the therapeutic relationship what is reinstated is the thrust to complete growth when the self is phase-appropriately supported.

As a latency-age child Tom seemed to have had a well-functioning cohesive self. He seemed to take pleasure in his schoolwork and was apparently a child whose attractiveness and skills elicited appropriate mirroring from the selfobjects of his expanding world. He enjoyed the companionship of a group of friends and schoolmates. It was only later that the intensity of his mother's merger with her son became apparent, and

Tom's lingering in that merger signaled deficits in his self structure as well.

The details of his mother's difficulties with his father can only be inferred from the glimpses of her competitive strivings with her more materially advantaged sister and her growing discontent. Unlike his wife, Tom's father did not feel discontented with the level he had reached. He had no burning desire to enhance his position or increase his possessions. From his wife's viewpoint, his lack of assertiveness seemed to be weakness; she wanted him to shape his abilities and productive efforts into more ambitious projects than the small business which he owned and managed. He tended toward passivity and delay in tackling new projects. There were intimations of this in the early consultation with the parents and from comments Tom volunteered in his sessions about opportunities which father had bypassed, though he centered his disagreements with father in the realm of politics.

In her increasing frustration, Tom's mother, to bolster her self-esteem, turned more and more to her son, overseeing his grooming, monitoring his school work more intensely at a time when his thrust toward adolescence dictated his need to free himself. Up to a point, he did not resent his mother's continued supervision until his own maturation and the intensification of her tenacious hold resulted in an explosive rupture. At the same time, Tom began to feel something amiss in the continued relationship with his eighth grade teacher; he experienced humiliation particularly when his classmates teased him about this relationship.

As he became more alert to his slower physical development, he sought more actively to disentangle himself from the merger with his discontented mother. Because of her own incompleteness and fragmentation fears, his mother could not release her hold and respond with appropriate acceptance and pleasure to her son's independent strivings toward new selfobjects; nor could his father, lacking assertiveness, effectively encourage his son's struggle to free himself.

Adolescents need selfobject peers intensely; they seek and use selfobject peers as alter-egos, partners in the process of sharing their anxiety about changing body structure, as well as of defining and experiencing pleasure in their new freedom and power. Their need of parents as selfobjects undergoes a transformation as they seek new symbols and idols for confirming a sense of greatness and expanding idealized goals (Goldberg, 1975; Kohut, 1977; Wolf, 1980). The symbols and idols of these years will go through many transformations and will bear little resemblance to earlier values and goals; this is a necessary process in firming and deepening psychic structure. Parents are still needed as available but not as intrusive selfobjects. In the failure of Tom's parents as selfobjects to respond to the whole self of this developing adolescent, Tom felt increasingly depressed, a sense of hollowness, emptiness. Left out and left behind by his earlier group of friends, to relieve his shame he turned finally to classmates whose feelings of low self-esteem matched his own. He turned away from former activities that had been an expression of his central nuclear self and sought to restore a sense of perfection and wholeness through a soothing drug.

Tom's therapist did not target the parents as culprits, nor Tom as victim. He viewed Tom's earlier sneering at his quarreling parents and his apparent boredom and flushing when his father reiterated his belief that Tom was going through a phase and would snap out of it as an expression of bitter disappointment in his formerly idealized parents. As his mother clung more desperately to Tom as a selfobject through whom narcissistic replenishment for her own undernourished self could be provided, Tom increasingly retreated. He found no strength in his father's easygoing acceptance. He withdrew from both parents and from the intense struggle to identify his own inwardly perceived and evaluated goals.

Through his understanding of the unfolding transference needs for affirmation, the therapist now provided Tom with the opportunity to experiment zestfully with typical adolescent tasks, to fill in missing functions of self-esteem regulation. There was a long period of need to have the therapist perform a mirroring function, rekindling his earlier pleasure in himself and his power. Tom exposed his reawakened grandiosity at first shyly and then rather imperatively to his therapist for confirmation. Small lapses or failures in his therapist's responses enabled Tom to deepen his capacity to soothe himself and to strive for and build in greater resourcefulness in regulating self-esteem. Along with a mirroring transference, there emerged an idealizing transference in which his therapist's calmness and understanding allowed Tom the "space" and time to experience and formulate his own needs and wishes. When these seemed amorphous and uncertain, he absorbed Tom's doubts and disappointments without censure, blame, or goading.

Goldberg (1978a) describes the need of adolescents to come to grips with the boundaries of their capacities. This was difficult for Tom. Overstimulated by his mother's intrusion of her own expectations and goals for him but understimulated in the opportunity to reflect on and forge goals for himself, he retreated to his longing for an earlier state of wholeness. But through the space and time provided by the new selfobject therapist, Tom regained a sense of himself as the center of his own perceptions, an initiator in defining and elaborating skills that gave him mastery over his talents and enabled him to use these to work toward reliable goals.

It seemed clear from the manner in which Tom was able to engage in therapy that the parents of his earlier years had provided an empathic milieu for their small son. They had been joyous and proud of his attractiveness and intelligence. They were pleased by his performance and the response of others to him. A child's success does enhance parental self-esteem. It is only when the fragility and incompleteness of one or both parents intrude on the forming, reforming, and firming self of the child, when a parent desperately seeks to maintain an archaic merger with the child that self disorders ensue. The transformation and the vicissitudes of the self in adolescence require a concomitant transformation of the parental self. While remaining available according to the adolescent's need, parents gradually learn to accept a less central role in the life of their child. This Tom's mother could not undertake until she entered psychotherapy herself.

In considering Tom's self pathology, his therapist might have viewed his problems as stemming from fixation at preoedipal level to avoid confronting his murderous rage at his father as rival. He may similarly have viewed Tom's reaction to his mother as a defense against, and retreat from, incestuous fantasies. But Tom's yearning for the mirroring archaic mother was a far cry from longing for incestuous union.

His therapist might have viewed Tom's fantasies about sitting in his lap and being closely held as an expression of homosexual longings. But a self psychological view permits us to understand his rage at his father's failure to perform the idealized assertive selfobject function of his earlier years, which then resulted in a too abrupt de-idealization, reactivating a longing to merge with the archaic selfobject father of his childhood. When these mirroring and idealizing needs met with failure to provide the nutrients by both parents, which the expanding and reforming self of adolescence required, he turned to self-medication to evoke a sense of wholeness and perfection. He chose as peers those whose similarly low self-esteem did not provoke a sense of discrepancy and fragmentation.

Viewing these transference needs as directed not to him as an incestuous object but to him as a new selfobject through whom interrupted self-development could continue, the therapist's response to Tom was to mirror and affirm his emerging pride in his physical and mental attributes. As new selfobject, Tom's therapist allowed himself to become the target of Tom's need to merge with and idealize his calmness and competence. It was not that the therapist was blind to or oblivious of oedipal issues, but that these could be resolved through his focus on Tom's mirroring, idealizing, and partnering needs. Through transmuting internalization Tom could acquire the self-function of regulating and shaping sexuality toward an effective relationship. Tom could become joyously alive to his maturing sexuality. His ability to form a responsive relationship with a young woman, his performance in school and other activities, his improved relationship with his parents and his sisters, and more importantly, his zest as he planned for college affirm the resiliency with which he could now respond to adolescent tasks.

The purpose of therapy was to reawaken the thrust to continue and complete development of an undernourished self. The therapeutic process enabled Tom to replace selfobject functions—missing functions—with self-functions. Through his therapist as new selfobject he could disentangle himself from the merger with his mother in order to define, savor, and claim his ambitions as his own. He could turn from his father's passive acceptance of the status quo to engage in a lively dialogue with selfobject mentors and peers, as he shaped his ambitions into his own realistic goals, both immediate and for the future.

This is a case of moderate adolescent disorder which yielded to twice-a-week psychotherapy over a three-year period. Anna Freud in a classic paper described adolescence as an interruption of peaceful growth. She noted that upholding a steady equilibrium during the adolescent process is in itself abnormal. Her description bears re-reading:

> I take it that it is normal for an adolescent to behave for a considerable length of time in an inconsistent and unpredictable manner; to fight his impulses and to accept them; to ward them off successfully and to be overrun by them; to love his parents and to hate them; to be deeply ashamed to acknowledge his mother before others and, unexpectedly, to desire heart-to-heart talks with her; to thrive on imitation of and identification with others while searching unceasingly for his own identity; to be more idealistic, artistic, generous, and unselfish than he will ever be again, but also the opposite: self-centered, egotistic, calculating. Such fluctuations between extreme opposites would be deemed highly abnormal at any other time of life. At this time they may signify no more than that an adult structure of personality takes a long time to emerge, that the ego of the individual in question does not cease to experiment and is in no hurry to close down on possibilities. If the temporary solutions seem abnormal to the onlooker, they are less so, nevertheless, than the hasty decisions made in other cases for one-sided suppression, or revolt, or flight, or withdrawal, or regression, or asceticism which are responsible for the truly pathological developments. . . . (1958, p. 275)

The crucial period of self organization which is necessary in adolescence (Wolf, Gedo, and Terman, 1972) may be accomplished with seeming ease (Offer and Offer, 1975) or may become a turbulent period triggering destructive behavior, empty depression, or hypochondriacal preoccupation. Kohut differentiated between those adolescents who "look schizoid during a particular period because the life task is so great, and those in which there is such pervasive hollowness in their personality that only prolonged work will accomplish any healing for them" (1970, p. 158). Less dramatic is the loss of ambition, the failure to establish goals and the toll of aimless drifting and waste, as in Tom's situation. Tom had been making futile efforts to overcome the threat of disintegration, to calm and soothe himself. The process of psychotherapy enabled him to regain initiative in undertaking adolescent tasks.

Psychopathology in adolescence extends from psychosis through borderline states to neurosis. Kohut described personality and/or behavior disorders expressed in severe substance abuse, delinquency, and suicidal depression as the attempts of an enfeebled, fragmented, chaotic self to overcome a sense of deadness, to recreate an illusion of wholeness (Kohut, 1971, 1977, 1984). Goldberg described:

> profound disturbances of catastrophic dimensions where self-fragmentation and deviant restitution challenge the therapist with the two-fold task of empathy with the suffering of the patient and the need to find a therapeutic intervention which may prove effective. . . . We allow ourselves to enter into a world of chaos and/or unreal resolution or restitution. We must let ourselves experience an alien and possibly hostile world which does not seem to offer sustenance or support to the patient or else to identify with a psychotic self which has managed to comprehend such a world via a delusional system or by way of a retreat from reality. . . . [T]here is an enormous range of pathology in this area but the methodology of empathic participation remains constant and, particularly with these individuals, profoundly difficult. An understanding of the self-fragmentation or disorganization or pathologic restitution allows a more rational choice of treatment. (1978, p.127)

Without being drawn into the chaotic disorganization of the adolescent, the therapist can then determine whether a controlled environment is necessary. He can determine whether the adolescent can tolerate an intensive psychoanalytic process, or whether psychotherapeutic intervention is indicated. "If the process of disorganization predominates, then our therapeutic activity devotes itself to putting things back together. If the new self is a damaged or injured one, then we work on the reparative aspect. If a total reorganization is called for, then analysis of an adolescent is prescribed" (Goldberg, 1978, p. 128). Essentially, Goldberg calls for a shift of emphasis from partial perspectives of personality, such as that of the Oedipus complex, to a total consideration of the epigenetic development of the self, as described by Kohut (1977, 1984).

9

Self Disorders in
Late Adolescence
and Young Adulthood

IN LATE ADOLESCENCE and young adulthood, we may assume a reasonably firm, vibrant self, capable of enduring broad ranges of emotional reactions and responses to the vicissitudes of life. Lesser disorders of the self, threatened fragmentation, loss of vigor, and dysynchrony may ensue in the face of disappointment. Common experiences, such as failure to achieve a cherished goal, the loss of a valued relationship, or the need to leave one job for another, shake up the constituents of the self; in the process of restoration, an individual will seek customary ways of soothing and calming himself as he strives for mastery of the task facing him. In this manner he will overcome his temporary disturbance as he once again seeks to elaborate his skills and talents in order to bring about the expression and direction of his nuclear ambitions in achievable goals. As Goldberg (1975) has pointed out, dashed hopes may lead to redirected aspirations.

The experience of success can also subject the bipolar self to overstimulation of archaic grandiosity, creating a state of anxiety in which doubt and a fear of helplessness threaten fragmentation. In such instances the individual draws upon his world of selfobjects—lovers, close friends, colleagues, groups, societies, books, new avenues of learning—as he seeks to restore an energetic and uninterrupted flow of ambitions. He defines his talents in skills which he now elaborates and redirects toward new goals.

These lesser disorders are common, bringing about an ever deepening and firming self structure by the manner in which increasingly diverse selfobjects are selected and employed. Moreover, in turn, serving as selfobject to others in similar need—friends, mates, colleagues—enhances

111

and strengthens self-esteem in the capacity with which one is able to meet their needs. When an individual has done something for someone and is thanked, both parties experience an increase in self-esteem. It is by no means vanity to feel good that one has been able to help another. It is vanity only when one continues to display oneself in the process, preventing the individual from translating a selfobject function into a reliable self-function. This may be seen most prominently in the experiences of late adolescents and young adults as they seek to find their way in work, in relationships, in lifestyle. Parents who have problems in relinquishing their central role in directing and overseeing the lives of their children cajole, threaten, and yoke the child with the ultimate reproach, "After all we've done for you!" This is different from a dialogue vigorously pursued, with resolution and acceptance, leaving the child free to try his way, to make his mistakes, and to work through his errors. In sustaining relationships, parents may then be available when needed or asked. Their affirming support, offered without vengeful reproach, may allow the child to absorb what he has learned in order to find new directions.

It is hard to recall that even college graduates one hundred fifty years ago seldom questioned a father's authority. When Charles Darwin was invited to go for three years without pay as a naturalist on the voyage of *HMS Beagle*, he was eager to accept but regretfully refused when his father objected. His destiny was to be a clergyman. His father offered his consent only if Charles found "any man of common sense" who *advised* him to go. Such a man he found in his uncle, Josiah Wedgwood, a successful founder of the pottery firm, who marshalled a list of arguments to overcome Robert Darwin's objections. Later he rode by horse 30 miles with Charles to put the case to Robert's father (Brent, 1981). The rest is history. Although framed in that earlier time, the incident reveals the 22-year-old Darwin turning to a new selfobject whom he idealized as he continued to forge and pursue his goals.

Like adolescence, late adolescence and young adulthood are crucial stages of transition. As the bipolar self struggles to balance internal and external forces, self-esteem is threatened by disturbing inroads into values, ideals, and goals. Most young people accomplish this transition, not without difficulty and suffering, but with increased strength, enhanced self-esteem, expansion of their values and guiding ideals, and a better delineation of their goals. Without becoming engulfed or overwhelmed, they appear to move into highly productive work in academia, the professions, or industry. They can involve themselves in those additional pleasures which enrich life, in a loving relationship, friends, various cultural and physical activities, sports and play. When they do become

deeply upset, they appear to be able to employ self-righting measures to restore their equilibrium.

Others suffer a profound loss of gratification in their work, family, friends, or activities. They seem unable to modulate internal needs and external demands, withdrawing from society or seeking out groups that lead them away from vigorous pursuit of solutions to their problems. They may engage in self-destructive behavior, such as substance abuse. They may experience psychosomatic illness.

The tasks of late adolescence and young adulthood may thus expose serious deficits in the bipolar self. Unresolved mergers with archaic selfobjects may result in a joyless pursuit of goals, a vertical split between ambitions and goals, in which the individual cannot trust his own perceptions, cannot initiate activities to test them, cannot define his own life goals. Perhaps nowhere is there so concentrated a population revealing these problems than in a university mental health clinic. Students at various levels who are seeking to define their goals in academic terms and to professionalize their talents seek psychiatric help when they reach an impasse which does not yield to the sustaining relationships with faculty, peers, or family. Particularly among new undergraduates vulnerability and narcissistic blows trigger immobilization and despair. The resultant self disorders may range from mild, transient moods through severe disorganization to suicidal states. Self deficits may be exposed requiring a broad range of intervention, from brief psychotherapy, to intensive analysis, and in some instances, to hospitalization. Deficits—missing functions of monitoring signal anxiety, calming and soothing themselves as they strive for mastery—may be found in one pole or another, or in both.

The transition from structured home and high school to relatively unstructured university setting exerts enormous pressure to deepen their knowledge in demanding coursework and to achieve a new level of relationship with parents, mentors, and friends. Under this pressure there is exposed a fragmenting, enfeebled self struggling to maintain cohesion through the employment of measures that seek to restore a sense of wholeness. These "immature personality distortions" may be temporarily regressive forms from which the individual can spontaneously recover.

Many young people achieve university admission with a background of substantial achievement in some field. Their promise of future greatness is fueled by the approval of parents, mentors, and friends. In the new social environment to which they have come, they expect a continuity of this approval, fulfillment of that destiny for which they have been prepared. In Blos's (1954) terms, their great future lies behind them. Competition with other equally well-prepared students comes as a sudden disruption of what has appeared to be a continuous course, well laid out,

and they are forced to reorganize their feelings and thoughts about themselves and their destiny. This occurs both in the lives of students whose grades continue at a very high level and those for whom grades indicate less preparation, less promise, or less interest in pursuing a course of study than anticipated.

These students suffer painful loss of confidence; they question their own worth and the value of long-cherished goals. They complain of emptiness, of feeling unloved, of being unable to respond to others. They may experience severe depression, disturbing dreams, immobilization or frenetic activity; they may have painful physical symptoms. In sum, under the impact of transition, deficits in the bipolar self system become painfully exposed and illness may ensue. The special aid in working with these young people is that, even for students with lifelong habits of loneliness and isolation, there is a great pressure to confide. Shorn of the customary supports of family and familiar surroundings, and faced by increasing demands of adult life, they experience a keen sharpening of the need for structure building. Everything they see, read, or experience, in waking or dreaming states, resonates to earlier stages of their development. The freshness of their experiences, the poignancy of their memories, the richness of their imagery allow the expression and identification of transference needs, whether mirroring, idealizing, or partnering, or elements of each. The urgency with which new selfobjects are chosen is uniquely endemic to late adolescence and young adulthood and is not evidence of shallowness of relationships but of a heightened need for sustenance and nourishment.

I shall offer a series of vignettes to illustrate how the thwarted thrust to continue development of the self is overcome, how the undernourished self, through the therapist, a new selfobject, finds the conditions under which healing can take place. The two cases I have selected range from mild disruption to more entrenched self disorder.

Henry

Henry, a 17-year-old first year student, came to the clinic because of an overwhelming feeling that life was meaningless. He noted that he would be 18 the following day and added that, if anyone could show him that it was worthwhile to go on living, he would try. The depth of his depression was visible from his slow speech, marked pallor, and dejected posture. It was only with difficulty that he would respond to the concerned questions of the therapist, revealing that he had been on campus for about six weeks. He had come from a small southern town and had very much looked forward to enrolling at the university of which he had heard a great

deal. No one from his community or his family had ever gone so far away to school. The dormitory in which he lived was huge, and he knew nobody even after six weeks. When he stood in line at the cafeteria, he was always alone. Sometimes he skipped meals because it was hard to join tables where everyone seemed to know each other but no one even knew his name.

The drudgery of his classes, normally the most intense interest of his life, led him to avoid them. Even physics, to which he had specially looked forward, had become dull. The instructor seemed "hellbent to get out of there" when class was over and simply pointed to a sign giving his office hours when Henry approached him. He would have liked to talk to his instructor, who was the author of the text they were using, but he felt that any questions he might ask this very busy man would be too trivial.

The therapist expressed an interest in hearing more about Henry's earlier enthusiasm for physics and Henry very hesitantly began to describe his long-term interest in astrophysics. His knowledge had been sufficient for him to place out of the first year into an advanced course in which there were a number of graduate students. At home, one of his high school teachers and he had worked together on a particular project which was then entered in a state competition, winning third prize. In view of the size of his high school and the unavailability of the sophisticated machinery he had needed, the judges were very impressed with Henry's work and his instructor's supervision. It was at this instructor's urging that Henry had applied to and been accepted by the university with a large scholarship. He felt, now, that he would never make it, that he would disappoint a lot of people who had helped him. Nothing seemed worthwhile. Troubled with disturbing dreams, he slept fitfully. From one of his dreams he awoke in a cold sweat. He dreamed that he had been climbing a certain ridge near his home town. He was tackling the vertical face when a thunderstorm broke out. Struggling, he could pull himself onto a narrow, sheltered ledge, but then could move neither backward or forward.

He recalled that something like his dream experience occurred when he was 11 or 12. He had gone with his parents and younger sisters for a picnic in a state park at the foot of a mountain near his home. After lunch he had wandered away and had begun to climb the steep side of the mountain because, through the trees, he could see an interesting formation he wanted to investigate. He had climbed quite a distance when, looking down from the height, he had become frightened. He could not move backward or forward. He heard his parents calling from a distance and kept shouting to them, "I'm up here!" A short time later his father appeared and after a moment calmly said, "You can make it, Henry," talking him down from the height by calling his attention to footholds below. When he reached the ground, his father hugged him and said, "You're quite an explorer." He never made fun of him or scolded him; in fact, he used to tell the story to friends and neighbors approvingly, emphasizing Henry's bravery and adventurousness.

His father was a farmer, well-known and respected for his ability and generosity. Henry reported that with neighbors his father stressed not his own role as rescuer but his admiration for his son's curiosity and exploratory interests. Thus, as an idealized selfobject, this father took quiet pride in his son. Henry's ability to respond to and work with his idealized high school teacher reflected a well-functioning cohesive nuclear self in which the development of idealized goals had been fueled by his appropriately nourished ambitions. The sudden disruption in leaving a community where he was well-known and admired, in which family and friends were available, to come to a large institution in which he had not one familiar, available friend, led him first to seek out a familiar kind of selfobject, his physics instructor. The latter's brusque dismissal left him without other resources to which he could turn. His dream reverberated to his early adolescent experience of danger, but in his dream there was no rescuer.

Henry's was not an empty depression but rather one of depletion, as he was unable to find available selfobjects in a new environment. He engaged rapidly in a mirroring transference with the therapist and even in the first session his marked pallor disappeared, as his speech became increasingly lively. Though he now looked forward eagerly to his birthday, when he was sure he would have packages and a phone call from home, he was fearful of returning to the loneliness of his room. He eagerly accepted the therapist's comment that it was understandable that he should have been lonely and upset, since he was undertaking his studies in a difficult university and in a challenging field without any friend nearby. Going ahead seemed dangerous yet going back seemed shameful and disappointing to others.

The therapist said that she was glad Henry had come to the clinic. It might be useful for him to talk over his experiences and his feelings about his move to a new environment until he felt more in charge. This plan Henry accepted eagerly. Over the next few months, with the therapist as a calm, listening presence, Henry poured out his youthful fantasies of his life's work, his anxieties as to his competence, his feelings of shrinking grandiosity as he recognized the strengths and rich backgrounds of some of his classmates, and his questions as to his native ability and deficits in his educational background. With focused empathic attention to his anxieties and concerns, his therapist enabled Henry to recognize that these were typical of college years. The twinship, partnering needs Henry now exposed became a prominent part of the transference in which his therapist, in response to Henry's questions, shared a bit of her own confusion in coming to a large institution as an undergraduate. She, too, had assumed that everyone was better prepared than she, with richer native endowment: a premise that had gradually given way as she learned to know her fellow classmates, to test out her abilites, and to find her own niche. Henry was struck by this, commenting, "You found your own niche, not a toehold on a ridge!"

It would be difficult to select out the mirroring, idealizing, partnering needs which Henry exposed in the transference to which the therapist responded. In the ensuing three months Henry, shyly at first, but then with increasing enthusiasm, developed several friends within his dormitory and within his classes. He was even able to meet his venerated physics instructor in a conference over a paper which he had been assigned and which Henry then tackled with energy and exuberance.

Returning from his Christmas holidays, he reported how excited he had been in sharing his experiences with his high school physics instructor. He had also been able, while basking in the comfort of being at home with his family and friends, to prepare them for the fact that the work he was undertaking now was far more difficult than anything he had expected. He was not at all sure of what he could accomplish. He distinguished between his mother's assumption that he would be wonderful at whatever he would undertake and his father's recognition that these were difficult years in which Henry would ultimately find what he was good at and wanted to do. "But I have four years for that!" He added with a grin that in between there was also time "for other things." He thanked the therapist for her help, shaking hands warmly, adding as he left, "I guess I'll see you around campus!" The sustaining selfobject function of the therapist had now "gone inside" (M. Tolpin, 1971) to become the self-function of easing his anxiety as he pursued new ventures.

This brief vignette offers a glimpse into the manner in which Henry, away from familiar, sustaining selfobjects, and rebuffed in his attempt to seek out a new selfobject, responded to a severe blow to his self-esteem. Although he arrived on campus with an action-poised program which would give expression to his ambitions in cherished goals, the absence of sustaining selfobjects resulted in a loss of hope, depression and dread of the future—a depleted self. The rapidity with which he experienced restoration through his use of the therapist as a new selfobject speaks for the essential vigor and wholeness of his nuclear self. His ability to use a new selfobject does not reflect shallowness in his relationships, an easy exchange of one for another, but, rather, the adolescent developmental readiness to find and use such selfobjects for sustenance. The disruption of continuity in familiar supports and his failure to engage new selfobjects exerted an enormous strain in which there emerged, with intensification because no immediate nourishment was at hand, his need for sustenance in three areas: "his need to experience mirroring and acceptance; his need to experience merger with greatness, strength and calmness; and his need to experience the presence of essential alikeness (twinship) from the moment of birth to the moment of death" (Kohut, 1984, p. 194). When response to these needs was provided through brief psychotherapy, continuity and cohesiveness were restored.

Goldberg (1977) describes the readiness for selfobject transference among adolescents that would otherwise be available only after much therapeutic work. The essential health of Henry's nuclear self is reflected in the manner in which he was able to use his therapist for further structure building. He could accept the possibility of his own limitations; he could endure the ambiguity as to whether he would be successful in a particular goal. This awareness allowed him to begin to explore what was needed to test his suitability for that goal. His was not a "grandiosity which admits no weakness or toleration of being brought down to earth" (Goldberg, 1975). On the contrary, with his father, his high school instructor, and now the therapist, Henry had demonstrated his capacity to transmute the calming strength and partnering functions of these selfobjects into self-functions through which he could progress to his own goals or forge new ones.

This case provides an understanding of the manner in which a mild disorder of the self, unyielding to the usual self-restoring efforts of the individual, can be addressed by a therapist employing an empathic understanding of the transference needs for mirroring, idealizing, and partnering. Applying the theory of self psychology involves a two-step process: empathic understanding of the transference needs followed by an explanation of their reactivation and childhood roots. The selfobject functions performed by the therapist are then transmuted into repaired and restored self-functions, which permit the individual once again to engage himself in his life tasks.

Andy

The second case demonstrates deficits in the goal-formulating pole of the self. Such deficits reflect an inability to define and pursue goals with meaning and value to the individual. They are pursued rather to retain a merger with an archaic selfobject and are in conformity with the ambitions and values of that selfobject.

Andy was a very tall, attractive, but solemn 20-year-old who had encountered an inexplicable loss of motivation in his studies. Although he had been planning to finish college in three years so that he could start medical school, and was only six months away from graduation, he had stopped going to classes. He spent his time reading or visiting friends in a dorm in which he used to live as a freshman. Usually he had been able to pull things together by the end of the quarter, even if it meant very intensive studying for a week or ten days. This time, as the quarter neared final exams, he knew he could not make it; he was struggling against enormous resistance. Indeed, he was filled with a "vast disinterest." What did it all matter anyway? To what end? Why bother? Although he had been embarrassed about asking his advisor for incompletes, nevertheless he approached him asking to withdraw from school. Because of his previously very high record, his instructor allowed him to take incompletes and suggested that he consult the clinic to see what he could make of this turn of events.

As he related what had happened to the therapist in a polite, interested manner, Andy conveyed the sense of an observer. He commented conversationally that he supposed the therapist would want to know something of his history and without hesitation proceeded to provide this.

Andy described himself as the oldest of three children. His widowed mother supported the family on her income as a dental technician. With almost fatherly pride he spoke about his two younger sisters and his plan to help them with their education, although he himself had been virtually self-supporting through his first three years at the university. His relationship with his mother had "always been a good one." She tended not to take an authoritative position with him but respected his judgment, leaving him free to make his own decisions. His father had died very suddenly just before Christmas when he was 12, and he recalled his bewilderment: out of all of the fathers in the world why was his father the one to die? Immediately after his father's death the family had been surrounded by his father's large family. Within a few weeks, however, his relatives had to return home and the family began to cope with the reality of their loss. They had always done things together, and he and his father had been particularly close in running the family store. The girls were still "too little"; they were four and six years younger respectively. He would accompany his father on various errands and work with him on repair jobs around the house. His father always emphasized the importance of education; indeed, both parents would refer to their own regret over having given up their educational plans.

With his father's death, the family had to sell the store, his mother went to work, and Andy continued to do a "man's job" around the house. He described, in simple manner but with quiet pride, how much he had been able to do, even, on occasion, helping neighbors who lived nearby. They "counted on me." He had always enjoyed school and had done well. His mother had always approved his activities and had never held him back from anything he wanted to attempt, but then, he "never gave her much cause to worry" about him. This was said with his one smile during the entire hour.

Currently, he was living in a house with five male roommates, a fairly congenial group who had known each other since their first year on campus. Two had now dropped out of school and were working. Over the Christmas break he had gone home to tell his mother his plans to drop out, too; though disappointed, she did not put pressure on him to change his decision.

He didn't quite understand why he "ran out of steam," but feeling as he did, he would not be able to complete the quarter. He had followed his advisor's suggestion that he at least try to understand his loss of motivation by consulting the clinic. Andy's manner was that of pleasant conformity without any real sense of urgency or involvement.

The therapist indicated that if Andy did drop out she would want to provide a treatment referral, since in her experience dropping out for a year removed the immediacy of the struggle but usually did not clear away the problem with studies. If he did decide to stay, the therapist would try to help him puzzle things out. She offered a tentative appointment for the following week and asked Andy to let her know his decision. The therapist was concerned and interested, and, though there was the risk of losing Andy by not saying flatly, "Stay and let's work together," (which might precipitate his departure in any case), the therapist felt it was important to leave the initiative with Andy.

Andy returned the following week, having decided "at least" to finish out the quarter. If he put out a great burst of energy he might be able to graduate at the end of the fall quarter, but he did not feel he could count on himself as he used to. Asked whether there had been any change in his relationships over the past few months, Andy began to talk about a resident head and his wife to whom he had been very attached in his first two years on campus. When they had left for another city, he and several friends moved away from the dormitory to set up their own apartment. Much of their time was taken up in athletic or social activities, very little in studying. Since Andy was the only one who would have been graduating a year ahead, the therapist raised the question of whether behaviorally, without conscious awareness, he was attempting to postpone the time when he and his roommates would have to go their separate ways. Andy said he had never given that much thought. Separation was "more or less expected and nothing much could be done about it."

The therapist asked quietly whether the loss of his resident head and the anticipated loss of his friends may have touched an old wound, the loss of his father. His eyes teared and he said softly he had not thought of that. What he had mainly felt was just a "whole lot of apathy," wanting some time off. If he left school he would be leaving his friends anyway. He had been pretty sure he wanted to go on to graduate studies, but maybe he didn't. Maybe he just wanted to be a businessman; maybe he just wanted to travel. The therapist suggested that there seemed to be many things pressing for his attention, which made studies seem dull. He nodded slowly and talked softly about the fact that his father was always so hardworking, had never really had much time for leisure. His father was responsible for his aging parents, and his mother had told him that it sometimes had made her very angry that his father had sacrificed his ambitions to stay near his parents. Andy wondered whether with an education his father could then have gotten into some line of work that wouldn't have been so hard on him as managing their store. In the end, they had to give it up anyway.

Therapy with this young man consisted of twice weekly interviews extending over two years. In the initial phase there was much evidence of his conformity, his wish to be pleasing and obliging to the therapist. There emerged not so much his fear of stating or presenting his own viewpoint as aridity and emptiness. He would fall back on such comments as "I don't know what exactly you want me to talk about" or a plea for the therapist "to get me started." The therapist was not withholding but rather suggested that Andy's loss of motivation had multiple roots. It would be memories, wishes, or fantasies that popped up in Andy's mind, rather than specific subjects or direction from the therapist, that would in the end prove helpful.

For a considerable period of time, Andy nostalgically idealized his relationship with his father. He repeatedly presented for the therapist's admiration his own ability to go on with his father's chores. The therapist commented that it was indeed remarkable for a 12-year-old to have developed such skills. Yet as a 12-year-old and later, weren't there tasks of his own that were pressing? It was here that Andy revealed a sense of emptiness, of deficit. The therapist's empathic attunement with an adolescent's needs gradually allowed Andy to recognize and verbalize interests of his own that had been overridden by his conforming behavior before his father's death. After his father's death his conformity had been an unconscious effort to perpetuate his father's presence. In addition, his mother's needs for solace and help obscured her recognition of Andy's need for comfort and support, for freedom to pursue typical adolescent activities. His ability to perform as the "man about the house" in various tasks was gradually taken for granted and expanded as he grew older.

At the same time, his mother "had made it very clear that she did not want to limit [him] in any way, that [he] was free to move about whenever [he] wanted and study whatever [he] liked." Andy could not remember, however, even as a small child, fantasying what he wanted to be when he grew up. He and his father never had any "real talks" about that; he supposed he was still "too young." He realized that his mother always regretted that his father, who had been in service when they married, had not taken advantage of the GI Bill to pursue an education. When interested friends later asked Andy what he was going to be, he would usually respond that he planned to study medicine, a reply which became routinized by the obvious approval of his questioners.

His concern and protectiveness of his younger sisters and his plans to provide for their education were much admired in the neighborhood. In fact, he had set aside a small inheritance from an aunt for this purpose, while working his way through school. When the therapist wondered whether it was not possible to give his own needs equal time, Andy was confused and then commented that he guessed no one really thought he had needs, "including me."

It was clear that Andy's parents had responded joyfully and with pride to their oldest child, encouraging his growth. He idealized his father, merging with him in a sense of power at the store, in work about the house, in an appreciation of the importance of education. With his father's death and the abrupt loss of their relationship, Andy took over as much of his father's tasks as his years permitted him to assume. It was not that the family had not grieved. They had, but the necessity to keep the family going meant that his mother permitted Andy to assume more and more of his father's chores. He performed well and took pride in his increasing ability. He received recognition and approval for this, and, as we have seen, was often in demand in the neighborhood for minor repair jobs. The information his mother shared with Andy about his father's failure to live up to his potential and her insistence that he not feel himself restricted to remaining close to her was an intrusion of her own goals, her sorrow, and her anger. She did not permit Andy to find a way of expressing his own ambitions through his own talents and skills in shaping idealized goals for himself. This he now had an opportunity to examine in the new self/selfobject unit created in therapy. Andy began to explore and reflect upon his own wishes. Moreover, the therapist's quiet, sustained interest allowed him to feel that these wishes had precedence and merit.

Andy was able to acknowledge his dejection over the loss of his resident head, whose personal interest in him, and even more important, excitement in pursuing his own studies in law had performed for Andy a function which his own father had been unable to perform. When the resident head left, zest in his studies died away. He recalled his own silent questions: What does it matter? What is it all about? To what purpose? Although externally he could participate in social and athletic activities, he could not put forth the burst of energy required to finish his work and had thus taken incompletes.

He now understood this loss of motivation as, in addition to the loss of an important selfobject, the absence of clear interest in his studies. Although he had arrived on campus with an interest in medicine and he could perform well in pre-med courses, he now realized that his burning interest was less in the material than in the men whom he could idealize. His instructors were always more important than the subject matter. A very personable adolescent, he was adept at involving his mentors and reflecting their views. He would always join in class discussion, interested as long as he had the attention of his instructors. Without this, he became subject to depression reflected in apathy.

His particular attachment to his resident head was not only to the latter's appreciation and responsiveness to Andy and his talents, but to the excitement the young resident had in preparing himself for a profession. Andy had begun to reorient his own goal toward law, but this shift appeared to be by way of identification rather than of genuinely experienced interest. It was his resident head's enthusiasm which vitalized his interests. With the resident's departure, Andy and his friends left the dorm and set up an apartment of their own. Although he was able to complete the fall quarter with good grades, by the second quarter apathy overtook his efforts.

It was not incidental that his apathy increased massively before Christmas, the anniversary of his father's sudden death, at a time when he also experienced the loss of an important new selfobject, who, in essence, provided mature psychic structure in place of Andy's missing self structure. What now became reactivated within Andy was the sense of loss and hollowness occasioned by the resident head's leaving, reverberating as well to his father's death. He found it hard to leave sessions, became quite depressed between interviews, questioned the value of therapy and its power to forestall loss. His therapist's empathic response to his feeling of helplessness, absorbing his renewed grief and allowing him to mourn, enabled Andy increasingly to metabolize the self-function of soothing and calming himself, recognizing that ''good things'' had remained from his experience with his father and with his resident head. He could examine ''my earlier self'' as one in which his sense of wholeness, his self-worth, proceeded from his responsiveness to goals which were not his own but borrowed in a merger with his father, perpetuated through his mother and later with his idealized resident head. What had stimulated him but

still could not heal the deficit was his participation in the vitalizing friendship with his resident head.

Unlike Henry, Andy showed a hollowness in the bipolar self, particularly deficits in the pole carrying idealized goals. The immaturity of his goals
went unrecognized until exposed in the sudden confrontation precipitated
by the loss of his idealized resident head. As this reverberated to the earlier loss of his father, life lost its sense of purpose. Then, barely pubertal,
he had been merged with his idealized father, performing tasks with him
about the house, feeling purposeful and meaningful as he did so. With
his father's death, he had been able to maintain that merger by his obliging, conforming performance of duties around the house and in the
neighborhood, for which, indeed, he was admired and which did support his self-esteem.

Out of her own needs, his mother had maintained a merger with her
conforming, complying son, unaware of his immature goals in pleasing
her. In keeping with his mother's wishes for him, he had chosen a university a good distance from home rather than attending a nearby state
university, superficially demonstrating for her that she was not, like his
father's parents, binding him to her. He recognized now, that, although
his mother had never held him back from anything he wanted to do, "[he]
never gave her much cause to worry about [him]." His father had been
a disappointed man, joylessly pursuing his responsibility for his aging
parents and for his young family. Although Andy would speculate about
what his father might have become had he continued his education, there
was never any substantive indication of ambitions which his father had
forsaken. With his mother as well, her sorrow and anger at his father's
blighted life and her own regret at giving up her studies had never been
detailed in actual interests and choices. Even where the vicissitudes of life
force abandoning such interests, there is usually some spark of excitement
about once cherished ambitions, and this was lacking in both parents. It
was the zest and enthusiasm of his resident head which had stimulated
Andy and obscured the hollowness of his shift to law.

It is not that, in the process of absorbing the special aspects of selfobjects, late adolescents and young adults do not in intermediate steps identify, even grossly, with those selfobjects. This does indeed occur, but only
as a small incremental process in laying down a self-function unique to
that particular adolescent. In Andy's case, the identification had a hollow
quality of imitation and served rather to satisfy a merger hunger. In his
classes it was not the substantive material which riveted his attention. He
could always join in discussion as long as he had the response of his instructors. He needed the affirming, mirroring interest of an idealized
selfobject to complete his own self structure. It was this which kept alive

his productive efforts. He did not lack goals altogether; rather, he suffered from a horizontal split—immature goals held under a repression barrier which prevented their maturation.

Self psychology directs attention to the self experience in relation to others and focuses on the affective reaction to that experience (Goldberg, 1978). Kohut (1984) has referred to this as the "I's experience of the you," which, transmuted as psychic structure, allows the creation, consolidation, and ultimately the sustenance of the self. Andy was clearly able to seek appropriate selfobjects, but these were needed to complete self structure. Merged with an archaic selfobject, he was not industrious in his own behalf. His industriousness was for the purpose of maintaining a confirming merger, rather than one through which he defined for himself a field of study which he could pursue from profound inner conviction.

From Andy's description and his later course, it would appear that his father bound Andy to him in the performance of various tasks in which they engaged, as he, perhaps, had been bound to his parents. With his father's death, Andy could continue this work, bound now to his mother's selfobject needs. Was it possible that his father had suffered from a vertical split, able to pursue goals in a conforming, dutiful fashion but without that lively zest which bespeaks a vigorous flow of ambitions in centrally perceived and initiated activities, shaping innate endowment toward realistic goals? Andy's earlier expressed interest in medical school was the kind of response that much younger children give to adults who ask what they want to become. For Andy, following the death of his father, it was a response his elders found pleasing. Yet he could now perceive that his interest in the pre-med courses he had taken, and in which he could perform well, was rote-like. When he began to consider the law, the burning excitement of his resident head vitalized this choice. There was, however, a hollow quality to Andy's choice, reflecting little exploration of the substantive nature of legal studies or his own centrally perceived initiative.

During the middle phase of therapy, Andy's clear aptitude and his capacity to perform well in a number of directions, rather than firming his self-esteem, engendered a sense of something missing. To what end? To what purpose? There were repeated episodes of dejection when he distrusted a new interest, questioning whether its source was genuinely his own or still another attempt to curry favor by joining in a new merger. He began to express anxiety over the therapist's health, to experience feeling drained of interest and depressed between interviews or over weekends, which seemed especially empty to him. One might speculate that Andy's very competence aroused castration anxiety, as he browsed through career possibilities which would take him far beyond his father's accomplishments, and that it was this which had earlier brought him to a sudden impasse. However, the choice of medical school had also been far beyond father's achievements, but that choice had been less Andy's goal than a means of maintaining a merger with earlier selfobjects.

His fears about the possibility of the sudden loss of the therapist stemmed not from competitive aggressive feelings which might destroy the therapist but from his continuing need for a source of strength and competence while he, in small increments, attempted to define and pursue goals that were his own. The therapist interpreted his anxieties that he had no ideas of his own, that he was an empty vessel, as reverberating to that earlier loss of his father at a time when it would have been necessary for him in any case to begin to make his own choices, to plan his own life work. The fears about the therapist's health also reverberated to that earlier time, but here represented his fear that he would be deserted just when he was in the process of understanding what he wanted for himself. He was exceptionally adroit at searching for clues to what the therapist might like him to be. In small increments, he became able to tolerate doubts and uncertainties as he sought to define interests that confirmed him. In small increments he transmuted memory traces of his therapist's calming acceptance of uncertainty as a necessary part of the work of establishing realizable goals. The specific functions that his therapist had provided—understanding and explaining—now became his own functions. Apathy and emptiness had covered over his fear and uncertainty in tackling half-formed wishes and fantasies. These he now began to test out, engaging in a realistic struggle to bring about their realization.

When one of Andy's instructors asked him to become a lab assistant for a stipend, he was initially very anxious about his ability to function in this capacity. However, he discovered a growing pleasure in helping first-year students tackle assigned problems. He read widely in a particular field of math to prepare himself; he found ways of presenting the material simply, winning the admiration of his instructor as well as the gratitude of the students who sought his help.

Was he now simply joined in a new merger with the therapist? Was his current interest merely sustained by the ongoing relationship with her? He subjected his experience to thoughtful scrutiny in therapy sessions. Zest and excitement seemed to characterize his efforts with his students; he would note that although it felt good when someone thanked him for his help, it no longer seemed "the main point." He was increasingly absorbed in the problems the material confronted him with and eager to pursue their solution. Andy felt "really turned on" by the particular field of math that now engrossed his attention.

The final phase of therapy was ushered in by Andy's new ability to identify and work through temporary ambivalent intervals which arose from problems engendered in pursuing a very difficult field of mathematical inquiry. Initially he had expressed dejection, depression, appeals to "get me started." This had given way to periods of doubt and confusion about his choice of a field. "Is this, too, going to be a dry hole? How do I know I'll really be good at it?" There occurred a shift in the manner in which he began to work with his mentors, in his selection of new courses. Now he could more purposefully direct himself to examining the content and substance of the field he had chosen, its problems and its limitations, his own difficulties with it, and a new definition of his aptitudes and limitations. For longer periods of time he could sustain his self-esteem in the face of uncertainties and disappointments. He differentiated his feeling good when people appreciated his work and complimented him on his progress from his present feeling of strength: "It's a different feeling. *I* feel good about me, my math, and I'm always *thinking ahead.*"

As termination of therapy approached, Andy felt saddened that his father could not have shared his excitement. He felt that his father's dedication to his work, plodding and dull as that work had been, nevertheless was a strength that he had absorbed and now stood him in good stead. "When there are potholes in the road, I don't quit driving. I find ways of going around them . . . or filling them in." For periods of time Andy would find himself in silent conversation with his father, remembering tough jobs they had "pulled off together." He regretted that he could not have learned more about his father's aspirations and shared with him his own sense of fulfillment in his present work. He recalled and could now understand the way his resident head had always been "fired up" when he returned from his law classes.

Andy now appeared to be fully engaged in work which had meaning for him, in place of his earlier immature goals, sought and clung to for the purpose of maintaining a merger with an idealized selfobject. Through a calm, listening presence, his therapist, not always in tune but striving to become so, through optimal frustration and occasional failure had provided the conditions under which Andy could endure the sense of emptiness and ambivalence in defining his talents for himself, in elaborating skills which would allow testing his capacities and limitations. His therapist had absorbed his fears and doubts as Andy metabolized the capacity to envision, set, and pursue goals that were intrinsically his own. These now proceeded from centrally perceived wishes and aptitudes, freeing him to initiate and sustain purposeful activities toward a realizable goal.

The struggle of the self to maintain cohesion is especially intense during the period of late adolescence and young adulthood. In Henry we have seen a temporary disorder which arose in the process of seeking appropriate new selfobjects in a community new to him and without customary supports. In Andy, the disorder arose not from his inability to find appropriate supports but in the way in which he used these supports to complete self structure. At the center of his difficulty was a defective self, a vertical split in which his ambitions were derived from his wish to remain merged with others; his goals were unfashioned except as they allowed him to please archaic selfobjects.

These two young men had an opportunity to work toward resolution of their difficulties, filling in psychic structure, while they were still in college and shaping themselves toward future goals. Other young people struggle with deficits while seeking their way in employment. They contend with disintegration fears which threaten their jobs and prevent them from achieving gratifying relationships with others. Feeling unvalued, they may turn to substance abuse, perversions, or forms of delinquency in an effort to stave off crippling depression, to overcome feelings of deadness, or to seek a sense of fantasied wholeness and perfection. These problems similarly afflict the college population, but let us now examine them in young people in the business world.

Disintegration fears arising from a defective self are often reflected in alarming symptomatology. Yet it is surprising to observe how this alarming behavior can subside and ultimately be dropped as no longer necessary when the focused, empathic attention of the therapist enables the individual to recognize the needs and longings underlying symptom choice.

Lilian

Lilian, on probation for shoplifting an expensive bag, was asked as one of the conditions for probation to seek therapy. She was a graduate of a nearby college, working as a secretary until she could accumulate funds for further study. This well-dressed, reserved young woman, initially coldly complying with the requirement, ultimately revealed a series of small thefts which had not been discovered. Some items she could have afforded to buy, others she could not. None of the items really had value for her, although momentarily they would satisfy some unidentified craving within her. Later she would experience remorse and guilt, and, with this most recent episode, a sense of horror and shame. Over a three-year period of therapy what was revealed was her deep-seated longing for admiration and confirmation, which in her childhood years had never seemed forthcoming from her parents, primarily her mother. No matter how well-groomed, how well-behaved or helpful she was, it was usually her tantrumming, demanding younger sister who became the center of her mother's solicitude. When occasionally she balked and attempted to assert her own demands, she would be sorrowfully rebuked and told how much her mother depended on her to serve as a model for her younger sister.

The work of therapy aroused and quickened Lilian's awareness that underlying her occasional theft was the inability to formulate or verbalize her longings and needs. Indeed, feelings and needs were what made her "unworthy." She could not seek response to these openly or with assurance that they would be recognized and met as appropriate. The items she took temporarily assuaged these longings but soon lost their power to console, leaving her once more prone to her driven need. It was initially in the ultimately intense merger with her therapist that she worked through the ability to recognize and assert her wishes. Her cold, reserved manner gave way in small increments to greater liveliness and pleasure in a sense of her own self-worth. The process of structure building was a slow one, fraught with episodes of vulnerability to fragmentation when she felt any lessening of the therapist's involvement, inevitable at occasional periods of fatigue (emotional absence) or interruptions in the steady course of appointments. As these episodes were understood and interpreted, they provided opportunities for working-through, that is, for her to make her own the ability to calm and soothe herself while seeking to understand and find appropriate means of satisfying her needs and longings.

As therapy terminated, Lilian was engaged in a number of responsive friendships, although her demeanor still bore the marks of control and reserve. Nevertheless, she was able reliably to recognize those feelings which earlier had led her to take what was not hers, and to find ways of expressing her wishes to appropriately selected selfobjects who could respond to her and to whom she in turn could respond. Further, she could indulge her own needs and wishes, on occasion, in pleasurable activities and attractive dress.

Carol

In certain cases the sexualization of needs may blind us to the origin of such behavior not in unresolved oedipal conflict but in neurotic-like behavior covering over deficits in the nuclear self. To illustrate, Carol, a 28-year-old computer programmer who held an advanced degree in math, was referred for treatment when her persistently seductive behavior offended her co-workers and threatened her with the loss of a job. Minxlike in manner and appearance, for a considerable time she fended off efforts of the therapist to engage her in a meaningful dialogue. She made heavy use of double-entendres and laughed off the concern of her employers and colleagues that had brought her to treatment. Assuming that her therapist "would want a rundown" on her sexual experiences, she proceeded to enumerate these while boasting of their number.

The pet of her grandfather, who had lived with the family throughout her childhood and early adolescence, she had been singled out by him for his special attention. Her natural liveliness and appeal stimulated in him a sexual playfulness bordering on abuse. Her parents, both employed, made use of his caretaking in their absence, only occasionally interfering with what they had begun to perceive as inappropriate encouragement of the child in her seductive ways. Ultimately her grandfather had moved to a retirement home; with his absence and her long unsupervised hours at home, her loneliness and emptiness precipitated a series of brief sexual relationships with classmates and neighbors. In her workplace, she continued these attempts.

In therapy she had an opportunity to recognize the depth of her depression, her sense of emptiness in "having nothing" to make people like her except her sexual behavior. Her natural wish as a child and young adolescent to be admired, to be confirmed and guided, had been exploited by her grandfather for his own stimulation. Although her parents found her behavior disturbing and they would rebuke her for "her forwardness," they offered little confirmation of her worth. Joyless and hardworking, as selfobjects they confirmed for her the emptiness of her life, an emptiness which could be momentarily overcome by sexual engagement. In her work, she was industrious, effective, and constantly seeking some response from her colleagues. She would misunderstand their praise as an invitation for intimacy. In this particular setting her behavior was viewed as disordered, but their genuine liking for her and their appreciation of her work skills had brought about the referral for treatment.

Therapy, continued over a three-year period, provided the conditions under which she could recognize and openly express her depression, at one point bordering on suicidal thoughts, as she confronted her sense of emptiness. Although in the initial period there were frequent episodes in which she sexualized her mirroring and idealizing needs, these episodes became the basis for her growing awareness of such needs. Her transference to her therapist as the same kind of killjoy as her parents and her efforts to make him the counterpart of her overstimulating grandfather yielded to an understanding of the childhood roots of her limited ability to engage in meaningful relationships that were not sexualized. Her therapist's genuine confirming admiration for her skills and her worth as a human being not to be exploited sexually allowed her in small increments to transmute and internalize the capacity to understand the childhood roots of her earlier behavior. This understanding reduced her anxiety as she struggled to engage in less one-dimensional relationships. Through the process of optimal frustration she gained the capacity to view herself as a competent young woman, attractive and interesting. By the end of therapy she was reliably engaged in establishing herself in a more demanding level of work in the computer firm in which she was employed. She had also been able to maintain a relationship with a fellow student in the night course in computer technology for which she had enrolled to broaden and improve her skills.

Essentially, these four examples of self disorder, ranging from mild to severe, are typical of late adolescence and young adulthood. Such disorders can be severely crippling, taking their toll not only in personal suffering but in the loss to society of potentially effective individuals, some of whom, in borderline and psychotic states, severely tax our knowledge and resources for treatment.

Further, vital statistics give silent testimony to the inability of the more vulnerable among late adolescents and young adults to master this crucial phase in development. Attention is most frequently centered on the rise in suicide rate in this age group, yet suicides are third after motor and all other accidents in contributing to death by violence (U.S. Dept. of Commerce, 1984). Deaths resulting from such accidents are commonly the result of daredevil activities, alcohol abuse, or lack of seasoned judgment in controlling a vehicle.

We view youth as a time of energy, strength, and vibrancy, yet these are also years when confusion, rage, and despair are not yet informed by depth of experience and the capacity to delay action. Deepening of the psychic structure is still in process through recognition and engagement of a broadening world of appropriate selfobjects. New freedoms in personal relationships have emerged which, when abused, seem to emphasize superficiality and transience not only among peers but also among older adults to whom young people look for support. For some, selfobjects, human attachments, necessary for growth, maturation, and well-being, have been unavailable or accessible only on a catch-as-catch-can basis. When this has been true from earliest infancy, significant deficits in the bipolar self are seen. For others, deficits may be reflected in numerous defensive behaviors and emotional states described as borderline. As we increase our understanding of self psychology as a theory of human development, we may be able more flexibly and ably to use ourselves as selfobjects through which the thrust to continue development may be freed.

SECTION III

Treatment in Adulthood

10

A Fragmentation-Prone
Single Mother

SOCIAL WORKERS IN PUBLIC and private agencies, in clinics and hospitals, in the educational and correctional systems, and in private practice are faced daily with individuals and families who have experienced neglect and abuse for generations. The effect of such neglect and abuse may be extensive, and the social worker may well feel inadequate and helpless in confronting the resultant severe deficits. Moreover, the expectations of the individual who seeks or who is mandated for assistance may be totally unrealistic. Those who refer such individuals for treatment may also be impatient for results and may be unable to understand or support the lengthy process involved in assisting such individuals.

Social workers have long occupied a position mediating between the individual and society. Later we will examine some of the ramifications of the theory of self psychology for social workers engaged in seeking to bring about broad societal responses to classes of individuals. But here we are concerned with the treatment of self disorders among individuals in adult life.

The fit between self psychology and social work practice lies in the capacity of self psychology to clarify experiences common to social workers engaged in responding to the treatment needs of individuals with severe deficits. Multiproblem families and individuals are found at all levels of society, but poverty and lack of educational opportunity are more common characteristics among individuals treated by social workers than by other mental health professionals. Self psychology clarifies the universal striving to secure a response to one's potential for individuality and significance. In even the most seriously deprived individual, underneath abrasive and cynical behavior, a vestige of the need to be confirmed remains alive to be rekindled. The very presence of the social worker may quicken this need. Many methods and approaches have been devised for responding to and controlling the relationship which ensues, but, regardless of method, how one orders what one sees and experiences, how one uses oneself on behalf of the individual, becomes more vivid through an explanatory system of human behavior that places the self of the individual at the center of one's observations and views the new self/selfobject unit as the medium for treatment.

In the broadest sense self disorders of adult life range across a spectrum of low self-esteem and loss of, or the failure to establish, goals. Earlier selfobjects, in their inability to respond to the mirroring and idealizing needs of the forming self of the child or the self in the process of consolidation, have rendered the individual prone to fragmentation and vulnerable to outbreaks of rage. Such individuals often lack the capacity to identify their affective needs, to cue others to such needs, and to tolerate delay in response to these needs. As we have seen in the case of Josie, the child discussed in Chapter VII, the function of the therapist was first to help Josie to recognize her affective needs and then to be able to express them, to modulate them, to endure delay as she sought response from those around her, from appropriate self objects. Structure building, the establishment or restoration of a cohesive nuclear self, took place by reason of myriad selfobject functions performed by her therapist. Optimal frustration—not perfect intunement, not immediate response—enabled Josie to develop self-functions such as the capacity to recognize what produced her anxiety and to calm and soothe herself as she sought mastery of a particular task. She learned how to engage appropriate selfobjects, which initially helped her to consolidate a cohesive self and laid the groundwork for the ongoing process of seeking and maintaining an increasingly sophisticated array of selfobjects as she grew to maturity.

Treatment of Josie's mother, whose undernourished self sought a merger with her young daughter both for stimulation and for support, involved providing the mother with acceptance. This acceptance of her as a mother bewildered by the increasing array of disorders Josie exhibited permitted a beginning empathic merger. The experience of being enfolded by the caseworker's understanding, of having a response to her own needs for mirroring of her maternal strivings, opened the way for that guidance she so desperately sought. This guidance did not entail direction and advice. Rather, through the experience of the therapist's calming presence, her responsive understanding of her distress, Josie's mother transmuted a bit of the capacity for calming and soothing herself. Engrams of memory of having been calmed and soothed permitted her to delay and reflect before responding to her small daughter's needs and wishes, which had been reflected in distressing behavior. As Josie's mother experienced acceptance and understanding, an idealizing transference with the therapist emerged, followed by a partnering transference, in which together Josie's mother and her therapist sought to understand what transpired between Josie and her mother. As a beginning dialogue, rather than a derailed dialogue, was established, Josie's mother enjoyed an increase in self-esteem. Through an increasingly firm, cohesive self, she no longer needed to use Josie as a selfobject but could mirror, confirm, and guide her small daughter in response to Josie's needs.

It is important to remember that parents whose rage erupts in punishing behavior towards their children are unable to monitor anxiety, cannot modulate the need for immediate response, and lack the capacity to employ soothing and calming resources in order to accommodate to the child's tempo in learning. As we have seen with Josie's mother, such parents use the child as selfobject to sustain their own faltering self and respond with rage to the child's inability to meet the selfobject needs of the parent. Social workers treating such parents are, of course, engaged in the process of increasing parental understanding of childhood needs. But this understanding in itself does not bring about change. Cognition alone provides only the antecedent condition for change.

Let us for a moment consider the classic analytic position. Rangell (1981, p. 119) outlined the process by which the ego is confronted with the possibility for change. Analysis of resistance exposes the contents of the id and demonstrates the dramatic conflicts between ego and id. The observing ego of the patient, allied with and spurred by the analytic activities of the analyst, comes into the possession of new insights. With cognitive insights and the accompanying affect needed to render them useful, the ego gains a less obstructed view into the nature of the compromise formations it has effected and the unconscious reasons for which it has brought them about. The ego is now confronted with the possibility of action. This possibility now presents an opportunity for a change in behavior, but such a change entails responsibility. Therefore, thought, as trial action, now becomes joined in the process of change.

Although social workers have not been engaged in analysis, these concepts have formed the basis of their understanding of the treatment process. Ego psychology, a theory of human development based on the tripartite structure of the mind, the psychosexual line of development, and the adaptive and organizing function of the ego, does not genuinely illuminate the spontaneously developing relationship between social worker and the individual she seeks to treat. What has been generic to social work practice has been the experience of the universal human need on the part of the individual to be confirmed, to be mirrored as worthwhile.

Human strivings may have gone awry; behavior may be self-defeating or self-destructive; hope of an effective relationship with the world may be buried under layers of cynicism. Yet through the focused empathic attention of the social worker there is rekindled the earliest need for mirroring, the earliest longing to merge with the strength and wisdom of an idealized figure. The transference needs and wishes that emerge can now be understood as an attempt to secure a belated response to the search for appropriate mirroring, idealizing, or twinship functions, through which structure building may be revitalized.

Mirroring is not a fatuous term, indiscriminately applied. It requires an understanding of the specific need for specific affirmation or guidance that had been unavailable from earlier selfobjects at a specific time. And it requires explanation and interpretation by the therapist of why it arises in the present and its childhood sources. Merging with an idealized figure is not simple dependency; rather, it serves the purpose of allowing the individual to achieve standards and values, to reach for goals which are defined and undertaken through the individual's own perceptions and initiative. Twinship or partnering—working together toward understanding difficulties that have stood in the way of establishing skills and identifying talents—permits the individual to establish partnering skills and to reach out and function as a group member when such group membership is sustaining.

The position of classical analysis fails to illuminate what actually takes place between the social worker and the individual in treatment. It is not that, with cognitive expansion and the accompanying affect needed to render it useful, the ego has a more unobstructed view into the nature of the compromise formations it has effected and the unconscious reasons for which it has brought them about. It is not that the ego, now confronted with the possibility of action, recognizes its accompanying responsibility and engages in preliminary thought as trial action. Thought as trial action is a self-function of a cohesive, vigorous, harmonious self free to become a center of its own perceptions and to initiate a program of action proceeding from the interplay of the metaphorical poles of the bipolar self. The concept of a bipolar self not only provides social workers with a theory of human development that directly informs their work with individuals, but also offers an explanation for their experience with these individuals that flows from reality of the relationship.

To gain access to an understanding of how universal and basic the need for mirroring is in the human organism, one need only watch the faces of a crowd over which a TV camera is panning. Not even the most sophisticated member of a crowd fails to respond with interest; others, with their grandiosity less tamed, smile and gesture. Few are impervious to the experience of being noticed, and some desperately seek this. The phenomenon of adulation of well-known individuals, the wish to be close to them, part of their entourage, offers us an opportunity to understand the deep-seated need to merge with the strength and competence of an idealized figure, to be enlarged by his greatness. And there is also the need to be part of a group, to feel strengthened and sustained through being surrounded by people who are in essence like oneself, doing similar work, sharing similar biases and predilections (Kohut, 1984, p. 203).

The problem-laden individuals with whom social workers are engaged have suffered from inconsistently or grossly unavailable mirroring and idealizing selfobjects. Circumstances may also have isolated them from the experience of group membership. These individuals expose not drive, conflict, and neurotic compromise, but the basic human need to have the emotional sustenance with which aspirations can be formed, revealed, shared, and shaped through the experience of a new selfobject in tune with such needs and wishes. The concept of the bipolar self enables the social worker to be a part of the psychic life of the individual as an element in psychic structure building.

When an individual comes to a social agency or to a social worker in private practice for help at a point when personal resources seem unavailing, there is set in motion a process through which the conditions for healing are in place. By a calming and soothing presence, the therapist evokes and hears the painful story. The questions raised are for the purpose of clarifying what has transpired, unlike earlier questioning which often was for the purpose of assessing blame or failure and meting out punishment. The self/selfobject unit provided in this manner is one in which time can now be allowed to determine the severity of the injury, to judge what is needed, to determine whether and how rapidly the individual rallies. It is not that the therapist, new selfobject in the present, will now undo the past misunderstanding or neglect of earlier selfobjects. It is rather that, through focused empathic attention, the individual has an opportunity to understand how the thwarted needs and wishes give rise to the driven behavior or thought which has brought about the present impasse.

Mrs. B.

When Mrs. B., a 26-year-old mother accused of child abuse, comes to the agency with her two small boys, one runny-nosed and clinging despite her efforts to detach his arms from their tight hold around her neck, the second solemn-eyed and clinging to her skirt, she is sullen and distrustful. Treatment has been mandated by the court. She sits on the edge of her chair, trying to disentangle herself from the children, who cling even more closely. As the therapist offers the children toys to play with, they look doubtfully at their mother. The older child, four, hesitantly reaches for a truck, but the younger child turns away and clings even more tightly.

At this point the therapist makes no effort to separate the children from their mother, but instead opens the way for discussion of what has brought the family to court attention by commenting, "I can see how important you are to your boys." This serves two purposes: It supports self-esteem, relieving the need for defensiveness, and stimulates the mother's observation of her experiencing self.

MRS. B.: They never give me a minute to myself.
THERAPIST: That can be hard.
MRS. B.: (Still sullenly and defensively) Drives me crazy.
THERAPIST: Would you like to tell me what happened?
MRS. B.: (With hostile undertone) I guess you know or I wouldn't be here talking. I guess they think I'm one of those mothers that beat up on their kids all the time.
THERAPIST: I know that Mrs. S. (court social worker) said she thought you had your hands full trying to manage two little boys and that we might be able to help.
(Again, the therapist extends her empathic understanding of the task this mother is struggling with.)
MRS. B.: Nobody gave my mother any help and she managed okay with six kids.
THERAPIST: Still, each mother has her own set of difficulties.
(The therapist offers affirmation of Mrs. B.'s uniqueness, which Mrs. B. resists at this point.)
MRS. B.: (Eyeing the therapist suspiciously) There's nothing much to tell. Besides, I don't see what good talking is going to do. I've got these two kids, and I've lost my job. Tommy here (jerking her head in the direction of the four-year-old) was kicked out of nursery school because he's always fighting with the other kids. I just showed him what it feels like to have someone beat up on you. That woman on the first floor thought I was killing him or something, and she called the police. I think she just wants me out of there because she's afraid about the rent. . . . I can't get out to look for a job or anything without dragging these two along. Tommy is always getting into fights, and this one is always whining.

Tommy is absorbed in setting up a garage with his truck and at this point the therapist asks whether he would like to play in the other room where there are more toys and other children to play with. He looks doubtfully at his mother, who gives him a curt nod and warns him not to get into any fights. When the worker returns, the younger child has relaxed his hold on his mother and has begun to doze off. There is a cot in the room and the therapist suggests the mother would be more comfortable if she could put the child down. As she does so, Mrs. B. eyes the worker and then returns to her chair.

In the course of the hour, sullenly at first and then with considerable anger, she describes how difficult things are for her and that Tommy is a real brat: He still wets the bed. He peels paint off the wall and eats it. He never stops talking or sits still. He ought to know how hard things are for her and show her some sympathy. He used to be some comfort to her, but ever since the baby came he's gone back on everything he used to do. (Mrs. B. views Tommy as a selfobject, expecting him to calm and soothe her.) She sees him as just like herself as a kid, always in trouble. Her sisters were smart and did well in school. She got tired of having teachers always hold them up to her. She began to truant, for which her mother was always punishing her. If she was hurt, or sick, or something, all she ever got was more scoldings.

> MRS. B.: But what could she do with a kid like me? Once I even cut my wrists and then I tried to hide it from her.

The cuts were severe enough to require stitches. At the therapist's expression of concern, Mrs. B. shrugs her shoulders.

> MRS. B.: I was always bad.
> THERAPIST: I think you must have been feeling very badly to have cut yourself. Was no one concerned with your wrist-cutting—not even the doctor?
> MRS. B.: Oh, I was just curious, I just wanted to see the blood.
> THERAPIST: Could it be that you felt hopeless because no one seemed to realize how much you hurt inside? That you cut off all feeling?
> MRS. B.: It wasn't like that; I was just mad all the time. Tommy is a lot like me, mad all the time.
> THERAPIST: I'm wondering what it must have felt like to be a little girl to whom no one paid much attention, who couldn't tell anyone why she was so angry all the time, or what hurt.
> MRS. B.: (Sullenly) Don't you think some kids are just bad?

Mrs. B. at this point indicates a structuralization of her tie to a primitive archaic selfobject. To let go of such an object at this point is too frightening until a merger with a new selfobject can become a reality.

> THERAPIST: I think some kids think they are bad because no one listens to them or believes they need anything.

MRS. B.: (Turning her head away. After a pause) Once I swallowed a half bottle of aspirin and had to have my stomach pumped. When we got home, my mother kept yelling at me, "How could you do this to me? Don't I have enough on my mind without this?" It was true. My Dad was out of work and sick. My grandmother was living with us and she was sick. Everybody else was doing well in school. I was the only problem. I got to feeling, I'd be better out of the way. (Bitterly) But I couldn't even do that properly. (Sullenly) What good does all this do? It's all over a long time ago.

Mrs. B. fears the resulting emptiness and chaos if she relinquishes her tie to the archaic selfobject—her primitive mother. Kohut (1984) points out that defense and resistance, initially needed to preserve a vulnerable self, dissipate through the therapeutic process of appropriate functions and responses performed by the new selfobject therapist.

THERAPIST: But bad feelings about the past are a little bit like an infection. Until it's drained off, it continues to fester and hurt.
MRS. B.: (With abrupt anger) What I need to do is get me a job and straighten that Tommy out so that he can get back in nursery school. That's a lot better than just sitting and talking. (Even a beginning relinquishment of her merger with the archaic selfobject frightens her. She goes to the cot and picks up the sleeping child. After a pause she says more quietly) I always could sass people.

This is the first bit of evidence of a beginning merger with the new object. Almost tantamount to an apology, it recognizes that she has begun to experience a minute bit of calming. Her resistance to empathic understanding on the part of the therapist is still in the interest of holding herself together, maintaining the merger with the earlier selfobject.

THERAPIST: I think we need to know, together, how much those feelings are still with you, whether there are still times you want to do away with yourself.
MRS. B.: Not that, so much, but I do get stoned, every now and then, when I can't sleep and everything seems to be getting worse.

(There's a commotion in the hall and Tommy bursts in, pursued by an indignant four-year-old, shouting, "He's got my truck!")

MRS. B.: (Trying to pull the truck away and giving Tommy a cuff) I told you not to fight!

TOMMY: She (pointing to the therapist) gave it to me!
THERAPIST: (Gently, to the other child) I did give that truck to Tommy to play with; why don't you run back and find another? (To Mrs. B.) Let's sit down a moment and make plans for our work together.
MRS. B.: (Sullenly) I guess you think I shouldn't have hit Tommy. But you don't know the kind of brat he can be.

Mrs. B. clearly here indicates almost a computer printout of the missing self function of monitoring tension and delaying reaction, a calming function which the therapist performs for her at this point. She attributes to the therapist her own observation ("I guess you think I shouldn't have hit him . . .") but this is an early preliminary step to transmuting the therapist's selfobject function into a self-function.

THERAPIST: I can see things come to a boil pretty quickly between you. You tell me you're medicating yourself when you can't sleep and things get pretty tense. Is there no one at home to relieve you when you need some help with the children?

The therapist continues to offer her mature psychic structure, empathically recognizing Mrs. B.'s burdens and isolation. Moreover, she affirms Mrs. B.'s needs for help as legitimate. In the past, it was not enough that her need and wish for comforting and help went unnoticed but that she was bad to have such needs.

MRS. B.: Nobody I can count on. Mom kicked me out when I got pregnant with Tommy. I showed her. I took care of myself. Tommy's father was in and out . . . left me as soon as Jimmy was born. Nobody sticks around me very much for long. (The individual who is unable to use and retain selfobjects views the world as a hostile place.) Tommy blames me that his dad left. I took a lot out on Tommy. At times I just hated him; that's how people must have felt about me, I guess.
THERAPIST: I think most people may not realize how much you hurt inside. It must have been hard for you to be a new mother without anyone around who knew how to go about things.

As the therapist absorbs the painful experiences associated with Tommy's birth, and with the present, Mrs. B. can increasingly reveal her early neglect and severe abuse of Tommy, showing remorse and concern about her current treatment of him and doubt about her capacity to mother both children. She reveals lack of knowledge and judgment about children's developmental milestones, stressing exaggeratedly early competence and a need to have Tommy perform a comforting role to her. This attempt to use her child as a calming, soothing selfobject signals the depth of her deficits. Her defiant comment, "Mom kicked me out when I got pregnant. I showed her . . . I took care of myself," is worlds apart from the experience of vigor and harmony in the self of a cohesive mother who can seek out appropriate selfobjects in times of need. Mrs. B. views independence as strength, but suffers the characteristic low self-esteem of individuals who are unable to find and elicit responses from appropriate selfobjects. Typically, she reflects guilt and misunderstanding about her own unattended needs in childhood. She is bad to have such needs. She lacks the capacity to soothe herself or to monitor the signal of anxiety, which rapidly becomes panic or desperation.

By absorbing her stress the therapist performs a pacifying role, much as the early mother provides her mature psychic structure to calm and soothe a troubled child. At the same time the therapist assesses the possibility of danger to the children, determining whether the selfobject functions she will perform can provide enough structure for this mother to enable her to accommodate herself to weekly sessions, whether it will be safe for the children. What is hopeful is the manner in which Mrs. B. is tentatively and tenuously responding to the therapist, who works out a plan with her for the care of the children part of the day in a supervised nursery where Tommy's behavior can be observed and evaluated. In addition, she has given the mother a phone number at which she can be reached, as the first step in a long process of helping his mother to identify the signal of anxiety before it escalates into panic and rage and thus to be able to seek out appropriate help. Mrs. B. openly expresses doubts about whether she can be helped, but reveals her hope inversely, "I don't mind coming back." This type of inverse communication is typical of the defensive, resistive individual who fears reopening the self to traumatic injury. What has taken place is that the therapist has offered herself as structure to this young woman, who reflects the typical loneliness and feelings of badness of the unmirrored child, viewing the world as peopled by hostile figures. Unable to have a meaningful image of herself reflected, she has covered her depression—depletion?—by a chronically raging and defiant manner.

Through the months that follow, in a slowly evolving process, the therapist comes to serve a mirroring, guiding function. Mrs. B.'s view of herself as a raging child, dumber than her sibs, kicked out of high school because of her truancy, has been giving way to recognition that her legitimate needs and wishes were obscured by the needs of others in the household. At one point, as she experiences with intensity the empathic merger that has been established, she shows the scars in her wrists to the therapist, eliciting that need for comfort which she had been helpless to elicit from earlier selfobjects. Mrs. B. views her mother as being able to comfort her sibs but never attempting to comfort her. Her early suicidal attempts were essentially viewed as bad behavior. Yet it was behavior, as Kohut indicated, to do away with an offending part of the self (1971, p. 181) and thus to become more acceptable. There is no indication that psychiatric evaluation was ever attempted for Mrs. B. The therapist, in responding, comments that she is glad that now Mrs. B. can allow, as she had not been able to earlier, someone to know her pain and to help her.

The therapist's intervention in arranging for a complete medical workup, including psychiatric evaluation, performs a responsive selfobject function in relation to Mrs. B.'s very real needs. She considers with her whether medication is indicated for her depression and sleeplessness. Further, the therapist's use of selfobjects, in the medical profession and in the supervised kindergarten, assists Mrs. B. in transmuting responsible health care into self-functions and affirming the importance and legitimacy of eliciting the care of appropriate selfobjects.

As they continue to work together, further depths of Mrs. B.'s deficit in monitoring anxiety and regulating self-esteem are exposed. Mrs. B.'s phone calls become frequent and inopportune as she demands almost immediate response to her needs. At times this has the quality of preverbal needs, the expectation that the selfobject knows the individual's wishes without the need to express these verbally. As she uses the therapist, seeking to complete her own psychic structure, she evidences little awareness of the therapist as a separate individual with needs and program of her own.

Therapists, particularly beginning therapists but even experienced therapists, struggle against a feeling of engulfment and sometimes withdraw in self-doubt. The therapist asks herself, "Did I fail to diagnose this young woman appropriately? Are my interventions contributing to her fragmentation?" Such doubts may indeed arise because there has been a misdiagnosis, or too great intrusiveness, or failure to respond appropriately on the part of the therapist that has blocked transmuting of selfobject functions. It is more freuquently the case that in an effective merger which establishes the conditions for healing, the individual becomes freer to expose at what depths deficits exist and the variety of missing self-functions. It is not that the individual has "become worse," but that the early, interrupted thrust to complete growth has been reactivated and now demandingly seeks the wherewithal (selfobject functions) to continue the process.

With Mrs. B. there follows an intense chaotic period in which she is driven to rage because of Tommy's demands on her. She complains of his hyperactivity, which is not confirmed by his doctor. She describes violent dreams of harm to the children. She identifies her hatred and rejection of Tommy with her own rejection by her mother and sees his behavior like that of her own. It is a slow bit-by-bit process through which the therapist helps her to bring order out of chaotic events. By her questions and comments ("How could it be otherwise? . . . Earlier there was no one at home who could help you . . . "), the therapist offers a soothing and calming selfobject function, which enables her to establish communication between her observing and her experiencing self, to build in the spirit of self-observation, the ability to delay and reflect.

Mrs. B. is unable to cue others to her needs, and the long history of unmet needs has confirmed her lifelong sense of being unworthy, bad. She is doubtful, suspicious, and quick to explode, lacking the capacity to monitor anxiety before it reaches desperation. The therapist helps her to identify her feelings; she opens a path toward the selfobject world, legitimizing Mrs. B.'s demands and bit by bit diminishing her unreasonable demands upon Tommy to serve as a comforting selfobject and her tendency to break into rage when he does not. This comes about through the therapist's meeting her needs and thus fostering Mrs. B.'s ability to be in tune with her own needs.

It is in this manner that the therapist, for a prolonged period, responds with calm and soothing understanding to a repeated cycle of injury, rage, and depression. The frantic phone calls at inopportune times comes under the influence of the capacity to tolerate delay without plunging into despair or punishing behavior with Tommy. She learns to undertake restorative steps.

What is presented here is only a fragment of a lengthy process—providing a new self/selfobject unit, allowing and maintaining an empathic merger succeeded by true mirroring, which allows her to accept her limitations without feeling destroyed. In tune with her needs, she can seek out sustenance appropriately from available selfobjects and institutions. She becomes more empathically in tune with the needs of her children.

To illustrate, at the beginning of one weekend, with the prospect of having both children with her and no relief, Mrs. B. cleans the apartment and takes care of the marketing and laundry. She feels she has a start, but her mood is brittle and tense. She becomes overly scrutinizing of Tommy's behavior. As she is preparing the younger boy for their dinner, she hears the refrigerator door slam.

MRS. B.: What are you up to, Tommy?
TOMMY: Nothin'.

MRS. B.: I heard you; don't go messing with stuff for dinner.

TOMMY: I'm not! I just wanted something to drink.

MRS. B.: You'll spill it!

(She hears a crash and dashes in angrily. A bowl lies in splinters on the floor and the half-jelled liquid is oozing in all directions. Tommy drops to his knees, trying to stop the flow, but Mrs. B. is in a rage. She cuffs Tommy aside, calling him clumsy and greedy.)

MRS. B.: You just can't wait! Now look what you've done!

(As she picks up the pieces of the bowl and mops up angrily, she continues to rail at Tommy, who is eyeing her apprehensively. She gets up, towering above her small son, who shrinks from her. She is startled by his fear, interrupts herself in the middle of her tirade, and then begins to cry. After a pause, Tommy moves toward her gingerly.)

TOMMY: Mommy, I'm sorry.

(As she hears these words, she recalls many times when she tried to appease her mother's anger. Echoes of her therapist's soothing voice reverberate and she cries even more bitterly and helplessly at her own unfulfilled longing for comfort. Mrs. B. puts her arm around Tommy. He snuggles, at first timidly, and then hugs her tightly.)

MRS. B.: I'm sorry, too. I guess you were just too hungry to wait. Next time ask me!

(Later, Mrs. B. described this episode to her therapist in great detail.)

MRS. B.: Suddenly I saw him. He's just a little fellow. He isn't even five yet, and here I was acting as if he had committed a federal offense. Afterward, at dinner, we both got a kick out of Jimmy. He was trying to use a straw but kept blowing in the wrong direction instead of sucking. Tommy tried to show him, but we got to laughing so hard we all began to blow in the wrong direction. (Looking up wistfully) You know, afterward we had a lot of fun. I wondered why it couldn't always be that way. We got through the weekend without many more squabbles and here I am.

Mrs. B. looks to the therapist for both approval and with fear of being disapproved of for her temper outburst. She expands and relaxes as her therapist focuses on her ability to recover herself and to interrupt her scolding behavior with Tommy. She affirms that Mrs. B. has taken important steps in being in touch with her own experiences and using them in understanding childhood needs generally. Mrs. B. gives many examples of her interactions with the children which do not erupt in angry outburst but in genuine playfulness and pride. She is more observant of other children and their parents and is pleased when a neighbor asks the family to join them in a picnic.

Mrs. B. has intervals of time for reflection and begins to see her environment as less peopled by hostile, vengeful individuals. The nursery and kindergarten teachers, the doctor who for a time provided medication, and neighbors begin to appear in her communications with the therapist not only as selfobjects but as people with responsibilities and activities. She moves toward securing employment and toward a more realistic evaluation of dependable qualities in those to whom she reaches out.

The area of involvement and intervention described in this case is typical of social casework. The social worker gathers information through her empathic intuneness with Mrs. B.'s unexpressed needs and wishes, her feeling states and behavior. She employs mature empathy in the service of her client and introspectively monitors feeling states aroused in her by Mrs. B. From these she winnows out what is personal and unrelated to the task at hand. She functions as a new selfobject through whom the urge to complete growth can be released, providing the opportunity to establish a more cohesively functioning, harmonious, and vigorous self.

The therapist's use of herself to monitor feeling states aroused in her by the individual with whom she works allows her to remain in touch with the inner life of that individual. In addition to what is being communicated verbally, she hears the omissions—for example, Mrs. B.'s disavowal of the despair that led to her suicidal attempt. Her desperate attempt to secure a response to her needs, a response her mother had no problem in according the older children, left her with a sense that her needs were bad, that unlike her siblings she was not a worthwhile person. It is not just the calming presence of the therapist which rekindles structure building. This alone is not curative. What is curative is persistently pursued and successful responses, which are empathically in tune with the specific transference need aroused in the present. Small failures of short duration allow the individual to respond by structure building, as should have occurred in childhood. The therapist does not respond by filling in needs but by helping the individual to understand her longings and aspirations, both in the present and in the driven behavior or thought that repeated failures to engage selfobjects perpetuated. The therapist helps her to understand what she feels and how she reacts, and demonstrates that these reactions make sense dynamically and structurally.

When an empathic merger is in full swing, the individual may respond with raging importunate demands, taxing the patience of the therapist. Prone to fragmentation and explosive rages, she uses others to supply missing structure. The intensity of these demands exposes the depth of the deficits of self-functions. "Manipulation" and "exploitation" are understood differently. Structure building or restoration is a slow process. It does not consist of steady progress but of innumerable derailings, which, if not too severe or too lengthy, allow the individual to engage herself in trying new activities which aid in structure building. With Mrs. B. the therapist performed the further selfobject function of empathically recognizing that she needed day care for the children not because she was an incompetent mother, but because she was overburdened and needed some freedom from the demands of her small children. She recognized, as Mrs. B. did not, her need for medical attention, and provided, as the earlier parental milieu had not, a response to her uniqueness as an individual with aspirations and potential.

In the course of their work together, Mrs. B.'s transference needs and wishes were first expressed in an intense merger and then transmuted into the capacity to use engrams of memory of having been soothed and comforted to monitor her anxiety and to regulate her self-esteem.

The episode with the bowl of jello (which had become something of a marker in the course of therapy) had been preceded by many sessions in which Mrs. B's fierce denunciation of herself and her problems with her sons had been modified by the therapist's ability to offer an understanding of her behavior. She pointed out that mistakes are inevitable; their importance lies in employing them not as a stick with which to destroy oneself but as a means to gain new solutions. Initially, Mrs. B. reflected that she often didn't really remember what the therapist said but rather her soft voice: "Just sitting here and looking at you and knowing that you really care to take the time for me makes me feel good. No one else ever did."

Later she recalled the actual exchange with Tommy and berated herself for her explosive behavior, but the therapist pointed out that Mrs. B. had actually caught herself in time to recognize what was happening. On several occasions Mrs. B. pointed out something she had done with the children that had worked out well, that had even been fun. And here she asked for specific confirmation; later she herself was able to explore what had happened and her feelings about it and then to assess whether her efforts had been effective. Then the experience of twinship, being like her therapist, responding with her gestures and indeed even her verbal expressions, "went inside" to become uniquely her own. She began to reflect, delay, and plan.

There ensued a mirroring transference in the narrower sense of the word. She felt better in the presence of the therapist but there was no longer the intense merger need to control the therapist. She could present for confirmation or guidance specific aspects of thought and behavior; the therapist's response, at times uncertain and speculative, became an element in structure building, because, although frustrating, it was not beyond Mrs. B.'s tolerance. She reached the point where she could say, "My understanding is better than my therapist's; my explanation is more to the point." This ability to claim perceptions as her own, to follow her own line of thought and experience, demonstrated a gain in the ability to maintain cohesion even in the face of trying events. Moreover, an idealizing transference established itself through which she transmuted a more reflective capacity and could aspire to and seek realizable goals. The selfobject functions of her therapist provided appropriately attuned responses, the wherewithal through which a more cohesive, vigorous, and harmonious self could be established.

Mrs. B. continued in therapy weekly for a little over three years. At times of particular stress, sessions took place more frequently, but Mrs. B. was increasingly able to plan ahead, particularly for weekends and holidays. Though these could be stressful, she learned to discriminate between necessary and driven tasks. For example, one snowy day when "the boys were standing with their noses pressed to the window, I just piled the clothes I was sorting into a basket, threw on our clothes and spent the afternoon with the boys making a snowman, complete with carrot for a nose." She reported a conversation with their pediatrician at the clinic when she was complaining about their getting into everything. He commented, "You've got a couple of live wires!" She confided that his comment made her feel good, that sometimes even when she looked in on the boys as they lay sleeping she could hardly believe how good they looked and that they were hers.

Eighteen months before termination, Mrs. B.'s old employer called her back. She returned to a better position in which she had supervisory responsibilities. Tommy was now in first grade and doing very well; the younger boy entered a junior nursery. In the initial period of managing both the job and her sons, Mrs. B. became tense, anxious that she was rusty at her work and might not last, and too tired to have much fun with the boys. She tended to be explosive at times and there was a renewal of her earlier self-punitive attitude. As her therapist enfolded her in her understanding that there were realistic difficulties in managing both her family and a job, particularly for a single parent, Mrs. B. began to seek out some parent groups attached to a neighborhood church. With considerable initial reserve, she began to participate in activities which also provided baby-sitting. She met a widower with an eight-year-old daughter with whom her boys and she occasionally shared outings. More of her time in therapy focused on her own reactions to what had gone on during the week, what she thought she had handled well and what "turned sour." She wanted to interrupt treatment for a while to see how things would go and, with a planned date for return, took a six-week "holiday." When she returned to therapy, she said that she felt she had been running very hard but was pleased, feeling definitely better about herself and about the boys. She had not reestablished much of a relationship with her family and at this point felt reluctant to do so. But she did look ahead to a time when the boys would certainly want some sense of family. Shyly she mentioned her friend and his daughter—a relationship "that was still on." She had brought a gift of a small crocus in bud. She wanted her therapist to know how grateful she was and that she would like to come back from time to time to let her know how things were going and "to kind of touch base."

11

Treatment for the Inability to Achieve a Goal

IN THE PURSUIT OF reasonable goals an individual may encounter difficulties which block his progress and defeat his aspirations. Instead of a free flow of ambitions through activities for which he has been trained, he encounters problems. He redoubles his efforts to forge ahead in driven fashion but again meets with disappointment. His normally cohesive self fragments and he begins to experience loss of purpose, irritability, fatigue, problems in sleeping. Not uncommonly, such an individual consults a physician. When no organic basis is found for this condition, he may be referred for exploration of the possibility that emotional difficulties are at the root of his dilemma.

The congruence between social work practice and self psychology lies in the manner in which the practitioner now becomes a new selfobject through whom deficits in the bipolar self can be explored and structure building resumed. Here, the self of the social worker provides the opportunity for the individual to use her presence and her strength to absorb his disappointment and chagrin. In so doing she provides the conditions under which he can endure the fear and trauma of exposure and his own questions about his adequacy. As together they examine his problems, her presence soothes and calms him. He takes into himself, and makes uniquely his own, the process of stilling his anxiety as he undertakes steps which may result in a renewed effort to assess his aspirations and to shape them toward an appropriate goal. As he encounters difficulties in the social worker's presence, he is somewhat better able to consider why they arise and to undertake steps to increase his skills or to modify his expectations and behavior.

The need to be noticed and valued, to be mirrored, and the need to merge with the strength and wisdom of someone viewed as having the power to uplift and set on course are old needs to which social workers have long responded. Self psychology now offers an explanatory system of human development that clarifies what takes place in the process. The social worker becomes that new selfobject whose presence and functions enable structure building to proceed. Her presence is soothing; her focused empathic attention is calming. She offers her understanding and her explanations of the feeling states or behavior that their work together elicits. Her minor failures in this process become the basis for stimulating and rekindling an individual's capacity for self-understanding and for providing his own enlarged explanations for episodes or events. Her minor failures thus become the stimulus for future growth. It is not that the social worker now actively soothes, actively calms, or actively gratifies. It is that her empathic intuneness, her focused attention, and her presence allow the individual to experience calming and soothing. What she gratifies is the wish to have his needs understood in the present and to realize that his needs do not make him unworthy.

The purpose in helping the individual to understand these needs is to enable him to identify the childhood roots of his inability to find a confirming response, which left him feeling unworthy. It is also to enable him to make them appropriately known to those who can respond or to recognize needs that can be best met by his own response. Transference needs help the social worker to identify where the deficits lie and what selfobject functions she must now fulfill to allow for their transmuting into psychic structure—self-functions. Through this process the individual is restored to or is provided with the capacity to experience himself as worthy, to establish and work toward goals that are his own, based on knowledge of what he can do. He enters a world of selfobjects whose responses he can seek and to whom he can be responsive. The following case illustrates the process through which this takes place.

Mr. L.

Mr. L. was referred to a family agency by his doctor, who suggested that his general fatigue, loss of appetite, and problems with sleep might be related to his difficulties in finding work that was satisfying to him.

> MR. L.: Dr. Mason is a good guy. I've known him a long time. He couldn't find anything specially wrong, but he gave me some stuff to take. I don't want to be a pill-popper . . . he wouldn't let me be anyway . . . so he thought you might be able to help.
> THERAPIST: What seems to be the problem with your work?
> MR. L.: I've been at this tool company for seven years; I'm a trouble-

shooter. They like my work and I like working there, but I'm in a rut. I always said it was temporary but here I am already 30! Computers are everything. I've been going to school part-time. (Darting a glance at the therapist) In fact, I got my degree last year and I've been taking some extra training. Everybody said I'd have no trouble getting a job. My work was tops. I even figured out a program for one of the professors . . . he liked it . . . in fact he said it was great . . . (Pauses, his face beginning to flush) The thing is, I've had about 15 interviews at different companies.

THERAPIST: What happens?

MR. L.: First, things go well, but then I get a thank-you-no-thank-you letter; no explanation. And it makes me boil! My wife and my kids try to cheer me up, but I just get mad and tell them to leave me alone. Sometimes I'd like to tear the place apart. I'm always boiling inside. Some of the guys who took courses with me have good jobs now and I know I'm better than some of them—probably all of them! You gotta have pull, someone going for you . . . I am good! But it's not enough just to be good.

The force and tempo of Mr. L.'s speech increase as he pours out complaints about the system: Everybody's out for himself; no one gives a hoot about anyone else; the guys who interview him don't know beans about computers; no one has ever helped him; everything he's ever gotten he got on his own. His rage seems endless, but after a time he slows down, fatigue takes over, and he looks at the worker in a somewhat shamefaced fashion.

MR. L.: I guess you think I'm off my rocker!

THERAPIST: I can see you're very upset. Have these feelings been present just since your problems in finding a satisfactory job or have they been going on for some time?

MR. L.: I don't know. (After a pause) I guess I used to be easier to live with; at least my wife says so. She's working part-time. With three kids and me, she's got her hands full, but she doesn't keep flying off the handle. She isn't pushing me. We both want the same thing: a house, a good school for the kids, something extra for holidays. (With a shake of his head) The kids are beginning to stay out of my way (sullenly) . . . like me and my dad . . .

The worker has provided her calming attention; she has been absorbing his rage. This process has allowed him to feel somewhat soothed and he begins to order his observations and to reflect. As we will see, it is only a beginning and his rage will return.

MR. L.: I don't know. Things have really been building up. Before, when we were first married, I used to feel excited about my plans. I was glad to be on my own. (With a return of surliness mounting to rage) My dad was something else. Always riding me, always comparing me with my kid brother. . . . Bob's still in school, into sports and always shining up the old man. . . . I couldn't wait to get out of there. Dad kept complaining about the money he was spending on me and when was he going to see any of it. He never rode my brother. . . . I paid every cent of my way. . . . I went to a state school and I worked part-time. I don't know what he was complaining about. Boy! Was I glad to get out of there.
I met my wife and we hit it off right from the start. She's a good kid; she really sets me up. But we both expected something better. This company I've been with is okay for a beginning but even the boss thinks I should be on to something better. (Sitting hunched forward, elbows on his knees and head in his hand) Fifteen rejections in a row! Something's gotta be wrong. You'd think they had me on a blacklist or something.

At this point Mr. Lewis views himself only as victim. Although there are glimpses of Mr. Lewis's attitude which may be infiltrating the job interviews, the worker internally begins to question whether the general economic climate may also contribute to Mr. L.'s difficulties. This must be cleared up.

THERAPIST: Is the sort of opening you're looking for in short supply?
MR. L.: They're not a dime a dozen, but there are openings and the school has no trouble in recommending me strongly and getting me interviews. I've got a lot of good ideas, but what's the use if I don't get to try some of them out?

As the interview continues the therapist observes states of alternating rage and depletion, indicating difficulty in regulating self-esteem. He has offered glimpses of earlier difficulties having to do with his younger brother's preferred position. Is this being repeated in some subtle manner in the present? Is there something in his way of presenting himself—or in responding to questions—that turns people off? There seems to be no reason to doubt that he is well-qualified and highly recommended by his school. What keeps him from getting beyond his first interview? Does the somewhat paranoid coloring to his reaction, his conviction that it is the system, signify deeper pathology than at present seems to meet the eye? Is there something that takes place between Mr. L. and the interviewer which expresses driven, repetitive, defeating behavior?

THERAPIST: From what you tell me, your experience is not only disappointing but also puzzling. Perhaps working together we may be able to understand what goes on that results in rejections.

MR. L.: What good will talking do?

Here Mr. L. reveals the intensity of his need for relief, his inability to tolerate delay, and his impatience with talking. The therapist offers her presence and her understanding, which affirms (mirrors) the fact that talk alone will not help. She gives "talk" purpose and function by her explanation. Moreover, the comment that it has helped others and it may help him allows him to accept himself as a human being among other human beings.

THERAPIST: It isn't that we just talk. It is that we may be able to make connections which aren't immediately obvious . . . to interrupt others that get in your way. It has helped many; it may help you. Shall we work out a time for regular appointments?

MR. L.: (After a frown and a pause) Dr. Mason thinks it may help. . . . I might as well give it a whirl. (A time is agreed upon and he waves a little sheepishly.) See ya.

As the therapist reflects on the quality of Mr. L.'s communications, she is struck by the intensity of his speech and his rage, which is close to the surface. The somewhat paranoid coloring to his views is open to further observation: Does it intensify and represent a fixed relationship to the world? Do the repeated rejections in job interviews reverberate to the old injury of father's preference for his younger brother and does he therefore ascribe his problems to the system? Is the younger brother's behavior sycophantic ("shining up the old man") as Mr. Lewis suggests or does it represent a natural pleasure and enthusiasm in a self/selfobject relationship that Mr. Lewis mistrusts and distrusts?

As Mr. Lewis settles into a routine of weekly interviews, the therapist often finds herself bracing for his appointment time. Although his voice is pleasant and his manner of expressing himself interesting, she is flooded by the volume and intensity of his speech. She cannot stem the tide or find an appropriate point to ask questions to elaborate their understanding of specific events he is describing. Yet he leaves the hour obviously refreshed and thanking her. He tells her that he is sleeping better, that he isn't so crabby with the kids. She is a mirroring selfobject attentively listening to the narrative of his experiences; at the same time she absorbs his anger and hurt.

MR. L.: I got to feeling I was behaving just like my dad . . . but I couldn't stop.

THERAPIST: In what way were you just like your dad?

MR. L.: (In a quieter, duller tone) Aw, I don't know. Any time I got really excited about something, he'd be too busy, or laugh and make fun of me. . . . I guess some of my ideas really were crazy . . .

THERAPIST: Was he always that way?

MR. L.: (With a frown, and after a pause) I used to trail after him when he was fixing things around the house or working in the garage. If he dropped something, I'd always be there to pick it up. If he needed something, I'd run and get it. (Here we observe Mr. L.'s intense efforts to merge with the power and competence of his idealized father, which, we will see, his father was unable to accept.) But . . . I don't know . . . he never really seemed to notice. I'd just hang around waiting . . . waiting for what, I don't know. One Christmas I got a really neat set of power tools. He told me to be careful . . . not to just mess around with them. I was afraid to use them. I kept reading the directions or asking my mom about them. She'd tell me to go ahead and ask dad, he'd know. But when I tried, he was always busy with his own stuff, or he'd say he'd do it later, and then he was too tired. After a couple of months, I still hadn't even started to use them. I heard him say to mom, "There's your genius; get him a good set of tools and he doesn't even know how to use them." I felt like crying, but I didn't. I just closed my door real quietly.

THERAPIST: That must have been very painful. (The therapist here not only confirms the legitimacy of his grief, but, as new selfobject, offers that enfolding understanding absent in the past.)

MR. L.: I guess I just got used to it. . . . With Bob, it was a different story—he always had time for Bob. I'd hang around watching them build things, trying to help, but after a while he'd look up and ask, "Don't you have something better to do than hanging around? Go see what your mother needs."

THERAPIST: Were you and your mother very close?

MR. L.: We used to be when I was little. My dad was in the service till I was almost five. We used to do a lot of things together. She'd read to me, take me everywhere with her. She used to tell me stories about my dad and me before he left for service. I was about two then. We used to go hiking and I would sit on his shoulders. Mom used to tell me when he'd meet friends . . . (with an embarrassed grin) I guess I was kind of cute or other people would say so and mom said dad would just puff out his chest as if I were a service decoration. She would go on about all the wonderful things he could do and how I would be at his heels wherever he went. (Here his mother appropriately encouraged idealization of the absent father.) I'd tell her all the things I was going to do when I grew up. . . . I had some imagination! She'd laugh and tell me I was her wonder boy. (At this point his mother was appropriately mirroring, confirming his grandiose ambitions.) I had all kinds of mechanical toys and I was pretty good with them . . . wasn't anything I couldn't figure out. When dad got back home, first off things went pretty well. Then mom got pregnant and it seemed like the next minute Bob was born. Dad took to him right away . . . mom, too. I guess I felt sort of left out. (Defensively) I wasn't jealous. I just figured there ought to be room for me, too.

Over the next months, Mr. Lewis described his gradual loss of a central place with his mother, and his sense of failure in ever being able to engage his father's attention, a failure at this point to find nurturance from early selfobjects for his longing and his need to be mirrored and to be allowed to merge with the strength and wisdom of an idealized figure.

He liked showing his little brother how to do things. It made him feel good. But they began to fall out when he'd come back from school and find that Bob had messed up his toys. He'd be in a rage; his mother would tell him not to be so selfish, to share his things, and his father would be angry. He'd go off to his room and sulk or read. No one seemed available with whom he could share his emotions. He recalled an episode which occurred when he was about eight or nine. His father had picked up a secondhand bike and given it to him, saying, "Here. See what you can do with it."

He had tinkered with the gears, oiling the parts as he had seen his father do. And then, with a burst of excitement which he could still savor, he rode the bike around the block several times. Taking it back to the garage, he got out some paint and gave it a shiny coat of black. He added the name of the bike in red and then ran to find his father to show it to him. His father looked it over silently and finally said, "Why didn't you wait for the black to dry, then the red wouldn't have run. . . . Clean up the mess you've made."

MR. L.: It was like the light went out. It wasn't only what he said, it was the *way* he said it . . . I could see he was right, but would it have killed him to say to a kid, "Gee! That's neat!" and then help me with what went wrong? That's what I do with my kids.

(After a pause.) We had a neighbor across the yard, Mr. Levy. He sort of took an interest in me when I was about 11. He'd let me work with him in his shop . . . try out his tools. Once I sent away for the makings of a rocking chair. I was going to put it together for my mom. When the parts came, I spread them all out in the yard, trying to study the directions. My dad came home from work and gave a snort, "What's it this time? Don't leave this stuff lying around." After he went into the house, I started picking up the pieces. Mr. Levy came to the fence and said, "Why don't you bring it all over to my workshop?" When we were there, he sort of put his arm around my shoulder and said, "Your dad's got a lot of trouble with his job right now. Don't feel too bad." He let me keep the parts there and I'd work on my own after school. Sometimes he'd watch me, and, when he could see the problem, he'd say, "Here, fellow, I think it might fit better this way." He never put me down. . . . He'd let me work with him. He didn't have any kids and I guess it felt good to him, too, to have me there. He sure had a wonderful way with wood, fixing things up, refinishing old stuff.

He turned to his schoolwork, a natural and important expansion of his selfobject world, but deficits in confident expectation of response, deficits in regulating self-esteem, robbed him of zestful absorption in his work. Elementary physics and math were his "big" subjects. One of his teachers at school let him wire up a project for class. Seeing his interest, his instructor mentioned a special summer course leading to a license in the field of electric circuitry. Although he was only 13, he was given special permission to enroll. All one long hot summer he traveled to class daily by bus, never missing a session. On the day of his final examination, his father, who had taken little interest in the project, drove him to school. He kept stealing glances at his father, wanting to express his gratitude, but was held back by the diffidence that had sealed off any spontaneity in their relationship. As he entered the examination room, to his horror his father followed and took the exam along with him. When the results came in, he and his father had both qualified. His father commented, "See? And I didn't have to take all the classes."

As the therapist absorbed his shame and humiliation, she helped him to recognize his longing to have his success noted and admired. Apparently some problem on father's part made it impossible for him to take pleasure in his son's competence. And now, for the first time, the realization dawned on him that his father, at the time of the incident, then in his late thirties, had served in the signal corps and was in a field that required competence in electric circuitry. His long-held awe at his father's competence, his ability to take the exam without study, broke into rage, and finally he gave up the struggle to choke back his tears, overwhelmed by a combination of the sudden de-idealization of his father and the full experience of his utter failure to have his own work rewarded by admiration and approval.

MR. L.: (After a time) He couldn't ever say a decent thing about what I did. He was always putting me down. It wouldn't have cost him anything. He always acted as if he was the greatest. . . . I thought he was, too. But it just seemed every little thing I did he found some way to criticize me. Once, I was standing before the mirror getting ready to go out. I kept brushing my hair first with a part, then straight up, and all of a sudden there he was right behind me. You should have seen his face when he said, "Why don't you quit pushing that mop of hair around and start shoving the lawn mower?" I was scared (fragmentation), my heart was pounding. I couldn't say anything, I felt sick. I heard mom say, "Why don't you leave the boy alone?" That's about as close as she'd get to taking my part. I felt like a fool . . .

THERAPIST: Your efforts to groom yourself were appropriate to your developing young manhood. It was too bad that your father, for whatever problem he had, deprived himself of the pleasure of admiring his son. Your mother's comment, "Leave the boy alone," made you feel foolish because you were no longer a boy in need of this kind of protection. Perhaps you longed for some sort of comment indicating that she liked the way you looked.

MR. L.: I think she did but she didn't say it much and certainly not when my dad was around.

THERAPIST: It's puzzling that he should have so consistently demeaned and belittled you.

MR. L.: Mom was always bragging about me. She thought I was smart. . . . She used to be surprised at some of the things I thought up. Instead of her telling me bedtime stories, I'd tell her about all the new inventions I was going to build. . . . It was pretty much, "Move over Buck Rogers." My kids are into Luke Skywalker and *Star Wars* and it's all pretty much taken for granted now but then it was all new. When dad got home, he'd keep teasing her, "Where's the little genius?" At first they seemed to be enjoying themselves; then it began to turn sour.

Over the next few months the work of therapy centered on understanding his sense of discontinuity with father's return. Earlier, when his father had left for the service, there had been an abrupt interruption of the merger with his father's idealized power and competence, through which he had begun to transmute self-functions representing a larval form of idealized goals. His mother's description of his father's puffing out his chest when his small son evoked admiration from others suggested, even at that time, some pathology in his father's response. Parents do take pleasure in the admiring response of others to their children, but there is a suggestion of something beyond that normal pride. "He wore his son like a service decoration." In his father's absence, his mother kept alive the toddler's idealization of his father. Perhaps, in her longing for her husband's return, there was an overdetermined quality in her attention to her small son, an overidealizing of his prowess. With his father's return and soon after the birth of his younger brother, the earlier admiring and stimulating sense of preferment provided by his mother's always available response to her small son terminated too abruptly and there was no one to replace her. He could not, in stepwise fashion, transmute the selfobject functions she had provided into those self-functions that would have enabled him to shape his grandiosity and to regulate his self-esteem reliably. Nor, despite his efforts, was he able to reestablish the merger with his father as an idealized figure, competent and powerful. He remembered clinging to his father's arm, trying to force his attention to some grand project he was describing. He had difficulty talking rapidly enough to maintain his father's interest, an interest half admiring, half belittling. He would soon be shrugged off, his father saying in an aside to his mother, which he heard and remembered, "He's got the know-how but does he have the go-how?"

THERAPIST: How that must have hurt you! You seem to have been a very imaginative little boy, and sometimes, for such a youngster, ideas crowd in too fast for words.

With comments such as this, the therapist would offer her mature psychic structure to provide a soothing and calming function, which enabled Mr. L. to examine the roots of his anxiety. The therapist speculated with him that as a little boy, with the return of his father from the service, he felt displaced, but more prominent was his longing to merge with the idealized strength and competence of his father, despite repeated rebuffs. It was not the return of a feared oedipal object which stimulated his anxiety, but, rather, the boy's intense need for an idealized selfobject, which, unmet, resulted in, at times, unbridled grandiosity.

There emerged better understanding of his vulnerability to being overstimulated by interested questions from, for example, a prospective employer. In that situation the floodgates of his long-denied yearning would open up—his yearning for appropriate admiration, confirmation, and guidance, exaggerated now by reason of its having been bottled up. His ideas would pour forth in such a torrent that the listener would be overwhelmed.

At one point an emergency session with another patient delayed the social worker in receiving him promptly. He observed the young man with whom she had been working as he left the office. She experienced some discomfort in not having managed her time well, at the same time that she felt some minor irritation with Mr. L.'s vulnerability to any diminution of her interest in him. His response to the incident was to begin talking at breakneck speed even before he sat down. He described in grandiose terms a project he was planning of such magnitude that the average person could not grasp its sophistication. As he began to run out of steam, he paused and appeared downcast, saying he couldn't understand what had made him shoot off like that. The therapist was able to share with him her understanding that her involvement with someone else had reverberated to an old wound, and that, as he pointed out earlier, it wasn't that he was jealous of his brother Bob, but that he had felt rightly that there should have been room for him. His response had been understandable in seeking to force her attention, as he had once sought to force his father to listen to his ideas. Perhaps he had felt her to be less attentive to him just at that point. Earlier in the treatment process the therapist had experienced such onslaughts, and these still could be triggered by inevitable failures in empathic intuneness on her part. The therapist provided an ordering process—unification—through which he could begin to understand the reverberations from the past to the present.

Mr. L.'s father never punished him physically, but his constant deflating and demeaning of the child's grandiose ambitions, coupled with his mother's dropping him emotionally from the center of her universe, left him with deficits in self-esteem regulation, in the capacity to soothe and calm himself as he strove for mastery in shaping his grandiose ideas.

Normally such pleasure in one's physical and mental powers, in the ability to pursue goals, takes form not only through the mirroring functions performed by the selfobject milieu but also in the opportunity to merge with the power and vigor of the idealized figures of childhood. What now emerged in the treatment process was a new understanding of his father's pathology. Returning from service, his father found that his formerly secure job had evaporated. The company by which he had been employed merged with another and he was less at the center of power, since his new job involved more menial work. Despite various efforts on his father's part to improve employment opportunities, no genuine advancement materialized. He turned to his younger son, apparently the embodiment of his hopes, whereas his older son represented for him his absence in the service and his lost opportunities. As Mr. Lewis reflected on his own situation, the sense of having been wronged and hurt persisted. For a period there was a sense of stalemate in the treatment process, essentially the structuralization of a deficit: preoccupation with failures in the system, avoiding opportunities that might have led to new job openings. He scrutinized the therapist's every comment, searching for failures in her understanding, her less-than-perfect responses to questions or experiences. He would comment, "It's all just talk!" searching her face for every nuance of expression indicating his underlying fear of the loss of the therapist as selfobject in the present.

The therapist was aware of countertransference reactions: of feeling exploited, of losing a sense of the goal of their work together. She was concerned, too, about worsening job opportunities, which might then make it impossible for him to find work in the field he was striving to enter. The sessions at this time were filled with his description of imaginative schemes for computer programs that would simplify and enlarge the capabilities of systems. At times she would find herself bewildered, overwhelmed, and somewhat impatient, speculating that her reaction was probably similar to that of interviewers who then rejected his application for work. Even when she allowed for the cyclical nature of the therapeutic process, that change and progress are not unidirectional, the persistence of this phase aroused speculation that the deficits in esteem regulation were deeper and more extensive than she initially had determined. It is true that the need for the understanding phase in empathic immersion in another individual's psychic life can be very extensive. But her concern was that a shifting transference might be more truly reflecting an oedipal conflict.

Did the stalemate reflect his fear of overtaking his father, being successful in improving his job situation as his father had not been, in effect demolishing a hated rival? Although not central to the work of therapy, his relationship with his wife and sons seemed enriching, fulfilling, and, except when his frustration and despair over work opportunities were at their highest, he took pleasure in strengthening their interests.

There was something reminiscent of the process which had set in with the father's return from the service and the birth of his brother Bob which now alerted the therapist to the meaning of his behavior and her need to brace herself for the interviews. She shared with him her concern about what might have derailed the therapeutic process, initially meeting with denial that anything had changed.

MR. L.: (After a pause, flushing) I keep meeting this guy coming down the hall from your office. I keep thinking anybody's got to be more interesting than I. I don't know . . . you must be getting bored hearing me go on and on. What happened to me wasn't the end of the world. My father wasn't one of those guys who beat up on his kids. . . . It's just . . .

THERAPIST: . . . that you felt again as you had when your father returned home and your little brother was born and the old feeling of being special was lost. That, as with your mother, I could not remain interested and concerned about you.

MR. L.: I feel like a fool. . . . I'm not a kid anymore. . . . I know that you see other people. . . . You're good . . . you make me feel good. I really am selfish like my mom used to say.

THERAPIST: It is not that you are selfish. These feelings rise to the surface when something in the present reverberates to an old wound not yet healed. And when that happens, you start to scold yourself and feel guilty, that you should be beyond such needs. As you pointed out earlier, it wasn't so much that you were jealous, which would be natural in any case, but that, rightly, you thought there ought to be room for you, too. We can understand how lonely and sad you must have felt at that time, how much you still needed your mother's interest, how eager you were to be part of your father's strength, to learn from him and to have him take pride in what you could do. But perhaps we can speculate that Bob's needs at that time were less demanding; with Bob your father perhaps felt less exposed in his own sense of helplessness at the impasse in his job opportunities.

MR. L.: (Choked up and struggling with tears) I guess I can see what he was up against, but it wouldn't have hurt him to let up on me once in a while. . . . I was lucky I had Mr. Levy to let me monkey around with his stuff.

The therapist as new selfobject cannot undo the past but she can offer her understanding in the present of his reawakened longings for confirmation. Her sense of pressure can now be understood as a response to his unspoken but insistent demands for her to perform appropriate, legitimate selfobject functions, which he can now transmute into the self-function of recognizing the signal of anxiety when issues of preferment are triggered. He is no longer the small boy whose mother had emotionally dropped him from his central position too abruptly and whose father had discouraged turning to him and allowing the boy to merge with his idealized power and competence; nevertheless, the incident of meeting another person his therapist is seeing reverberates to the past and signals the need for further filling in of deficts. He is beginning to strengthen the regulation of self-esteem, calming, soothing, self awareness: to reflect and delay —when . . . then.

The therapist returns to the silent question she had put to herself: is this indeed an oedipal conflict, a fixation which will then require more intensive treatment in analysis if he is to be successful in functioning in a vocation that is satisfying to him? She has deferred her conclusion until there is further opportunity to examine Mr. Lewis's progress in his job hunt. His current employer, a friend for over seven years, and his co-workers find him helpful. They seem to come to him for advice, recognize that there is not a great future for him in his current work, and are eager for his opportunity in a larger field.

In the course of the next sessions Mr. Lewis confides that he has had another interview which went fairly well. He answered the questions put to him briefly. Only once did he find himself being carried away in describing a project, but he was able to interrupt himself and get the interview back on track. He isn't sure that the slot he is being considered for is the best opportunity, but the company is large. There are many projects going, and he has the feeling that once on the job he'd be able to demonstrate his abilities. He just hopes it materializes.

The following week he comes in with great excitement. He has received a job offer from the most recent interview. His anxiety seems appropriate, centering on questions about the opportunity for advancement and development. Nevertheless, there is a surge of confidence; he does not go off into flights of ideas, but is thoughtful and reflective about his next steps. There is also another job interview coming up. He is afraid to let himself hope too much from it. It is a smaller company of three partners who are looking for someone with precisely his skills. There is an air of suppressed exhilaration as he describes the outfit, mentioning that his professor thinks it has great possibilities.

MR. L.: If only I don't get carried away. (Here Mr. L. recognizes his struggle to manage his grandiosity.) It just sounds great. They're about to get into the field of equipment for biophysics. I'd just love to have a whack at it. Boy!

THERAPIST: (Absorbing his excitement, which in the past has usually been the opening to flights of imaginative ideas) Let's try to understand your anxiety.

MR. L.: (After a pause) If they like me, do I really have what it takes? Is it just again what my dad used to say to me, "You think you know everything. You have the know-how but you don't have the go-how."

THERAPIST: You've mentioned that more than once. What led him to make such a comment?

MR. L.: I guess I used to have a whole lot of things going at once. That's what used to make me so mad when Bob would barge into my things. Some things were half-finished. Others I gave up on. But

a few were special and took a long time to figure out. Sometimes
my dad would come in when I was working and stand behind me.
It made me jumpy. I think he knew what the problem was sometimes, but he wouldn't say anything and I was afraid to ask. I didn't
like him hanging around. I'd wait around after school and ask Mr.
Avery [high school instructor]. He didn't always know the answer
but we'd look up stuff together in his library. (Looking up with a
clear direct smile) That felt great! We were like partners.

Some comments led the worker to put aside the question of the oedipal
conflict for later consideration as the therapeutic process continued. At
this point it was her empathic savoring of his experience which led to her
conclusion that he worked well with his male colleagues and with his
superiors in a partnering relationship. He seemed to have no difficulty
either in taking direction or in going off on his own when that was indicated. His relationship with the neighbor, Mr. Levy, his earlier work
with his high school instructor, his ability to follow through on the special
course when he was 13, his response to his co-workers in the small company where he was employed as a troubleshooter—all seemed to support
this impression. It was in his move toward the fulfillment of an idealized
goal that he seemed to have encountered difficulty. His father's failure
to realize his own ambitions and Mr. L.'s fear of besting an old hated rival
were not the cause of Mr. Lewis's failure in interview after interview. Such
failure seemed, rather, to proceed from an inability to contain and shape
his brilliance of mind and imaginative play of ideas to the needs of the
moment in a manner that would allow the interviewer to assess his abilities. He could not stem the flow of the unfulfilled longing for admiration
and confirmation. It was not his rage at an old rival whom he wanted to
defeat, but rather the wish to compel admiration from someone whose
full attention he now had. It was the father's pathology, his empathic
dullness to the affective needs of his growing son, that Mr. Lewis sought
in driven fashion to undo.

When the therapist found herself repeatedly bracing for his appointment, she was able to share with him her own sense of being flooded by
the intensity, speed, and volume of his communications. Together, they
could understand the childhood roots of his driven need to compel her
attention and admiration as, in the past, he longed to but could not regain
his mother's interest nor compel his father's interest in his imaginative
undertakings. That hope nevertheless was there to be aroused, as exhibited in his response to his neighbor, Mr. Levy, to his high school instructor, Mr. Avery, to his co-workers, and to his professor who even now
was forwarding his interests, suggested that the beginnings of a cohesive,

vigorous, harmonious self had been acquired in the first two years before father's departure. His capacity for allowing himself to be taught, to "work alongside" in a partnering relationship with another more knowledgable than he, indicated how important twinship and alter-ego selfobjects had then become.

A phrase, "There I go again," began as a shared recognition of his tendency to burst into expansive, untamed exhibitionism. But it also represented growing strength in his capacity to recognize signal anxiety. "Little shame signals" (Kohut, 1978, Vol. I, p. 441) alerted him to the threatened reactivation of his grandiosity, to which his mother in his early childhood responded with such open admiration. Initially it would seem that she had communicated to her husband her joy in the skill and creativeness of their small son. His father may have responded with a gently teasing effort to stem her uncontrolled enthusiasm. But as his own struggle to improve his vocational opportunities met with stalemate, he became increasingly demeaning of the child's efforts. Mr. Lewis described and worked through numerous desperate attempts to merge with the strength and competence of his idealized father, to work in partnership with him on his projects, to secure even minimal response to his needs for admiration. He came to recognize that his tendency ("there I go again") to spill over into prolonged, uninterruptable descriptions of plans and projects was to enforce the listener's unrestricted attention to him. The therapist, too, learned that such avalanches of ideas could be triggered by an occasional drop in her attention in a manner which repeated his earlier experience of being dropped from the center of his mother's interest. She shared this with him and, further, described her problem in absorbing the intricacies of some of his projects. The therapeutic process was reinstated, the derailed dialogue was once more on course. Through this optimal frustration a further minute transmuting of self structure took place.

He began to reflect more on his contemporary father and his brother Bob's relationship with him.

MR. L.: I've watched them together (with an embarrassed grin). I guess it isn't so much that Bob is always shining up to him. I just remember how good it used to feel to me when someone would work with me on a project and that's what Dad could always do with Bob.

In the closing phase of therapy, Mr. L.'s communications took on an exhilaration and yet a moderation which was striking.

MR. L.: I find I don't need to lay out the nuts and bolts of every idea I have. It is enough that *I* know them and feel good about my proj-

ects. When I have to go into detail, I find I no longer have such a
head of steam. I wait for questions.

In what had been agreed upon as their last interview, Mr. Lewis had
come in with an air of quiet pride.

MR. L.: I guess I've got the "go-how" as well as the "know-how".
Those guys in the biophysics outfit called me back for another interview. They showed me a problem they were working on and I
was kind of bewildered at first. But then I could see it was something
like what I had worked out for my professor that time. I showed
them what I thought might work and they let me try it. They really
want me to work with them but they've got to figure out how much
of my time they can afford. And then my wife and I have to sit down
and figure out whether we can afford them! They're a real good outfit. My boss where I work now says he could probably keep me on
part-time until they get squared away. I'd sure like to be on the
ground floor with that outfit! (After a pause) I feel like I've come a
long way. I think I've got a kind of handle on myself and I think I'm
ready to go along on my own for now. . . . I guess I'd like to come
back in if something comes up.

The therapist accepted his assessment and treatment terminated with
her assurance that she would be glad to hear from him. She experienced
some uneasiness over the still ambivalent issue of whether this opportunity would materialize in an ongoing job which was satisfying. But she
reflected that initial referral had been for fatigue, loss of appetite, and
problems with sleep. These had long since vanished and had not recurred.
Moreover, there was evidence that Mr. L. had, through myriad experiences of optimal frustration, transmuted self structure which he could rely
upon to regulate self-esteem, to tolerate anxiety and ambivalence, and to
right himself through appropriate calming and soothing. He could turn
to and elicit responses from family and colleagues and could in turn respond to their needs.

In the therapeutic process, what had been exposed was the manner and
the point at which deficits had developed. To the therapist as new selfobject he could pour forth the torrent of his longings, leaving the hour
refreshed and sleeping better, less irritable with his children. He could
reveal his longings and he was comforted. He could describe his interests
and accomplishments and he was stimulated by the therapist's attention.
For the period of their time together, he had the experience of appropriate
preferment and learned to recognize his anxiety when he felt himself less

central to someone's attention. For his excesses in interviews that led to rejections, he could learn to understand and forgive himself, rather than to destroy himself with shame and humiliation. He became increasingly able internally to alert himself, "There I go again." Past driven thought and behavior yielded in the present to that transmuting internalization which stimulates the growth of self-functions in monitoring anxiety, regulating self-esteem, calming and soothing himself.

About six weeks after terminating, he telephoned to advise that he was working three-fourths time with the biophysics concern, another quarter of his time with his old outfit. He added, "I want to thank you for all your help. I guess Dr. Mason knew what he was doing when he referred me to you."

12

Resolution of a Merger
With a Depressed Mother

I N THE FOLLOWING case we will examine the manner in which a merger
with a depressed mother perpetuates a vertical split, which gradually
yields to intervention.

Jennie

Jennie, the 26-year-old mother of a four-year-old son, was referred to
a family agency by a fellow worker who occasionally took over her work
as a secretary when Jennie had to be out of the office to care for her son.
Jennie was known as a hard worker but grumpy and irritable. People in
the office leaned on her for help but she was repeatedly passed over for
advancement. A colleague had suggested she get some help, as she herself
had, and recommended a family agency. Jennie commented, "I thought
she was off the wall, but things couldn't be worse, so here I am."

Jennie, a rather plain young woman, explained that she had married
a fellow student while she was an undergraduate. She had become pregnant and had then dropped out of school to care for their child. In addition she had taken a job while her husband continued his graduate work.
Her husband was her first boyfriend, not a very interesting person—but
then, who would be interested in her "except for a free ride?"

Jennie's bleak recitation of her life led the therapist to feel doubtful about
what could, indeed, be done to overcome the sense of joylessness she conveyed. Yet Jennie's comment that people were interested in her only
because she could provide a free ride suggested there was more to her
than that. Encouraging her to tell more about her discontent and sadness,
the therapist asked:

THERAPIST: A free ride?
JENNIE: Yeah, Jim just expected I would drop out so he could go on.
He didn't think much of my courses.

THERAPIST: What were you studying?

JENNIE: (With a grimace) Nothing earth-shaking. Some philosophy and some sociology.

THERAPIST: But did you enjoy them?

JENNIE: I guess. I had a professor in sociology who could really make us sit up and take notice. He really made it interesting. Philosophy was tough, but dad was a teacher and that's all he ever talked about, so I guess I kind of found it natural to hear about (with grim sarcasm) virtue, the virtuous man, and all that junk.

THERAPIST: Junk?

JENNIE: Yeah, I used to do a lot of typing for dad. I could take dictation straight on the typewriter and he liked that because he could read it right away even if there were a lot of mistakes. But every now and then he'd ask my opinion about something he had written. I'd tell him what I thought, but he would act as if I had made a foolish remark. Once he said, "I'll ask your brother. He has a man's head!" That burned me up; here was I sitting and typing and not having any fun, and my brother was out playing baseball with his friends!

THERAPIST: Did you say anything to your father?

JENNIE: To dad? You gotta be kidding.

THERAPIST: He was difficult to talk to?

JENNIE: (Rolling her eyes and almost sneering) Difficult? He would have said, "Don't be so emotional." So, I'm not emotional, but he certainly listened to my brother whenever he worked up a head of steam about anything!

THERAPIST: How did you feel about your father's way of treating you and your brother?

JENNIE: I don't know. I really like Bob. He was really a good kid. Stormy, but a good kid. (After a pause) I really helped him a lot.

THERAPIST: You helped him. Was it a two-way street?

JENNIE: (With a sarcastic snort) Help me? No one ever thought I needed anything.

THERAPIST: Why do you suppose that was?

JENNIE: I don't know. . . . There were just the two of us and I was four years older. . . . Mom always thought I should help him out. I used to get mad sometimes and go and sit in my room. But no one would ever come after me the way they did Bob to see what was wrong. I guess after a while I didn't care and didn't expect it. (After a pause, suspiciously) Say what's all this for anyway?

THERAPIST: You've told me you were irritable and lonely, that your friend suggested you might find some help for this here. We go about it by getting to know what's been troubling you.

JENNIE: Yeah, but all that's stuff in the past.

THERAPIST: But apparently your feelings about it are very much in the present. Perhaps as we talk about these things we'll be able to see some links to what's been going on and you may come to feel differently. I would like to help you . . . would you like to try?

JENNIE: I guess. What else is there to do? I've tried everything else (sarcastically)—aerobics, choir. I'm not doing too well with Billy, and I feel up against a wall in my job. Whoever thought I'd end up being a secretary for a law office! Whoever thought I'd be coming to anybody for help! (After a pause) How do we start?

THERAPIST: It seems we've already made a beginning.

As the therapist sets up a schedule of weekly appointments, Jennie gathers her coat and scarf, gives a curt nod and leaves. As the therapist reflects about what she has learned, even at this early phase, she finds it tempting to speculate about Jennie's relationship with her family. Does she suffer penis envy? Does this envy now afflict her relationship with her small son? Has an unresolved oedipal conflict dictated an unhappy marriage?

But self psychology offers another view of Jennie's strivings. Almost from the first moment what has emerged is a lonely, unmirrored individual who expects nothing to change. Each parent has been presented as responding only to her younger brother's needs. We have only an oblique view of her husband's response to her. He's not a very interesting person, but then who would be interested in her except for a free ride? She is willing to try therapy less out of hope than out of desperation.

When an individual comes in for the first time and is doubtful about whether psychotherapy will prove effective, one may overreact by proceeding with a prolonged discussion. At this point we really don't know whether psychotherapy will help. Briefly stating the agency's or clinic's purpose and area of work or the conditions of one's private practice is sufficient. One responds to questions about one's competence and training courteously and informatively. It is the individual's right to know and accords him the respect he must come to feel in everything we do and say. It is not infrequent that questions about the competence of the social worker to respond effectively to the needs of a troubled individual will be broached at the outset. What does a clinical social worker do? How is it different from what a psychiatrist or a psychologist does? What is the difference in training? These are legitimate questions, spoken or unspoken, which reflect a natural anxiety at opening sensitive or extremely painful areas to the scrutiny of a stranger.

When does a background of training in medicine become indispensable? When does the systematic study of the psychology of the mind become vital? And when is an understanding of psychosocial process across the life cycle (the person-in-his-situation (Hollis, 1964)), the individual as problem-solver (Perlman, 1957), an appropriate and effective means of relieving stress, allowing for change and growth?

It can be reassuring to an individual to find that such questions are received and answered without defensiveness. It can also be reassuring to have it understood that the clinical social worker is competent to help the individual determine if his needs dictate referral and stands ready to help with such a referral. As the work of therapy proceeds, however, questions of competence and differences in training offer an opportunity to explore and understand the self/selfobject need which prompts such questions.

Although this is a fragment of an initial interview, we can see that the therapist has moved from her initial state of feeling imposed upon by this seemingly dull young woman. Her initial feeling—an echo of the client's feeling of being someone whom others exploit—serves as a focus for her empathic attention. The work of an agency may be available without fee or at a very low fee. On a hierarchical scale the clinical social worker may be viewed as having a lesser position. This may arouse feelings of being devalued, which can be usefully and silently explored through introspection as one then reestablishes a sense of pleasure and integrity in one's work—unlike Jennie, who at this point feels only a sense of being exploited for a free ride.

In her second session, Jennie sits on the edge of her chair, waiting for the therapist to begin. The therapist believes that at this point it is premature to wait for Jennie to initiate the hour and asks how things have been during the past week.

JENNIE: Oh, the usual thing. Billy's had a cold and I've had problems with my sitter. I had to take time off and that's rough because things just pile up at the office. Billy's a handful, especially because he's feeling better but can't get out. He just messes everything up as if all I've got to do is pick up, pick up. I got so fed up I put him in his room and told him he couldn't come out till he said he was sorry. He kept pulling at the door but I was so mad I just hung on to the doorknob and wouldn't let go. Suddenly it got awfully quiet and I saw his hand come sliding under the door where it doesn't meet the floor. I yelled, "You can't come out till you say you're sorry." He said, "A hand under the door means I'm sorry." "Nope," I said, "say you're sorry!" He's gotta know who's boss. Anyway, he finally did, and I was still mad."

At this point the therapist is inwardly distressed at Jennie's rebuff of her small son's creative effort to reestablish contact with her. Although the therapist would like to make some comment about the child's cleverness and appeal, she is aware that this deflection of her empathic focus from Jennie reflects the history of Jennie's inability to secure appropriate responses to *her* needs. Noting and commenting on Jennie's weariness and frustration, the therapist encourages her to go on. The process of responding to one who seeks relief from emotional pain or unrewarding behavior, who searches for a way out of loneliness and isolation, requires the disciplined use of oneself. Within the period of partnership toward a mutual goal, the needs, feelings, and wishes of the individual in whose behalf one employs introspection and empathy also stimulate needs, feelings, and wishes in the therapist. But these echoes of human likeness and difference are now employed for the purpose of understanding and healing another.

Jennie continues with many instances of "cleaning up someone's mess." She cleans it up but somebody else gets the credit. Most recently she straightened out "a real disaster" on one of the computers, but the girl whose work she corrected was promoted over her. Her manner was that of a sulky child rather than someone who could ask for an explanation about what was involved in the lines of promotion.

THERAPIST: Has it always been this way for you, Jennie?

JENNIE: Oh, I don't know. Mom was sick a lot and I was always trying to think of things to do for her. Sometimes she would say I was a real help. That felt good, but then she'd pretty much take it all for granted. I guess I did, too. What's the big deal?

THERAPIST: I was wondering how you must have felt as a small girl when so much of what you did was taken for granted. You must have felt very lonely and sad.

JENNIE: (Her eyes fill with tears. She wipes them away angrily.) Oh, it's just your job to say things like that!

THERAPIST: Perhaps it felt strange to have me understand how you must have felt and to let you know. This feeling that people just use you for a free ride clearly has a long history. You and I together are trying to understand how this came to be and what keeps it going even now.

Jennie has been quick to reject the therapist's gentle initiation of an opportunity for Jennie to enter an empathic merger, but the therapist ventures a little further, tentatively recognizing that for Jennie such understanding seems strange. Although the therapist does feel her effort has been demeaned ("It's your job to say things like that"), she feels no need to defend herself or her interest and pleasure in her work. Rather, she seeks to engage Jennie in an empathic merger which may provide the conditions to initiate change. If this can be established, Jennie will be able to use the therapist as a new selfobject in the present, allowing her responsive functions to be transmuted into self-functions: monitoring stress, seeking new goals, and regulating self-esteem as she encounters inevitable setbacks. But we are just at the beginning of the process.

Over the next few months Jennie is regular in keeping her appointments. She is a close observer of the therapist's dress, the furnishings of her office, and people she passes in the building on the way to and from her appointments—she is curious about them but full of caustic comments. At the same time her therapist has noted that, despite a sallow complexion and no makeup, Jennie is far from plain. She has good features, and although her posture is often tense and awkward, her body is well-formed.

In the first few months of therapy she has continued to describe repeated episodes of being exploited, cleaning up other people's messes. She usually rebuffs the therapist's efforts to absorb her anger at feeling unappreciated, tossing such comments off with, "Oh, you're so emotional. It's no big deal!" At an opportune moment the therapist recalls these as Jennie's father's words, reported in the first session. Jennie becomes thoughtful and silent, finally saying with a half smile and a quick shy glance at the therapist, "I guess you're right. Who would have guessed it!"

A softening of her mood has begun to emerge; the sneering and snorting prominent in the earlier months have subsided. She has begun to talk of Jim and his work. His field of study is an obscure branch of math, one at which he is quite good but which doesn't make for social chat. In this he is very different from her father, who was very charming with people though not so with her. The family always revolved around her father and his activities. Bob is like that, too, but she is more like her mother in being less obtrusive. Her mother is an attractive woman, very capable when she isn't "sitting around being depressed." Jennie feels, bitterly, that she is going in the same direction. She is quick to say that it is not that she has such great abilities, but she always did well in school and she'd like to get back into it—see what she can do; find out what's in *her* head. Instead, here she is stuck in this old job, everlastingly cleaning up other people's messes.

The therapist points out that Jennie frequently uses this expression and wonders about its origin.

JENNIE: (After a pause, flushing) I can't believe what I'm thinking. It's
    just that . . . it's just . . . oh, never mind . . . it's just a silly old
    memory.
THERAPIST: But a memory that pops up in your mind now must be
    pretty powerful.
JENNIE: (After a pause) Oh, what's the use of digging up old stuff?
THERAPIST: Sometimes old stuff can help us understand what's going
    on now.
JENNIE: Oh well, it's just that . . . one time Bob was down for his nap
    and I was playing in my room. Mom was lying down, somewhere,
    in one of her crying spells. My father came storming in from some-
    where yelling, "Why didn't you get him up in time. Now he's gone
    and made a mess in his bed . . . get it cleaned up before your mother
    gets up. She's got enough to do." I guess I was about eight and I
    didn't usually get Bob up . . . I guess he didn't usually make a mess.
    Anyway, I was crying and Bob was crying and my father kept shout-
    ing, "Don't be such a baby." In the middle of all this mom came
    in and started to take over, but dad shouted to her, "Let her take
    care of it, let her learn to take some responsibility around here." I
    guess I got it all cleaned up somehow. When dad was on one of
    those rampages, mom just kept quiet and did whatever she could.
    (After a pause) The thing is, part of me felt he was right, I was just
    being a baby.
THERAPIST: But it must have frightened you to have your father burst
    in on your play in a temper. You didn't know Bob had made a mess,
    and his mess wasn't yours to clean up. To cry or complain seems
    babyish to you, but you were still a little child.

Jennie looks uneasy but says nothing. The therapist wonders if she has
gone too far. Should she have waited longer for Jennie to recognize these
feelings for herself? But her comment has been prompted by Jennie's
description of a number of such incidents in which neither parent seemed
to recognize their child's overwhelming feelings. As earlier selfobjects
failed to do, the therapist now in the present is performing that function
usually performed by the empathic selfobject: helping the child to identify the feelings appropriate to the event. As the therapist provides this
understanding now she is aware that Jennie has become anxious.

THERAPIST: (After a pause) Is it so babyish to cry about feeling hurt and
    misunderstood?
JENNIE: (Sullenly) Oh, well, for me it was.
THERAPIST: For you?

JENNIE: I don't know, people just seemed to expect more of me. And besides, you don't know all the things I could do. I could read and write a little before I went to school. Mom was a teacher before she married dad, and she used to teach me things.

Jennie presents her competence and ability to perform beyond her years for the therapist's validation, fearful of being overcome by her longing to be comforted and preferred. She has had to disavow these needs particularly under pressure of father's disapproval.

JENNIE: Mom used to be proud of all the things I could do, and I helped her a lot, especially when she got into one of her crying spells. Then everything was terrible. She'd lie around in her room for days; the house would get all messy. Dad would come home and be in a terrible mood, too. Bob and I would try to keep out of his way. In the morning when I'd get ready for school, right away, right out the front door, I'd put a big smile on my face. I wasn't a baby, people didn't have to feel sorry for me.
THERAPIST: But how would you be feeling?
JENNIE: All through school I'd be scared inside, not knowing how things would be when I got home.
THERAPIST: And how were they, Jennie?
JENNIE: (Her eyes beginning to brim with tears) Oh, it wasn't so terrible. I got to learn how to do a lot of things. But . . . but . . .

After a struggle she bursts into tears which she tries angrily to stop, finally giving way to uncontrollable sobs. When these subside, she describes coming home and finding her mother face down on the floor. She tried unsuccessfully to rouse her. Her father, who had apparently been called by the sitter, burst into the house. He shouted to her, ''Go take care of Bobby.'' A short time later an ambulance came and her mother was taken to a hospital. She recalled her father coming into her room at night and sitting down to explain that her mother was sick and would be away for several months. She'd just have to shape up and take more responsibility in the house and take care of Bobby.

JENNIE: He sort of patted my head and I tried to take his hand but he got up and went away. He said sort of out of the door, ''Don't go saying anything to anyone.''

Afraid to cry, her tentative effort to catch hold of her father's hand rebuffed, Jennie turned to the wall. (The therapist is struck by the similarity of her rebuffing her small son's effort to reach out his hand to her and her father's rebuffing of her tentative effort to establish reassuring hand contact with him. At this point to draw her attention to this similarity could deflect focus from her needs.)

THERAPIST: How frightened and lonely you must have been.

Jennie continued to cry and then began to describe her struggles to keep up a good front at school. Once the little boy next door asked where her mother was and, when Jennie didn't answer, said, "They say she's off her nut." Jennie fled, fearful of tears, fearful of falling apart.

She described her relief when her mother finally returned home. For a time things went better, but her mother began to lie around the house again, crying, and had to return to the hospital. It was in response to the therapist's comment that to be frightened and lonely and not to have anyone to talk to about these painful feelings that Jennie sobbed violently, and then, after a time, drying her eyes, looked up and said, "I smell chocolate chip cookies baking", as described earlier (p. 37), reflecting her longing for the food-giving empathic mother who, when she was well, could mirror her little daughter's pleasure in her activities. This the therapist clarified. The incident also reflected Jennie's use of the therapist as a selfobject in the present who could absorb her grief and help her to bring order to her world.

She spoke sadly of her mother's condition, believing that she should have helped her *more* than she did when she was growing up. The therapist pointed out that she was viewing what might have been from the vantage point of a young woman of 26. At the time of her mother's greatest illness she had only been approaching adolescence. It sounded as if she had done a great deal and all that a child of that age could have done. How painful it must have been to have no one help *her* with *her* feelings and her own tasks in growing up! At such comments Jennie would dry her eyes, look up, and once, with a mischievous smile, said, "Chocolate chips! Chocolate chips!" Such comments gave evidence that Jennie was beginning to be able to calm and soothe herself, to regulate self-esteem, but that she still recognized her need of the therapist to help her fill in this selfobject function.

In the months of work that followed, Jennie described many incidents of confusion and embarrassment when, during her school years, neither parent was available for special events. She learned to sign up for activities that involved behind-the-scenes work, but she resented the amount of attention that some of her classmates received for "walk-on parts" or "mickey-mouse" tasks she could turn out in short order.

Pretending that their noisy laughter as they carried on with each other interfered with her work, she would surreptitiously eye her classmates.

JENNIE: After school they'd be off to someone's house. . . . It wasn't that they didn't want me, too. But even when mom was feeling better, I was afraid to be gone too long. If anything happened, I'd feel I should have been there.

Jennie would always cloak in ambiguity what was keeping her so busy at home. Occasionally she would be asked to a movie or school dance.

JENNIE: But the guys who asked me were so . . . so twerpy! Like me!
THERAPIST: You don't seem so twerpy to me, Jennie.
JENNIE: (Flushing and lowering her head) You should have seen me then. You should have seen what I wore.
THERAPIST: Tell me about it.

Jennie described her efforts to dress like the other girls, always feeling awkward and plain, or too fussy.

JENNIE: Other girls went shopping together. I just felt out of it. Once I bought a lipstick and practiced using it. Mom saw me and seemed so sad when she said, "Oh, Jennie, there's time to grow up." I guess she didn't realize I *was* growing up. (After a pause) Dad noticed, though. Once when he saw me with lipstick, I thought he was going to say something, but he just turned away and mumbled, "It's not what you put on your face that makes you look good. It's what's inside that counts." (Sullenly and yet with some pride) Mom's complexion was peaches and cream; she didn't need makeup. *I* could have used it. Jim thinks I look great anyway. . . . I wonder if he really notices me. (Jennie began to weep.) I missed so much fun. Jim was my first boyfriend. Other girls went through three or four boyfriends and some are still at it. (Defiantly) I guess I could be, too!

Jennie went on to describe her brother Bob's escapades, the girlfriends whose hearts he broke, and those who broke his.

JENNIE: We had a lot of fun together and I think he really got a kick out of talking to me and getting my advice. *My* advice! What did I know? . . . But I guess I learned a lot from watching and listening to kids at school.

THERAPIST: Weren't your parents at all concerned about your not going out?

JENNIE: I guess they didn't really notice, or after a while they thought it was just the way I was. After a while I guess it really *was* the way I was!

THERAPIST: But inside?

JENNIE: Inside?

Jennie was silent and thoughtful, gradually flushing and darting her eyes from side to side. The therapist was aware that her question had reverberated to a part of herself Jennie had previously disavowed. She had described her courtship in a dull, dry manner: her husband was her first boyfriend, not very interesting, "but then who would be interested in me except for a free ride?" Her lack of zest and joy was marked. All the accumulated evidence pointed to the failure of her parents (her mother out of depression, her father out of a puritanical, duty-bound view of his daughter) to respond with pleasure and support of her legitimate needs to be affirmed and guided as she traversed the period of adolescence into young womanhood. Jennie had already signified her readiness for some shared work in this area by her reference to her surreptitious surveillance of her classmates, her help to her brother in support of his developing manliness, and her own frustrated attempts to take pleasure in her physical attractiveness. Her comment that some girls went through three or four boyfriends and are still at it also revealed the breakthrough of assertiveness in this area: "And I guess I could be there, too!"

During the next few months Jennie struggled with intermittent rage at her husband for taking her so for granted, for plodding on in his dogged, determined way with his research, with her sense of being exploited and unappreciated. She continued to struggle with the pain of the fun she had missed. She described a recurring fantasy of her earlier years in which she would return to her high school for something—"any old something" —which had made her famous. And as she was standing before her classmates holding forth in authoritative manner, all eyes would be on her, but she would look *smashing*. Her clothes would vary from severe to off-the-shoulder blouses as she pursued her fantasy, gradually focusing on a particular athlete whom she had worshipped from afar. But as she sought to give the relationship a narrative course she would become depressed, find some unfulfilled task, and discard the fantasy. The therapist was struck by her inability to play even in fantasy and shared this observation with her.

JENNIE: I don't know. . . . It felt like cheating.

THERAPIST: Cheating?

JENNIE: (After a pause, beginning to drip slow tears) Mom never had any fun. You probably think like everybody else she was just nuts. But I remember her from when she was really well. She could get really excited about things we did together. She was really fun and I used to be very proud of her when she came to school. (Pause, sadly) But I remember once there was a meeting, and all the kids and their mothers were there. I had a best friend and I kept tagging after her and her mother, wanting mom to keep up. But there were too many stairs and she kept lagging behind, and then saying, "Oh, they don't really want us! I'm too old." I was mad at her for spoiling my fun and making me feel so out of it. But, you know, looking back I think she was right. My friend's mother looked . . . looked young and sharp. Mom's clothes just sort of hung. She was prettier, but it didn't matter. I think that must have been when she started to get depressed. And afterwards when she went to the hospital and all, I didn't want to . . . let her fall behind. I felt if I let go of her, she'd really go to pieces. (Jennie weeps.)

As the work of therapy goes on, the intensity and depth of Jennie's merger with her depressed mother are exposed bit by bit. There are discouraging cycles of despair, questions about "whether therapy really works . . . it isn't doing any good." Periods in which the therapist, too, finds herself discouraged but uses such feeling states to recognize the depth of Jennie's despair and the slow process of healing deficits incurred so early.

THERAPIST: Could it be, Jennie, that you felt "deserting" your mother caused her illness? And so you killed your own fun, or pretended you didn't need any. You had "grownup" tasks and didn't need to do any other "silly things your friends were into."
JENNIE: (Weeping) Even now . . . I feel good, when I'm with you, when we talk things over . . . I feel sort of more whole, not so empty inside. But then I think, "Poor Mom, what fun did she ever have?" And I feel sad all over again.
THERAPIST: But you've let me see that when your mother was well, Jennie, she rejoiced in your pleasure. It was only after she became ill that she feared your growing up and leaving her. And so part of you remained joined to her in all those sad and lonely feelings . . . so when you let go of them, you begin to feel you're deserting her all over again.
JENNIE: (Nodding) Anyway, it's too late now. I've missed all that fun and I'm never going to get those years back.
THERAPIST: How old are you, Jennie?

JENNIE: (Surprised, and then with a grin) I get it. You *know* how old I am. I guess 26 isn't over the hill! Jennie and her therapist break into laughter.

THERAPIST: It is true that the years can't be lived over again, but isn't it possible that you're clinging to that feeling, postponing fun now as another way of not letting go of your mother?

Jennie is thoughtful but does not respond.

There followed now a period in which Jennie reminisced about the parallel lives of her mother and herself. When Jennie was four, as Billy now was, her mother had been 40. Her mother had married late and embarked on motherhood late—"not late for now" when women defer mothering because of career lines, "but late for then" and among the mothers of Jennie's friends. Her father had renewed his studies when he was in his mid-forties, but Jim, her husband, like herself was *only* 26.

In the next few months Jennie's manner continued to soften, and she experimented with new hairstyles. Aerobics and singing in the choir, which she had mentioned belittlingly in her first interview, now became the scene of amusing incidents which she shared with the therapist. On one afternoon she came in with a soft glow and very becomingly dressed. The therapist responded with an admiring comment.

JENNIE: Not so twerpy, huh? (Joining in the therapist's laughter) I've been chosen for a solo part in the spring concert. It's hard but it's fun and it's just right for my voice. Some of the guys are beginning to notice me. I used to turn that sort of thing right off. But you know, it's fun! (Darting a mischievous glance at the therapist) Don't worry. I won't get carried away!

At this point the therapist silently wondered whether she should engage Jennie in exploring the origin of the remark but opted for viewing it as Jennie's way of regulating her own grandiosity, something that should not be intruded upon. This proved a wise abstention, since Jennie embarked on an exploration of why it was she and Jim had never played around, either before they met each other or after. As she increasingly viewed the various options of housemates, roommates, playmates, and relationships that were ambisextrous, what struck her about many of these individuals was the joylessness that proceeded from their "playing around." She came to the conclusion that she and Jim had been good for each other and good to each other. She was amused that some of their friends looked at them as being afraid to get off the "straight and narrow" and mused about whether this could be so. She recognized that among Jim's colleagues and their friends they played a helpful role and she took pleasure in being idealized.

Jennie began to discuss plans for the future. She became aware that her fellow workers at the firm where she was employed were really appreciative of her efforts.

JENNIE: It's really different from clearing up other people's messes— or their using me for a free ride. I really feel good about what I can do, and it makes me feel—I don't know—really happy, not dropped down.

Jennie thus indicates that she has achieved cohesiveness that can be relied upon. Helping another no longer is joyless drudgery but proceeds rather from pleasure in her competence, enhanced empathy, and increased self-esteem in the experience of being idealized. At work she was offered a supervisory role with an increase in salary, but this led her to consider whether she really wanted to continue at what essentially was, for her, a dead end.

She began to talk with Jim about the possibility of returning to school. His own work was going well now. She was more appreciative of the respect his work was given by his department. She experienced pride when she witnessed his excitement in his discussion. She wondered about a field for herself and reflected sadly on her mother's experiences. Her mother had always enjoyed her teaching but had given it up to marry and have a family.

JENNIE: I think she enjoyed it all at first; I don't know why she started going downhill. We've been talking some about it when I go over to visit with Billy. Dad really likes Billy. (Sadly) He gets a kick out of him the way he used to with Bob. Why didn't he ever with me? (Weeping)
THERAPIST: We don't know what his problems were that kept him from enjoying his bright and competent little daughter. Did he never show an interest in you?
JENNIE: Mom says he did before Bob came. But then he began to go to school nights. He wanted to get to be a principal. I guess he worked round-the-clock . . . he used to say that all the time. Maybe that's why mom got so sad and lonely. She was an only child and her mother lived on the West coast. We never got to see grandma much. In fact it seems we never saw anybody much.

Jennie reflected on the course of her parents' lives, realizing now that hers did not have to take the same course. The merger with her depressed mother was yielding. To her therapist she began to describe the many activities she had been interested in but had never really tried. She glowed as she recalled some of her fantasies and began to report, too, incidents of Billy's creativeness.

> JENNIE: He does get things in a mess, but he's fun and he gets good ideas. I used to have to be too careful and keep everything neat. It got so what I'd mostly do is line things up and keep them that way. Now, I get down on the floor with Billy a lot and I watch to see what he's going to do and if he wants me to help him. (With a mixture of sadness and pleasure) With mom, she was a good teacher but she didn't know when to stop. Pretty soon it was her thing and not mine. And dad! Mr. Critic! (After a pause) I've been carrying them around inside me too long and it's just gotten too crowded!

Sharing her observations of Billy's responses, not in an intellectually dry manner but with warmth and zestful pleasure in the phases of childhood through which he was passing, she continued to look back sadly on her own experiences, but to reflect on these with an increasing grasp of the reality of her parents' personalities and the differences from her own and Jim's. But she found likenesses as well in her quickness and her ability to order her ideas.

Over the next few months Jennie enrolled in a class on human development, sharing her excitement in what she was learning. As she considered the new direction her interests might take and the coursework they would dictate, she came in boundingly one day to remark:

> JENNIE: You know, in a few years or so I could be sitting in your chair! I think I'd like to go into social work and I can go for a master's degree straight from a B.A. What do you think of that?

Such a comment could be viewed as competitive but we have a deeper understanding of the healing process if we recognize that she had moved from an empathic merger with her therapist to a twinship transference. For months, Jennie has had back-and-forth stirrings as she struggled to let go of the merger with her depressed mother without feeling that she has abandoned her. With the therapist as new selfobject in the present, she has been able to savor her own wishes and needs, to trust that in fulfilling them she is not deserting her mother. Not only can she recognize the need to act independently, but the therapist now responds with appropriate mirroring and confirming, which her fragile mother was unable to provide. In response to Jennie's question, "What do you think of that?" she says:

> THERAPIST: If it proves to be what you really enjoy, I am very pleased for you!
>
> JENNIE: (Revealing her need for the therapist's continued mirroring by her anxiety) But what if I'm not good at it?
>
> THERAPIST: There's no reason to fear that possibility. That's what learning is all about, finding out what you really want to do and then whether it's the field for you. The two go hand in hand.
>
> JENNIE: When I'm with you, you really make me feel good; you make me feel I can try anything.
>
> THERAPIST: And so you can, and change directions if you find you must.
>
> JENNIE: Jim says he thinks we can swing my going back to school full-time. He's got a good grant to finish his work and he's interviewing for jobs. (With a sudden gasp) But that may mean we have to go out of town. And I don't feel ready to stop this yet.
>
> THERAPIST: We have time, still, and when we do decide our work together has come to a satisfactory point, you'll probably feel ready.

In the next months Jim's job offer came through but for a college within commuting distance. Jennie continued in her job and enrolled for another course. She found her studies exhilarating, but she wasn't ready as yet to venture everything for the sake of her goal. She commented that she used to be described as a grouch, but not now. One of her friends asked her where she got all her energy. There were periods of anxiety, however, which the therapist shared. Was Jennie's interest in social work an identification with her profession? Did it proceed from a strengthened, cohesive self, a center of her own perceptions and initiative? Jennie's announcement of her interest in social work ("In a few years I could be sitting in your chair") was open to interpretation as springing from oedipal rivalry. But self psychology offers a more integrative view: Jennie has been transmuting the capacity to monitor anxiety and regulate self-esteem, self-functions that have been missing or enfeebled. The therapist accepted and reflected a meaningful image of Jennie, a competent young woman who in the past joylessly functioned at others' behest. She had been driven by an old need to have confirmation from a withholding father. She had been merged with her depressed mother whose need of her as a selfobject perpetuated Jennie's perception of herself as providing a "free ride" for others, of "cleaning up other people's messes."

In the earlier months when the regularity of weekly interviews had been interrupted by holidays, Jennie had retreated into sullen reenactment of her earlier drudgelike relationship with others. She became demanding with her small son and depreciative of her husband. When, on one occasion, it had been necessary to skip two weekly sessions because of the therapist's illness, Jennie returned anxious and frightened. A certain spunkiness and liveliness had disappeared.

JENNIE: I began to think I'd have to get myself one of those downtown therapists, that if you were really any good, you'd be working in private practice and not in an agency setup!

Although the therapist felt her efforts and abilities were being demeaned, what stimulated her empathic response was the recognition that Jennie's fears sprang from the intensity of her need of a dependable, idealized selfobject. In the earlier months her need was for an almost unrealistically perfect union. Through absorbing Jennie's anxieties and helping her to identify the feelings and emotions these stimulated, the therapist helped her to order the events that led to her anxiety. The way was opened for expansion and greater flexibility in a cohesive self. At unavoidable interruptions and holidays, Jennie recognized the childhood roots of her fears and was able to bounce back more readily when she was frightened or upset.

In the remaining months of their work together, Jennie decided that she would enroll in a master's program leading to a degree in social work. The wish seemed to spring from genuine interest in the field, and this had been intensified by her ability to offer effective help to a neighbor undergoing hospitalization. She had met and talked with one of the social workers on the service. She explored her reactions and reported with a certain intense pleasure witnessing the response to her efforts and the total absence of a feeling of being exploited or unappreciated on her part. The therapist, knowing the difficulties that beset the field of social work, experienced anxiety at whether she should point these out to Jennie in advance, but felt it would be an unwelcome intrusion. It was Jennie herself who, coming from a lecture describing the broad range of social work practice, reported that she knew there were a lot of difficulties but she didn't feel she had to protect herself from their reality. What she really had to do was keep her eyes and ears open to the possibilities that were available and to find something she really could enjoy.

As the time of termination approached, Jennie had a profound surge of anxiety. She brought her first and only dream to therapy. In the dream she was getting ready for a party. Her clothes were all laid out for her, but she didn't like what she saw. She went to the closet to see what choices there were, but there was only one dress, a kind of shabby house-dress. Still, the dress on the bed was too fussy; she turned to the mirror and saw her mother's weeping face. She woke with a start that wakened her husband, to whom she told her dream. She laughed, still a little anx-ious, as she reported his comment: "Go ahead, wear the fussy one; if no one likes it, I will, and let's get some sleep!" She was profoundly moved by the symbolic condensation of her struggle which this dream repre-sented.

Over the course of termination, Jennie described past events to which she was invited in grammar school and high school. She never felt she had the right clothes, and her mother was often reluctant to have her leave, needing her presence. If she went, she felt lost and empty; when she stayed at home, similar feelings overwhelmed her, but at least she didn't feel terrible about deserting her mother. The themes that found ex-pression now increasingly freed her from the sense of betrayal of her mother and the recognition that, had her mother been well, she would have rejoiced in her child's activities. Was the weeping mother also the therapist? Jennie was able to express typical sadness at termination. The therapist recognized the sadness she, too, felt at her leaving, but felt pleasure in what Jennie had accomplished and the energy with which she approached the next phase of her life. With a mischievous grin that had now become characteristic, Jennie commented, "I guess from now on I'll be baking my own chocolate chip cookies. Mom gave me the taste, but you gave me the recipe!"

In her valedictory comment, Jennie has signaled pleasure in her own competence and her readiness to reach out for new goals. Her humor, her playfulness with her son, her satisfaction in her marriage, her capacity to explore options for professional training—all reflect the filling in of deficits—missing functions—in a previously depressed self. The joyless, driven behavior that characterized her relationships and her activities has yielded to a sense of zestful interest.

The self/selfobject unit established with the therapist initially enabled Jennie to expose the depth and extent of her loneliness, her drudgelike existence as "she cleared up other people's messes." As a new selfob-ject, the therapist allowed her mature psychic structure to serve a calm-ing and soothing function responding with understanding to the needs and wishes of Jennie's younger self and their reverberations to the pres-ent—other people use her strengths for their needs, they don't see her needs. As repair proceeds, the work of transmuting internalization con-tinues. She begins to take pleasure in her appearance—"not so twerpy." She feels readiness to explore her talents and interests, not in her previous joyless fashion, but with energy and curiosity. With an increase in her own capacity for empathy, and her ability to envision different goals for herself, Jennie weeps both for the lonely child she was and her parents' joyless lives. She tries to understand her father's inability to take pleasure in her growth and development, watching his pleasure in play with his grandson, recalling his different response to her brother. She no longer seeks such response from him, accepting his deficits. The past cannot be undone, but the focused empathic attention of the therapist in the present performs a healing function.

It is difficult to characterize the transference that emerged as mirroring, idealizing, or twinship; each was present in the evolving therapeutic process. Jennie idealized the therapist's calmness, her wisdom, her capacity to work with so many different kinds of situations. As she merged with these idealized qualities of the therapist, the experience of being soothed and calmed permitted Jennie to transmute empathic awareness of others and allowed continuity in which her already developed skills of responding to other's needs now became an expression of her own pleasure in her attributes. Just as the therapist's response—"you don't seem twerpy to me, Jennie"—had given Jennie a realistic reflection of how others might see her and enhanced her self-esteem, so too the response of her friends and colleagues to her freely given assistance and understanding allowed strengthening of idealized values and direction to her pursuit of goals she could enjoy.

Evidence that her choice of social work as a profession did not reflect merely a gross identification with her therapist can be seen in the care with which she examined her choices. She tested out her capacities, derived pleasure from her talents, and prepared to professionalize her skills with realistic confrontation of problems in her chosen field. Throughout the termination phase, Jennie confronted episodes which initially triggered earlier feeling states of being "used for a free ride," but from which she rapidly recovered, exclaiming with one such episode, "It just doesn't feel like that anymore. I know what I *want* to do! I know what I *can* do and I *do* it!"

Her playful reference to chocolate chip cookies—"Mom gave me the taste but you gave me the recipe"—signals that self-awareness now functions independently: it has been transmuted as a self-function.

In examining the course of this therapy, we would say that the initial period provided the conditions for an empathic merger in which transmuting internalization of selfobject functions could take place. Jennie's doubts and caution gradually yielded to the healing experience of having both her childhood hurts and their reverberations to the present understood and responded to with appropriate description of previously disavowed or unrecognized affect.

The middle period exposed the intensity of her need for the selfobject functions of esteem regulation, of her inability to recover from hurts and slights and her readiness to retreat into joyless, driven behavior without the therapist's intervention. Increasingly during this period, Jennie began to "work with" the therapist; together they would confirm the onset, the course, and nature of her behavior in response to trauma. And Jennie worked over and expanded her understanding of internal or external events, interweaving past and present experience.

In the phase of termination, there were intervals of anxiety and doubt, a genuine sense of loss at the thought of proceeding without therapy, without the therapist. She would recall the therapist's voice, particular phrases, but this self-conscious self-awareness yielded to pleasure in new associations she was making, new selfobjects with whom she experienced mutuality of interests and pursuits. She felt herself ready to move ahead on her own.

13

Self Psychology and the Aging Process

I N ADULT YEARS, the nuclear self maintains cohesiveness through self-righting functions, which continue to involve human selfobjects as well as symbolic selfobjects. Their variety reflects the vigorous pursuit of a life which is meaningful and worthwhile. Yet it is the nature, availability, and depth of such relationships which provide confirmation and sustain continuity. Some individuals are able to maintain a responsive, reciprocal relationship with many individuals. They find fulfillment in a host of cultural, philanthropic, and social activities. Others live more in the mind, perhaps in greater solitude, but nevertheless with a sense that their lives and activities are rewarding. Whatever the size of one's circle, to feel human, to be confirmed and sustained in one's human attributes, we continue to need selfobjects until the end of life.

Depression is more prevalent among the aging because it is a period in which the tempo of loss quickens. All the familiar vicissitudes of illness, separation, divorce, death, the loss of one's powers, whether physical or in one's sphere of influence, may trigger fragmentation. Despite reduced vigor or disturbance in harmonious balance, the sturdiness of the nuclear self and its capacity for self-righting will determine the capacity of the individual to seek new solutions.

We differ in our ability to find sustenance in abstract symbolic selfobjects such as the arts, literature, philosophical concepts, religion, or government. Most of us require a combination of these and human selfobjects although, as we have said, some individuals, with greater strength in the idealizing and value-setting pole, will turn from disappointment to pursue with renewed vigor the elaboration and acceptance of universal ideals for mankind. Even when the life span, the time ahead, becomes increasingly foreshortened, certain individuals find sustenance in the renewal and affirmation of beliefs and standards which have sustained them in the past. If cultural and social values alter and shift broadly, they can accomodate their views if, in doing so, they are not compelled to sacrifice continuity and integrity.

Other individuals turn increasingly to human selfobjects, and it is here that the process of aging exacts its toll in depression and depletion, as inevitably the circle of selfobjects shrinks. The opportunity to seek restoration and regulation of self-esteem diminishes, but the task now becomes one's acceptance of the human condition, transience, even though in minute experiences this process has been at work throughout the aging process.

Aging brings increasing pressure to bear on one's ability to regulate self-esteem. Kohut has described the evolution of self-esteem, healthy narcissism, from its most primitive form to its most mature, adaptive, and culturally valuable forms in empathy, creativity, wisdom, humor, and an acceptance of human transience (Kohut, 1966). He viewed the mature form of narcissism as an integral, self-contained set of psychic functions rather than as a regression product (Kohut, 1978, p. 618).

Interviews with six individuals in their eighties, all highly successful in their careers, seem to confirm these functions. Of those interviewed three were women: two were leaders in the field of philanthropy and volunteer social services; the third was a training analyst and educator. Three were men, a historian, a training analyst, and a surgeon, all still functioning as consultants in their fields. Looking back over the long course of their lives, all except one individual, who tended to idealize a past that would come no more, reflected a remarkable capacity to examine with humor their own growth and development and that of the professions they had chosen.

The interviews were conducted with a view to exploring their experiences in leaving home for college in comparison with that of today's entering college students and to learn how they had come upon their choice of profession. In general, they described themselves as curious, in no hurry to close down choices. What was striking was the role of their mentors. The quirks and competencies of these mentors were reviewed with a combination of wisdom and humor, which they also turned upon themselves and their work.

The comments of one, a surgeon, will convey the general tenor of the comments of all six. The surgeon, asked when he had first felt security in his choice of profession, replied:

> I'm not sure I have it now! All my life I was filled with self-doubt, but I covered it up! Throughout a medical career, one is always afraid one may do wrong—afraid of errors in judgment, making mistakes, all of it! Medicine is full of such

possibilities. But I think my controlling belief was that the patient is the reason the doctor is there. . . . Learning and teaching is part of the process, but the patient is not there for the purpose of aggrandizing the doctor's skill. It is the patient's pain and suffering which require a medical response if a response is humanly possible. When relief and improvement follow upon the doctor's interventions, and enough evidence accumulates about the procedure, one shares one's knowledge, one's doubts, the area for further research with one's colleagues and students. The same is true when one is unsuccessful. There is a healing process for the doctor as well in this interchange.

Along with these sober reflections, he revealed a quiet elation in aspects of his work that had confirmed his competence. But he was also able to view admiringly the work of younger colleagues in his field who were operating at a level and in areas beyond those he had reached. Implicit in his comments is Kohut's description of mature forms of narcissism as an integral, self-contained set of psychic functions: empathy, wisdom, creativity, humor, and an acceptance of one's own transience.

These individuals were at the closing years of their lives. An example of an individual just in the process of relinquishing an active life may be more instructive. In the following vignette we may observe the manner in which a 70-year-old man responded to a severe narcissistic blow and to loss. The intensity of his devotion to his profession and its importance to him as a selfobject, as well as his ability to turn his empathy to a younger generation, are poignantly illustrated.

Ray Meyer

Ray Meyer was a basketball coach who had for 42 years led his team through the ups and downs of victory and defeat. In the final game of his career, through a basket made by the opposing team in two seconds of overtime, his team lost a regional championship. It was the last game of his coaching career. Responding to reporters he remarked:

I lost a good friend in basketball. It's sinking in rapidly now. I've lost a real close friend that's been with me for so long. For three-quarters of my life, I've been in basketball. . . . I walked down that gauntlet of newspapermen and I saw the lights flashing and I knew it was the last time I would ever make that walk. . . . I have to accept it. I'm not going to die because we lost a ballgame. . . . I'm very disappointed I went out this way but I feel worse for the players who made the bad plays. They're taking it very hard. . . . They should just forget it. It was only a basketball game. We tried and we had a fine year, and I don't think the boys are losers because they lost this game. . . . I don't blame them. . . . Next year they'll be back and they won't make the same mistakes.

But it will be a sad day for me when the boys go out on the gym floor again and I'll hear the ball bounce and I'll wish I were down there to help them. I'll talk to the coaches and realize then that I'm no longer a part of them. I'm no longer a part of the game.

Besieged by autograph seekers, among them a small boy who asked if he could have his signature, Ray Meyer answered, "You sure can, son." Then, turning away from his admirers, the requests of photographers and reporters, he expressed his concern about keeping "his boys" waiting for him on the bus and went to join his team (*Chicago Tribune*, 3/25/84, Sec. 2, p. 1).

We can see in his response, his beginning efforts to accept a less central position in his profession and the quickening of his empathy for his team. Despite his pain, he does not express the narcissistic rage with which more vulnerable individuals respond to blows; rather, he begins to move toward relinquishing his central position and extends his empathy to those whose careers he has helped to guide.

To feel pain, to mourn loss but to turn creatively to the future, is the hallmark of a cohesive nuclear self. Whether grief becomes a secondary disorder of the self, requiring professional intervention, will be determined by the sturdiness of the nuclear self. At a time when one's powers, including physical powers, are waning, longstanding deficits may be exposed or exacerbated. Aging or aged individuals then require others to become supportive rather than sustaining. Helplessness in the aged, unlike that of the young, does not carry the promise of ultimate strength. It carries only a future of greater helplessness and, with good fortune, the ability to meet death with a modicum of dignity and respect. In those situations in which an individual's family, friends, and financial resources have dwindled, emotional difficulties weathered in the past become exacerbated. Aged people particularly may suffer from a loss of continuity, of a historic sense of self, and therefore may have a great need for past memories to sustain them. Such needs may drive others away. Countertransference is not limited to the therapeutic milieu alone. Children, burdened by many years of caring for an aged parent, may experience a frightening quality of annihilation (Grunes, 1981a). In some instances, individuals to whom the aged may turn behave as if old age is catching and avoid their aged parents just at a time when their needs are the greatest. Old age is indeed catching; that is, it catches up with all of us!

Where children have contended with difficult, demanding parents throughout their years of development and must contend now with responsibility for them when they are aging and infirm, negative expectations may intensify the tempo with which such parents then lapse into dependency, ill health, and helplessness. As we will see in the following examples, an understanding of the concepts of self psychology may permit interventions which interrupt the downward course or limit its extent. Several examples will illustrate the manner in which this may take place.

The needs of older people have much in common with those of every age group. For the elderly as well as the young certain essentials are required in order to live with full dignity: an acceptable home, economic security, social status and recognition, a meaningful purpose in life. As difficult as it is for many people of all ages to fulfill the conditions necessary for optimum adjustment, the aged often have the hardest time of all. (Hollis and Woods, 1981, p. 62)

When widowed and having to make a home with a child burdened with work and family responsibilities, an individual may feel, and indeed may be, shunted aside and tolerated in a duty-ridden manner. Resentment then accumulates on both sides, as reflected in the following vignette.

Mrs. D.

Mrs. D., a 75-year-old widow, was referred to the social service department of the hospital in which she was recovering from surgery. The nurse had reported that whenever her daughter visited, quarrels would erupt and the mother would banish her daughter from her room. Since Mrs. D. was due to return to her daughter's home in a few days, the nurse was beginning to question her readiness for discharge. Mrs. D.'s physical recovery was without incident, but she had become increasingly demanding and difficult.

Her daughter, divorced and the mother of two teenaged children, worked full-time at an exacting job which left her little free time; her visits to the hospital were sandwiched in with other household tasks. When interviewed, the daughter confessed that she felt little able to deal with her mother at this time of her life; her mother was never easy to please, but since her surgery she had become even more difficult. Although she was ashamed at having "an outsider" help her in dealing with her mother, she was at her wit's end. She could accommodate her mother in her home; there were no physical limitations on her mother's activities. But Mrs. D. had become intrusive and domineering in her behavior with the family. The children were increasingly resentful and unwilling to spend much time with her. They were "good kids" but they had their own lives to lead and she could understand; her mother could not.

Mrs. D. was a bright, "peppery" woman who initially resented the "interference" of the social worker. She didn't need her daughter; she could find other accommodations. "With kids, they take everything you do for granted as long as they need you. When they're through with you, out!" Mrs. D. railed for some time at the selfishness of "this generation"; her own treatment of her mother "could have taught her daughter a thing or two!" She herself used to do a lot of visiting with her mother's contemporaries as they grew older and ill. "Now you get *paid* for the work I used to do just because it was the right thing to do." The caseworker was a aware of a sense of fatigue at this comment. She recognized it as a countertransference reaction to Mrs. D.'s demeaning description of her work. This recognition enabled her to extend an empathic merger to Mrs. D., whose need now was to overcome her sense of helplessness and to reestablish continuity with that past when she had functioned at a higher level.

Absorbing the rage and resentment which Mrs. D. expressed, the caseworker encouraged Mrs. D. to describe some of her activities in the past. Mrs. D., initially suspicious, countered, "You don't believe me, but you should have seen what I used to do with those old women." As she recounted some of her experiences, and the caseworker responded with genuine admiration, her peppery manner diminished. She told about weekly knitting parties for which she would find interesting projects. Ultimately she had arranged an exhibit of knitted garments in a storefront which later became the basis of a thrift shop for a welfare organization. She recalled with tears the home she and her husband had provided, "nothing fancy but everyone liked to come to us." But then her husband died and her son moved to the East coast. He and his family remember her on birthdays or Mother's Day. "I'm lucky there's something to remind him that he has a mother!" At the same time she pointed with embarrassed pride to a large flowering plant that was there to greet her when she returned to her room after surgery.

She had been living with her daughter for some 10 years. "I know I'm hard to get along with; I like things just so. When the children were little I gave my daughter a lot of help. She couldn't have hired better. . . . and they still like my cooking. But then it got so everyone was busy . . . this one band and basketball, that one drama and debate." She began to cry. "You'd think they'd have a little time for me. Everyone says what a beautiful girl my granddaughter is; you should have seen me at her age. They say how smart she is, but you should have seen my report cards."

The caseworker recognized this less as competitiveness with her granddaughter than as an effort to secure a confirming response to her earlier pleasure in her attractiveness and in her intellectual capacity. The caseworker's interest and attention performed an affirming selfobject function which enabled Mrs. D. over the next few days to achieve a restored sense of continuity with her earlier, more cohesively functioning self. She began to greet the caseworker with a bright, "There comes my lady!" On one occasion, as she was returning to her room where the nurse awaited her, she said brightly, "She's my shot in the arm . . . it's different from the shots you give me!" Yet, more than a "transference cure" was at work. Mrs. D., in her weakened condition after surgery, needed to reestablish a sense of continuity with her earlier, more energetic self. This she accomplished through the opportunity to use the caseworker as needed psychic structure. Her demanding and quarrelsome behavior proceeded from a driven need to have mirroring confirmation of her useful and even creative life. And this selfobject function her caseworker was able to perform by her genuine interest in Mrs. D.'s earlier life and her understandable emotional distress in her present circumstances. The caseworker's understanding and acceptance confirmed Mrs. D.'s sense that she was a dignified, worthwhile member of society. The calming and soothing effect of this understanding performed a restorative function.

With her caseworker Mrs. D. began to review her daughter's experiences in her marriage, which had ended in divorce. She recognized retrospectively that both she and her husband had focused their attention on their son, a somewhat demanding and indulged youngster. They had taken advantage of their daughter's sweetness and easy adjustment. She could see now that her daughter had chosen a demanding and indulged man as her husband. In her marriage she had continued to be the accommodating one, but when her husband eventually become unfaithful, her daughter had refused to accommodate any longer to an intolerable situation.

Mrs. D. revealed her sorrow over failing to respond to her daughter's needs earlier, in not being alert to her sweetness and compliance as a means of avoiding burdening her mother with her problems. She wept over lost opportunities to help her develop assertiveness. As the caseworker absorbed her grief, she began to accept the fact that it is not always possible to see such problems until too late.

With the healing understanding of the caseworker, she was able to forgive herself and to take satisfaction from her ability to help her daughter with her children during the years it had taken her daughter to equip herself for a profession. She could now see that, in the period before her illness and during her hospital stay, she had once more fallen into the pattern of expecting a compliant, accommodating daughter, without regard for her daughter's needs. She began to note how tired her daughter looked when she visited and to encourage her to take some time off. With this change, her daughter brightened and confided that she had begun to date a colleague. Mrs. D. caught herself in the middle of fault-finding, warning her daughter about pitfalls in a new relationship. Later, reporting this to her caseworker, she commented, "I thought of you. After all, you don't tell me what to look out for or what to do. How can I know what is really a good relationship for my daughter? She has to be able to judge this for herself and what I'm doing is only burdening her with my anxieties."

Mrs. D. wondered whether part of her beginning intrusion stemmed from her own fears about a change in her situation if the relationship led to marriage. Nostalgically she reflected that, although she knew her daughter was lonely as a divorcee and she had been genuinely concerned for her happiness, nevertheless her own life had been given purpose and meaning. Was she so selfish a mother that she could think only of herself? Life had changed for older people—children move away; grandchildren grow up and move out, too. Only, what was going to become of her?

Her caseworker encouraged her to understand that her preoccupation with her own needs was appropriate and timely, a necessary step to finding new solutions. Once again she was confronting change; how had she met it in the past? Offering evidence of her restored cohesiveness, Mrs. D. used her last interview before discharge to share earlier memories of activities she had undertaken in the past. One or two she might be able to take up again. She thanked her caseworker for helping her to "find" herself and asked if she could remain in touch. Her caseworker assured her of her interest and commented that she had learned a lot from Mrs. D., too.

Several months later the caseworker received a card from Mrs. D., advising that it looked as if her daughter were going to be married in a few months. She was glad for her and liked the man she had chosen. Although everyone wanted Mrs. D. to remain with the family and she had not entirely closed out the possibility, she had begun to feel a need to have a quieter spot. There was a nearby apartment building in which several of her friends lived; this might be the best of both possible worlds. She was also pleased with some volunteer work she was doing with a group of elderly women at a nearby settlement house. "The pros think I'm a pro, too! Thanks again; it really helped to sort out my feelings with you. Keep up the good work!"

Mrs. D. used the caseworker as a new selfobject to avert fragmentation. Her retreat into narcissistic rage was stemmed by an empathic merger through which her anger at her temporary dependence, helplessness, and isolation could be recognized and absorbed. This process freed her to accept the caseworker's interest and attention as a means of reestablishing a sense of continuity with her earlier productive and performing self. Stimulated by her caseworker's genuine interest, she offered for her admiration and confirmation activities she had undertaken in the past and the important function she had served in helping her daughter. This provided her with a further opportunity to share what had been a silent mourning over her failures with a selfobject who gave appropriate recognition to her painful feelings. Her caseworker's empathic understanding enabled her to forgive herself and to focus more clearly on her own and her daughter's needs in the present.

The relatively rapid pace at which her cohesiveness was reestablished emphasizes some of our misconceptions about the aged. Gutman (1981) has called our attention to the prevalence of a deprivation and loss theory in treating the elderly. He suggests that there are special endowments, the fruits of . . .

> later life developmental advances that are exclusive to older individuals. . . . For example, the uniquely positive aspects of the older person's response to outpatient treatment go unremarked in the geropsychiatric literature. . . . The older patient can be maintained in the community through infrequent, glancing contact with the therapist. Despite minimal "dosage" the older patient will idealize the therapist, internalize him, and derive from him a sense of constancy and self-esteem. On the face of it this goes contrary to the depletion doctrine: it suggests that the aged patient has a capacity, relatively unavailable to younger individuals, to generate a fixed and sustaining object out of brief and irregular meetings with a relative stranger. . . . [T]herapists who use and observe this phenomenon persist in assimilating it to the ruling doctrine of deprivation. As they see it, the aged patient who converts a relatively anonymous therapist into a sustaining internal reality is not demonstrating a developmental advance; rather he is giving further evidence of childish, regressive dependency. Emergent capacities do, admittedly, contain the outlines of earlier structures but the point is that the therapist treating the older person automatically notes the early structures that betoken regression and fails to observe—or denies—the matured components that may well be unique to the older individual. (p. 491)

We believe that this phenomenon is better understood and explained through the lens of self psychology. Rather than "the capacity to sustain a fixed and sustaining object out of brief and irregular meetings with a relative stranger," what is being demonstrated is the ability to use the functions of a new selfobject to restore and sustain a self-function. The capacity to cue others to our needs may be weakened in illness and aging, but a new selfobject reawakens that earliest need for mirroring, for merging with idealized strength. And as that need is met, resiliency is restored. One has only to visit a geriatric unit to observe how a friendly word or a smile will bring a glow to a vacantly staring face. Moreover, in certain instances, that human response may provide the difference between living meaningfully within one's own community or being shuffled off to an institutional setting which may intensify the rate of disorganization and withdrawal. The following case illustrates this point.

Mrs. R.

Mrs. R., widowed for many years, lived alone, taking pride in her ability to participate in community activities though she had passed her 75th birthday. Her children were married and she was proud of their accomplishments. Scattered as they were throughout the United States, their relationship was a warm one, though limited to occasional telephone calls and yearly visits. She always turned aside their expressions of concern: "I'm fine, don't worry; I don't need a thing."

The reverse was true. With increasing restriction because of dizziness, a heart condition, and diabetes, she had been staying at home and withdrawing from her usual groups. Her doctor had changed her medication but her response seemed to fluctuate. To a visiting niece she said that she didn't like to bother anyone, she would be all right. There was mute evidence of her deteriorating capacity to care for herself. Scattered through the apartment were half-opened letters, bills, checks, and stale food; a burnt pot sat on the stove. She complained that her air conditioner would not work, not realizing that, with her failure to respond to notices, her electricity had been turned off.

Her niece restored order and talked to the doctor to establish the rate and order of medication. He thought it likely that her aunt was on a downward course; further, he believed that things would not improve. He did not mean to be discouraging, but these eventualities had to be faced. Her niece was reluctant to accept this. In any case, an interim plan had to be worked out.

Supervising Mrs. R. over the next few days, her niece discovered that her aunt was disoriented in time and could not follow instructions for medications, although these were laid out for her in orderly sequence. On one occasion, Mrs. R. insisted on going down for her mail, but then could not remember the number of her apartment. She wandered up and down in the elevator until a neighbor rescued her. Accepting the fact that it would be "just for a few days," she allowed someone to come in regularly to prepare meals and oversee her medication.

Her disorientation in time continued. On waking from a nap, she would assume it was the next day and time for breakfast. All the familiar signs of deterioration accumulated: forgetting what month it was, wandering unresponsively in her replies to questions. She brightened considerably when her favorite son came to visit. In his presence and with his help, she recaptured her ability to tell time. A congenial housekeeper was employed on a regular basis, though against her initial protestation, to provide supervision of medication and regular meals appropriate to her diet. Her family rallied to her, calling frequently and writing often. Although she could not return to community activities, her friends visited frequently.

Over the next few months, the deteriorating process was reversed. Her capacity to monitor hours returned. In phone calls and visits she was immediately responsive and on target in her comments. One year later, these gains had been maintained.

Mrs. R. had grown up as the oldest in a large family, ministering to their needs. Her character had taken form in providing for others. This continued with the family she and her husband had reared until her medical condition had worsened and she experienced waning of her powers and the expectation of decreasing ability to fend for herself. There is no question but that the combination of medication and appropriate preparation of meals improved her physical condition. But what stemmed the downward course was that she was enfolded in the responsive selfobject milieu of her family. Their presence affirmed her worth, mirrored the strengths of her more vigorous years, and offered her now the opportunity to merge with their strength and generosity.

We do not mean to minimize the difficulty in treating the elderly who, in addition to severe emotional or physical illness, may be without funds and without family or friends. That this is a growing population is well-known. Its very numbers make the problem of intervention unwieldy. Yet the enlarged vision of human striving that self psychology has provided permits us to be more in tune with their needs. Societal measures—small shelters, group involvement, stimulation by means of planned outings—provide that empathic response which may prove at least minimally sustaining. We know further that certain individuals are more capable of responding to the needs of the elderly ill than others who feel engulfed by the profound merger needs which are stimulated in even minimal contact. In the face of such demands, out of a need to protect their own integrity, they withdraw and label individuals as unmanageable or untreatable. Others are able to make themselves available in a manner which minimizes the intensity of merger demands. They recognize such behavior on the part of the individual as a driven need to complete missing structure by using the mature structure of the therapist. Although these demands and this behavior may be burdensome, it need not be categorized as manipulative or exploitive. Here again it is instructive to observe the manner in which a smile or a nod, a word or two, a hand on the shoulder, will forestall an explosive reaction. Moreover, such individuals seem to enjoy the reminiscences which provide for the elderly that necessary sense of being alive when customs and circumstances have so profoundly altered within their lifetimes.

Mr. S.

Without patronizing, individuals who understand the important role reminiscences play for the elderly are also able to provide modest, realistic goals, one of which may be to allow the individual a sense of connectedness, of being a human being among other human beings. The experience of Mr. S. is illustrative. He wandered into a family agency carrying a duffel bag. He buttonholed one of the caseworkers as she passed through the reception area, saying, "You people must have someone who can take the time to talk to me; that's what you're here for, isn't it?"

As it happened she was free and invited him into her office. His complaints were varied and numerous. He had lived alone since his wife's death several years ago. The two or three friends he had were no longer living in the city; the guys he used to work with had no time for him. He felt angry and rejected by people in the community who couldn't take two minutes to pass the time of day. His memory was going—for example, that morning he had mislaid his dentures; it took an hour to find them even though he lived in one room, with a small alcove for a kitchen. When his wife was alive and he was working, he felt all right. Life wasn't great but it was okay. Now he couldn't seem to understand what was happening. Nothing was the way it used to be. The caseworker, thoughtful and attentive, communicated her understanding by nods or brief words. His rage and truculence diminished and, though disheveled and musty in appearance, he made some efforts to straighten his tie and brush food spots away. He excused himself to use the restroom. When he returned he explained that he had been suffering from diarrhea and hadn't been eating well. In response to her question, he replied that he had not had a medical checkup in some time. Trying to control himself, he added that she was the first person who had taken 10 minutes with him in a long, long time.

The caseworker suggested that as an initial step in determining what they might accomplish together, it was important for him to have a general physical examination. This he agreed to when she assured him that he would not, as he countered, be given the runaround. The clinic to which she was referring him was busy, but he would be seen that day. At the same time she gave him an appointment with her for later in the week. As could be anticipated, Mr. S. did not wait for the scheduled appointment but dropped in. He was kept waiting and, when she was free, she could see him only briefly. Yet she listened without impatience as he described his new diet and his medication.

Over the next few weeks, Mr. S. came regularly, garnering hurts and slights which he then poured out in a torrent. By the end of the session, he would leave in a calmer mood. He took to making friendly comments to people in the waiting room, occasionally accepting a cup of coffee. People in the office knew him and called him by name.

Although still somewhat musty in appearance, he was less disheveled. He was living on his Social Security benefit and a small pension from his previous work as a tool and dye maker. Displaced by computer technology, he shared his painful feelings at having been discarded. Earlier he had done some carpentering and he used to be pretty handy, but his old shop had no place for him. He couldn't blame his boss; he had to meet the competition. In small steps the caseworker shared with him her knowledge of several projects she knew about in his neighborhood. Would he care to take a look at one of them? He was anxious at first, fearful that she was "firing" him. She absorbed his anxiety, at the same time assuring him that, together, they would recognize when their work was accomplished. She had been thinking about ways he could continue to use his skills.

Initially slow and guarded in exploring these projects, he finally visited a storefront workshop in which a group of older men were repairing various items for a neighborhood church. He "hung around till he saw one of the guys going at it all wrong." Modestly, but with a twinkle, he said he had been able to give him a hand. He was going back. It was an open workshop; you didn't have to sign up; you could come and go as you liked. Mr. S. became a dependable fixture at the workshop. His visits to the agency were less frequent and ultimately terminated.

The essential function the caseworker performed for Mr. S. was that of recognizing him as a human being in search of contact, enabling him to overcome a sense of oblivion. As new selfobject, in tune with his sense of loneliness and isolation following his wife's death and the termination of his employment, she extended her understanding, which served a partially restorative function. He was an individual who, by his own report, had lived a constricted life. He did not demand a great deal. As the caseworker listened to him purposefully, called him by name, and recognized what he had been in the past, her interest reestablished continuity and stemmed a downward course toward fragmentation. She provided affirmation that his needs were legitimate; she confirmed his rights to have them responded to; she guided him to practical resources, such as the medical clinic and the workshop. She used her recognition of his restricted lifestyle not to dispose of him hastily but to make it possible for him to find sustaining selfobjects beyond that of the therapeutic relationship. As this was established, she could withdraw in steps commensurate to Mr. S.'s strengthening ability to find sustenance at this phase of his life.

Self psychology enables us to respond to those who are aging in a flexible manner. As we have seen, certain individuals pursue a constricted pattern in their lives. Others live their lives in the shape of a cornucopia, finding sustenance in expanding symbolic selfobjects and in themselves, providing sustenance for those selfobjects with whom they can maintain contact. As life departs they can allow those who minister to their needs the expansion of self-esteem which flows from allowing another to merge with one's own strength. In working with aging individuals, the earliest need for mirroring, for confirmation, may be reawakened and responded to. The need to merge with idealized strength at a time of waning strength and vanishing goals can be met with empathic understanding. Being enfolded in this understanding allows the individual to feel soothed and strengthened in his own sense of continuity, even though that continuity is with the human condition and ultimate death.

SECTION IV

Broader Perspectives

14

Self Formation and Cohesion in the James Family

W E HAVE THUS FAR examined treatment of individuals for a variety of emotional and behavioral difficulties across the life cycle. Except in biography, we rarely have an opportunity to explore the vicissitudes of self formation and cohesion over the entire life course. Cases drawn from family therapy focus our attention on the subjective and interactive experience of family members in a given period. These are valuable, but, as Kohut has pointed out, specific events or memories of such events serve only as crystallization points for later disturbances. Rather than specific events, it is the impact of the parents' total personality on the particular child and his unique strengths and vulnerabilities that will determine the course of self formation.

Although the distinguished James family and its individual members have been the subject of many biographical studies, Edel (1985), Matthiessen (1980) and Strouse (1980) to name a few, my interest is in the opportunity their experiences offer us to explore the vicissitudes of self formation and cohesion in the very words and writings of the parents and children. The children were born in the mid-1800s and their lives were spun out with the death of Henry James, Jr., in 1916. This was before Freud described the tripartite structure of the mind and his theory of the drives. And it was more than six decades before Kohut formulated the theoretical concepts of self psychology. Yet what the Jameses have to say about their parents, themselves, and each other offers instructive insight into the formation of the nuclear self, its vigor, its vulnerabilities, and its capacity to initiate activities that culminate in meaningful life work.

Henry James, Sr., and Mary, his wife, were devoted parents, thoroughly involved with the care of their children. Their relationship with each other was regarded as ideal by their four sons and daughter born within a span of six and a half years.

Their father's views on womanhood were well-known, publicly avowed and privately discussed. In essence, "(W)oman is inferior to man. . . . She is inferior in passion, his inferior in intellect, and his inferior in physical strength. . . . Her aim in life is simply to love and bless man" (Strouse, 1980, p. 45). He would have it that women had all the virtues, but man must struggle to overcome his naturally vicious nature.

Henry James, Sr., presented these views often, and not infrequently with wry wit, as when he contemplated children born to a marriage in which husband and wife were equals: "Alack! alack! what litany would be long enough to recite their abominations! A sprinkling of girls . . . might slip into the first generation, but every successive one, . . . would be boys alone, boys of both sexes" (Strouse, 1980, p. 46).

It would appear that Mary James accepted these views; at least there is no written evidence that she disputed them. Her children saw her as self-effacing and self-sacrificing, but Leon Edel, who described Henry, Sr. as a "maternal man" and his wife, Mary, as "a plain unimaginative woman . . . gubernatorial," suggests that "this masked a strong will and a vigorous guiding hand" (1964, p. 3). At her mother's death, Alice would recall that from the "essence of divine maternity, I was to learn great things, give all but ask nothing" (A. James, 1964, p. 221). The encomium which Henry James wrote after his mother's death was part of the family myth to which all the children subscribed: "It was a perfect mother's life—the life of a perfect wife. To bring her children into the world—to expend herself, for years for their happiness and welfare—then, when they had reached full maturity and were absorbed in the world and their own interests—to lay down in her ebbing strength and yield up her pure soul to the celestial power that had given her this divine commission" (Strouse, 1980, p. 27). His fictional mothers represented the reverse of these qualities.

Henry, Sr., was the son of a highly successful businessman and strict Calvinist. In adolescence he had suffered severe burns, necessitating the amputation of his leg and a long convalescence. Upon recovery, he undertook the study of law to please his father, but he soon dropped out and for a time gambled and drank to excess. Later he completed his degree, "cured of his alcoholism but not of religious doubt" (Strouse, 1980, p. 12). Although a truce was in effect between father and son at the time of his father's death, Henry and an equally rebellious brother, were left small annuities, a condition they remedied by overturning the will. Thereafter, Henry, Sr., possessed an estate that made work unnecessary. His marriage at 29 to Mary "allowed [him] to become a man . . . solely by the presentation of her womanly sweetness and purity" (Strouse, 1980, p. 5). This difference between men and women was repeated frequently both verbally and in his writings.

After the birth of William and Henry, Jr., he took his family to Europe. There he suffered a "vastation" which filled him with a recurrent dread of a nameless evil shape. Rest cures prescribed by his doctors proved less helpful than his studies of Swedenborgian philosophy, studies which were to lead to his writings and lecturing over the rest of his lifetime. His son, William, later would write of his father's works, "Probably few authors have so devoted their entire life to the monotonous elaboration of one single bundle of truths . . . the true relationship between mankind and its Creator. What he had to say on this point was the burden of his whole life, and its only burden" (Matthiessen, 1980, p. 139).

Alice was the youngest child and only girl in this close-knit family. We must ask what care a mother could give five children born to her in a span of six-and-a-half years, even with the available assistance of her sister, her servants, and her husband, who worked at home as a writer and theologian. Some sense of the spirit in which she saw their needs may be grasped from her own description of her third son's plight. He was only a little over a year when her fourth son was born. She wrote to a friend:

> Seeing that he was about to be shoved off [he] concluded to let us see how well he could take care of himself. He began to walk when the baby was two weeks old, took at once into his own hands the redress of his grievances which he seems to think are manifold and has become the *ruling* spirit in the nursery. Poor little soul! My pity I believe would be more strongly excited for him were he less able or ready to take his own part, but as his strength of arm or of will seldom fails him, he is too often left to fight his own battles. (Matthiessen, 1980, p. 24)

Struggles in the nursery apparently went unaided. Alice, in particular, because of her vulnerability as the youngest James, seemed to suffer from "mild torture" imposed by her two younger brothers, for by then William and Henry, the oldest two, were in school. Struggles outside the nursery also went unaided. Alice reports in her Journal a drive of which she recalls only a "never ending ribbon of dust, stretching in front and the anguish of Wilkie's and Bob's heels grinding into my shins" (A. James, 1964, p. 128). There is no indication that she protested or expected protection. Perhaps she had already absorbed one lesson of femininity—"to endure all and ask no aid."

An interesting glimpse of the family in action is reported by a visitor. Henry, Sr., initially moderator between the children, would enter the fray: "When, in the excited argument, dinner knives might not be absent from eagerly gesticulating hands . . . Mrs. James would look at me, laughingly reassuring, saying, 'Don't be disturbed . . . they won't stab each other.'

This is usual when the boys come home.' And the quiet little sister, ate her dinner, smiling, close to the combatants" (Strouse, 1980, p. 66). Had she even now made quiet endurance the unique trait of her femininity?

Robertson, the child for whom Wilky was "shoved off," 50 years later would himself write that he "wondered if I had really been as little appreciated as I fully remember feeling at that time. I never see infants now without discerning in their usually solemn countenances a conviction that they are on their guard in more or less hostile surroundings" (Strouse, 1980, p. 24).

When Robertson's son, the first grandchild, was born, Mary James wrote to the parents that she did not believe in "letting the 'little tyrants' rule too soon. . . . if he has such broad shoulders and deep chest, let him bawl a good bit, that is if you are sure that his stomach is full and there is no pin running in him" (Strouse, 1980, p. 24).

Yet both Robertson and Alice also described their early childhood years nostalgically as "full of indulgence and light and color and hardly a craving unsatisfied" (Strouse, 1980, p. 24). What this seems to suggest is that, because of the many pressures on her, Mary James may have been unable to offer, with any degree of consistency, her comforting presence. Although their father, an aunt and servants were also available, rather than optimal frustration through which psychic structure is acquired, there were apparently gross failures that resulted in deficits in all of the children in their capacity to soothe and calm themselves. To Alice, the youngest and only girl, no special protection was offered.

Alice describes her father as a "delicious infant" (A. James, 1964, p. 57). He had no known occupation which the children could claim in the usual exchange with friends. In his autobiography, Henry, Jr., reported constantly plying his father with the question, "*What* shall we tell them you are, don't you see?" His father would reply, "Say I'm a philosopher, say I'm a seeker for truth, say I'm a lover of my kind, say I'm an author of books if you like; or best of all, just say I'm a Student" (H. James, 1913, p. 278). What seems to color his response is his own zestful amusement at his small son's dilemma rather than an empathic understanding of the child's need to have a father with a clear-cut role. Unlike an envied friend who could say that his father was a stevedore, Henry, Jr., could report only that his father worked at home at his studies.

As his five children grew to school age, Henry, Sr., searched for the perfect combination of educational experiences for his sons. When Alice was six, he again took his family across the Atlantic, one of many crossings to various capitals in search of schools, governesses, and tutors that would meet his standards. But it was his own search for perfect wholeness rather than the children's needs that dictated these sudden breaks. There were countless uprootings. William, Henry, and Alice each were to write of the hardship of being "hotel children." Alice, in particular, wrote to William with reference to the education of his children, "What enrichment of mind and memory can children have *without continuity* if they are torn up by the roots every little while as we were . . . of all things don't make the mistake which brought about our rootless, accidental childhood" (Emphasis supplied; Strouse, 1980, p. 43).

Ultimately disillusioned by what the continent had to offer, Henry, Sr., wrote to a friend that his sons were "getting to an age, Harry and Wilky especially, when the heart craves a little wider expansion than is furnished by the domestic affections. They want friends among their own sex and sweethearts in the other, and my hope for their own salvation temporary or spiritual is that they may go it strongly in both lines when they get home. . . . One chief disappointment . . . has been in regard to Alice, who intellectually, socially, and physically has been a great disadvantage compared with home!" (Strouse, 1980, p. 59). This is one of the rare comments in which her needs are considered undimmed by his own display.

Upon their return to the States, Alice rode horseback, swam, sailed, and walked with her brothers, an apparently energetic little girl as yet untroubled by repeated prostrations which were to plague her later years. Her father set about finding the perfect school for the two youngest boys, but, though the boarding school he selected was coeducational, there was no apparent thought of including Alice, then 12 years of age.

Although there is mutuality in the self/selfobject unit of parent and child, for Henry, Sr., his children were a necessary protection against fragmentation. His comment made when he placed the two younger children in boarding school supports this view: "I buried two of my children—at [school in] Concord, Massachusetts and feel so heartbroken this morning that I shall need to adopt two more instantly to supply their place" (Strouse, 1980, p. 64).

Unlike parents who take quiet pleasure in their children's growth and development, Henry, Sr., needed his children to protect him from fragmentation. For example, Alice, in a letter to her brother, described his state upon his unexpected return after less than two days from a trip which was to have taken a fortnight: " . . . Mother beside him holding his hand and we five children pressing close around him as if he had just been saved from drowning and he pouring it out as he alone could the agonies of desolation through which he had come" (A. James, 1964, p. 58). On another occasion, she wrote to her father, "We have had two dear letters from you and find you are the same dear old good-for-nothing-homesick papa as ever" (Strouse, 1980, p. 56). As a letter by an 11-year-old to her father, her observation is striking.

This "delicious infant" used to let his sister-in-law take the children to the dentist while, later, he would take them for ice cream treats. Regularly, he used to spoil the surprises of Christmas by first giving broad hints as to the nature of the gifts to be bestowed and later taking the children to see their gifts with instructions to maintain secrecy. Alice, writing of this later, described herself as an "ungrateful wretch" but added, "How I wish he hadn't done it!" (A. James, 1934, p. 124). His inability to delay his own pleasure robbed his children of anticipation and delight.

There are but glimpses into the intensity of the family relationships set forth in the brilliantly realized biography of Alice James by Strouse, in the *Diary* of Alice James, in the autobiographical writings of Henry James, Jr., and in the letters of William, Henry, Jr., Wilky, and Robertson. To detail with accuracy and completeness the interaction of these individuals is beyond the scope of our purpose.

The spirit of the household was characterized by teasing, boisterous dispute into which Henry, Sr. entered as one of the children. Through this household, Mary James and her sister moved ordering the details of daily living. Mary James performed a calming and soothing selfobject function both as wife and mother extending herself to try and cover everyone's needs.

But such quiet ways provided little interest for Alice. Excitement lay in the lives of her father and brothers. And to them she was the object of playful overstimulation. Thus she had both a sense of being special and yet of being the subject of witty mockery. Henry, in his autobiography, described an occasion on which Alice, eight years old and dressed "after the fashion of the period and the place," was seated next to the famous author, Thackeray. Suddenly, in the middle of dinner, Mr. Thackeray turned to Alice, "laid his hand on her little flounced person and exclaimed with ludicrous horror, 'Crinoline?—I was suspecting it! So young and so depraved!'" (Strouse, 1980, p. 52).

Henry described this joke as "lingering long in the family lexicon." For Alice it repeated one of the many instances in which she was singled out for special attention and then playfully ridiculed. It takes no great insight to imagine the reaction of an eight-year-old, dressed for a special occasion and given a place of honor at a distinguished guest's side, to the sudden burst of laughter about a comment she could not understand. We do not have to fictionalize the account in order to understand that she longed, though she may not have expected, to have her emerging femininity admired.

This combination of overstimulation and teasing letdown is perhaps more blatantly set in relief with reference to another episode that entered the family lexicon, with Alice as the butt of William's extravagant wooing and the well-documented family hilarity over his performance. She was 11 at the time William described the episode to his father in a letter. He had written a "sonnatte" to Alice and the whole family was assembled in the parlor to hear it. In rhyme and song he protested his love for her, her coldness to his wooing and his despair. The last four lines will suffice to convey the spirit:

> Adieu to love! Adieu to life!
> Since I may not have thee,
> My Alice sweet to be my wife,
> I'll drown me in the sea!
> (Strouse, 1980, p. 53)

William reported that Alice had taken it coolly but Wilky added that the song "excited a good deal of laughter among the audience assembled." That she did not enter into the laughter and fun about William's flourishes is understandable since it was William who was on display and she the butt of his "gallantry." Again, to an 11-year-old, this must have been confusing. As Strouse writes, Alice had "learned to take William's flourishes coolly, it was exciting to be singled out for this flirtatious attention, to be appreciatively catalogued and cast as proud fair lady pursued by an ardent admirer. It was also confusing and embarrassing. Was William complimenting or making fun of her? Did the idea of sweet little Alice as a desirable woman seem ridiculous? Did only boys have inflamed hearts? Did brothers marry sisters? The poem celebrates an Alice who is the object of male dreams, a fatal child-woman whose refusal of her entranced suitor-brother condemns him to suicide. Were girls supposed to be cool and superior to desire and despair?" (Strouse, 1980, pp. 53–54). Although Alice learned to tease back, doubt about her attractiveness is very much in evidence, as we shall see from later writings in her diary.

This teasing quality appears frequently in William's letters home when he was away at school, with such expressions as "kiss Alice to death" (W. James, 1980, p. 20) or remarks that her letter to Henry and William "inflamed [them] with an intense longing and desire to kiss and slap her celestial cheeks" (W. James, 1980, p. 7).

Teasing and twitting were as natural to the family as breathing. Her father, writing to Alice from a New York shopping spree, regretted that although he had picked up "half a hundred foreign photographs for William they were too expensive to allow him to buy any fancy ones for [you]; I shall go into Stewart's this morning to enquire for that style of ribbon for you. If I had only brought a little more money with me! I went into Arnold's for a scarf for you, but the clerks were so rapid with me I couldn't buy and bought two pairs of gloves for myself one of which turns out too small for me but will suit Harry. . . . Goodbye, darling daughter, and be sure that never was daughter so beloved. Keep my letters and believe me ever your lovingest Daddy" (Strouse, 1980, p. 47). In all likelihood her father's teasing covered purchases he had indeed made for her to be presented on his return. But he appears oblivious to the combination of expectation, envy and deprivation the letter might sadistically have aroused.

His ability to overstimulate her appears most strikingly in an episode which was a harbinger of her later illnesses. William, away at college, had written that the Emerson daughters were eager to have Alice visit and he "would take most lofty pride in promenading the streets of Boston with her [he] the observed of all observers for manly strength and beauty and [she] for feminine grace and gentility" (Strouse, 1980, p. 67). When the invitation came, her father wrote William that he "gave the palpitating Alice carte blanche to go at any expense to her health and got her expectations so exalted that her more affectionate and truly long suffering Mama found it one of the trials of her life to reduce her to the ordinary domestic routine. All I know is that I am hopelessly wicked and cheerfully postpone myself to the world-after-next for amendment. I tell Alice by way of makeup of the delights of heaven. . . . I think, however, the tears still trickle in solitude" (Strouse, 1980, p. 68).

There is a combination of mischievous overstimulation of his 13-year-old daughter and teasing promise that although, because of her excitability and fragility she must postpone her pleasure, this would later be fulfilled in the delights of heaven. Rather than genuine remorse over the tears she shed in private, he makes humorous play of his wrongdoings in his letter to William.

Both her father and William used Alice's femininity as foils to display themselves. William often protests exaggerated affection for her and susceptibility to her charms. It is only much later, in letters to friends who are beginning to look toward marriage, that Alice discloses her feelings about her appearance. She confides at one point her hopeless crush on a young man whose eyes are elsewhere: "the young woman to whom he is attracted is, I am forced to confess . . . not bad looking, its (sic) painful but true. I refrained from looking in the glass for sometime after I got home . . . " (Strouse, 1980, p. 166).

But plain women do marry, and Alice's features suggest that she was not unattractive, but that she *felt* herself to be unattractive. In a photograph taken in Paris at age nine, she appears to be a somber child, dressed in stiff clothes which, even allowing for the styles of the times, one senses were poorly chosen. At 22, except for her large and luminous eyes and expressive brows, the same solemnity and stiffness are present, yet she is not unattractive. At age 19 she writes to a friend, "I wonder if you are ever torn by the pangs of envy and cry aloud as I did, 'Why am I not made as one of these?' Or rather, why are they not my gowns, for my features I have long since ceased to question as the work of inscrutable wisdom, but I can't get reconciled to the *peculiarities of my clothes* so that when I see a maiden arrayed as I am not, I am greatly visited by hankerings which I am sure no woman's breast is quite a stranger to" [Emphasis supplied] (A. James, 1934, p. 61). On another occasion she asks enviously, "[B]eing arrayed in a Paris gown, who wouldn't have a pretty figure?" (A. James, 1934, p. 54).

Yet if Alice experienced such deficit in her ability to take pleasure in her appearance, to enjoy her attributes unambivalently as a girl and a young woman, what of the opportunity to develop and take pleasure in her intellectual capacities? Here, too, the teasing quality of her father's relationship with his young daughter is in evidence. When she was nine, he wrote to his mother, "Our Alice is still under discipline, preparing to fulfill some high destiny or other in the future by reducing decimal fractions to their least possible rate of subsistence" (Strouse, 1980, p. 57). It is one thing to write in this teasing vein of a nine-year-old, but there is no evidence (except his one expression of concern that Europe was a failure for Alice, socially, intellectually, and physically) that he was concerned about her intellectual development. This is only partially explained by the mores of the times in which women's education was constricted and secondary to that of men. For her father was constantly on the lookout for educational opportunities and novelties for his sons, yet he overlooked similar opportunities for Alice even when available in the coeducational school he chose for his two youngest sons. She did attend a girl's school, but the family interest in her limited studies was never at the same pitch as the interest in her brothers' schooling.

A strong factor in this failure may well have been her father's need of Alice to be his "darling daughter." Her desperate effort to secure recognition of her intellectual capacity bursts forth in her diary, begun in 1889 when she was 40 with the hope that her writing might "help her to lose a little of the sense of loneliness and desolation which abides in me." She comments with reference to a "small joke" she had made which had appeared in a volume of Oliver Wendell Holmes but which she had never read, "As great minds jump (together) this proves conclusively what I have always maintained against strenuous opposition, that my Mind *is Great!*" (A. James, 1964, p. 61).

Later, after writing a ten-line letter to the *Nation* published in its European Edition, she exclaims with delight, "A *European Reputation* at the first

go off! How fortunate for the male babes that I am so physically debile!''
(A. James, 1964, p. 139). This must be seen not as evidence of penis envy, competitiveness with her brothers, but rather as a deeply rooted longing for mirroring, confirmation of *her* intellect.

Her efforts to secure some response to the liveliness of her own mind
is reflected in another diary note: "In the old days, when William's eyes
were bad and I used to begin to tell him something which I thought of
interest to him from whatever book I had been reading, he would usually say, 'I already glanced at that yesterday.'" (A. James, 1964, p. 127).
Even Henry fails her in affirming her fine mind. He of all the family was
genuinely responsive to her needs and able to perform for her a calming
and soothing function. Yet she writes " . . . Henry, by the way, has
embedded in his pages many pearls fallen from my lips, which he steals
in the most unblushing way, saying simply that he knew they had been
said by the family so it didn't matter" (A. James, 1964, p. 212). Later, upon
her death, he would recognize her great ability and wonder to what
heights she might not have risen had she been given the opportunity for
appropriate education.

Alice was often her father's companion, closeted with him in his study
while he pored over his writings. She wrote of this experience:

> As I used to sit, immovable, reading in the library, with waves of violent in-
> clination invading my muscles, taking some one of their varied forms such as
> throwing myself out of the window or knocking off the head of the benignant
> pater, as he sat with his silver locks writing at his table, it used to seem to me
> that the only difference between me and the insane was that I had not only
> all the horrors and sufferings of insanity, but the duties of doctor, nurse and
> strait jacket imposed on me, too. (A. James, 1964, p. 149)

Looking back upon her younger self, it was in this way she described
her desperate efforts to maintain cohesion, struggling with profound fears
of fragmentation. Her wish to throw herself out of the window or to knock
off her father's head was a desperate attempt to seek a response to her
growth into intelligent young womanhood not as teasing foil to others'
display but in her own right. Again, retrospectively she describes her
14-year-old self:

> How I recall the low grey Newport sky in that winter of '62-'63, as I used to
> wander about over the cliffs, my young soul struggling out of its waddling
> clothes, as the knowledge crystallized within me of what life meant for me,
> . . . I had to peg away pretty hard between 12 and 24, "killing myself," . . .
> absorbing into the bone that the better part is to clothe oneself in neutral tints,
> walk by still waters and possess one's soul in silence. (A. James, 1964, p. 95)

Her *Diary* reveals her lively mind; it also reveals that she was capable of towering passion and searing wit. She writes, however, that she "is not of a rebellious temperament, having early perceived, fortunately, that the figure of abortive rebel lent itself much more to the comic than the heroic in the eye of the coldblooded observer" (A. James, 1964, p. 119), suggesting thus that her anger provoked laughter and may have been belittled in the family. Instead, she expressed what she was unable or not really permitted to express verbally through a variety of bodily dysfunctions. Twenty-year-old William, describing his disappointment at still another visit she was unable to make, wrote to his 14-year-old sister, "I hope your neuralgia or whatever you made believe the thing was has gone and you are going to school instead of languishing and lolling about the house" (Strouse, 1980, p. 69). William wrote frequently to Alice, giving passing recognition to her illnesses but quickly returning to his own. In a letter which is typical of his playful use of her, he writes of a youth wandering " . . . displaying a row of teeth like orient pearls, muttering 'Alice, beloved child . . . that Alice was none other than . . . Thou! . . . [He had been ill] and crying all the time for to have you sitting by me stroking my brow. . . . Whole dialogues did I frame of how I wd. work on your feelings if you were there, and longed to cleave the Ocean once more to press you in my arms" (Strouse, 1980, p. 124). As Strouse points out, William would move between concerns about her illness to prescriptions for true femininity: "Let Alice cultivate a manner clinging yet self-sustained, reserved yet confidential, let her face beam with serious beauty, and glow with quiet delight at having you speak to her; let her exhibit short glimpses of a soul with wings . . . let her voice be musical and the tones of her voice full of caressing, and every movement of her full of grace, and you have no idea how lovely she *will become*" (Emphasis supplied; 1980, p. 124).

The affectionate yet teasing and seductive quality of his letters continued, with William writing from Dresden when she was 25, "Thou seemest to me so beautiful from here, so intelligent, so affectionate, so in all respects the thing that a brother should most desire that I don't see how when I get home I can do anything else than sit with my arm around thy waist appealing to the (sic) for confirmation of every thing I say, for approbation of everything I do, and admiration for everything I am, and never, never for a moment disappointed . . . " (Strouse, 1980, p. 181). Once more, what is foremost is his use of Alice as selfobject to his mirroring and confirming needs. Her mother wrote to Henry, Jr., that "Alice's health, spirits, wit, intelligence and personal charm had greatly impressed William on his return from Europe. . . . He is very sweet upon her, in his own original way, and I think she enjoys very much his badinage" (Strouse, 1980, p. 182). But his use of her is to confirm and admire *him, his* wit, *his* charm.

At age 19 Alice broke down severely, in a state bordering "insanity and suicide" (Strouse, 1980, p. 185). Her illness bound her father to her side night and day and dictated family comings and goings. Although his devotion to his deeply troubled daughter is everywhere noted, again his response is colored by his own display. In response to Alice's question whether it was a sin to commit suicide, her father replied that it was absurd to believe it sinful, if Alice wished release from her suffering. He gave her his fatherly permission to end her life whenever it pleased her, "beseeching her only to do it in a perfectly gentle way in order *not to distress her friends*" (Emphasis supplied; Strouse, 1980, p. 186). In letters to his sons he placed in the forefront his shrewdness in taking this approach and the relief it afforded his daughter.

From the period of her adolescence, Alice was repeatedly subject to fainting spells, and various organic illnesses in response to excitement of any kind. These repeated fragmentations grew more severe, although interspersed were periods of restored cohesivenss and an active life in social and community affairs. Her illness bound everyone to her in a manner that the role of rebel could not have. Her patience and uncomplaining acceptance of her suffering were extolled by the James family in numerous comments in letters to her and to each other. That the loss or threatened loss of important selfobjects, emotionally or in reality, may have been the key to her repeated fragmentations is suggested by her most severe breakdown in the spring of her 29th year, when William fell in love and subsequently became engaged to another Alice.

Strouse points out that

> Whatever agitation William's flirtatious attentions caused his sister, they also flattered and excited her—and they were the only consistent, overt, amorous attentions she ever received from a man. To this brother whom she admired and loved, she seemed at times the most important woman on earth. She returned his mocking banter, and undoubtedly, in a suppressed way, his sexual curiosity. His engagement to a paragon of health and virtue was a profound betrayal. (Strouse, 1980, p. 182)

Henry, Jr., wrote to Alice, "[I]t seems rather inconsiderate in William to have selected such a moment for making merry" (Strouse, 1980, p. 183).

By the time of William's subsequent marriage, Alice was almost 30. She had experienced long periods of illness, had endured and partially recovered under various regimes and health cures prescribed for her according to the state of the art. By the time of her first breakdown the word "neurasthenia" had been coined to describe the various illnesses from which women suffered and for which no physical diagnoses could be established. William, too, would seek to define the psychic suffering of women in his time, but it would be a year after Alice's death in 1892 that Freud's paper "On the Psychical Mechanism of Hysterical Phenomena" (1893) would be published.

In many ways the James family fulfills the close-knit, intense family structure in which the infantile neurosis arising from oedipal conflict described by Freud flourished. Kohut would some 80 years later describe the changes in family structure which provided the conditions under which a shift in psychic organization was taking place (1977, p. 280). The structure of the James family, particularly the manner in which its forces impinged on each of the children and the matrix it provided for gender definition, is more clearly examined through the theories of self psychology than through drive and conflict theory. It is self psychology, rather than oedipal conflict, that defines Alice's experience of the oedipal phase. The response of her father, seductive and sadistic by turn, and that of her uncomplaining, hardworking, overburdened mother prevented her from resolving her oedipal longings in a manner that permitted the integration of sexuality. Her maturing selfobject needs went unnoticed. She was unable to find confirmation as a loveable, intelligent female. And William's teasing, his exaggerated and inappropriate description of her "irresistible charms," reinforced her difficulties.

Many years later, when she was already within a year of her death at 43, she described with wry wit her need to be admired both in her physical and mental attributes. She was half-mockingly aware of the inadequate selfobject she used for this purpose and her struggles to secure adequate mirroring for her needs: " . . . [I]f you saw the paces through which I put poor little Nurse; in the winter she has to applaud me mind, in summer me beauty." To restore her depleted self-esteem, which she characterizes as "my moments of modesty," . . . "I consult her about my letters and you may be sure she knows too well which side her bread is buttered on to do aught but admire. In the summer when we pass an old frump more sour than the last I throw myself upon her mercy and ask her if I am as dreadful to look upon as that. When she comes up to time with a reassuring negative I fall back on my cushions . . . pacified for the moment!" (A. James, 1964, p. 76).

Her struggles to have her own mirroring needs responded to are repeatedly thwarted by the selfobjects from whom she most sought affirmation, her father and William. For them it is she who serves as selfobject, she through whom they can display their wit, their intellect, oblivious to her struggles for affirmation in her own right. Even Henry, who of all the brothers was most in tune with her needs, fails to see her longing for confirmation of her intellect by the manner in which he uses her "pearls" in his written work without acknowledging their sources and compounds this by adding that he knew it was said by the family so it didn't matter. Yet she is lonely and homesick for him when she is ill and he is away, "[A] friendless wisp of femininity tossed upon the breeze of hazards . . ." (A. James, 1964, p. 130).

We have little information about the forming self of Alice in early childhood except as we can derive it from her later writings and those of her family. She was mirrored as her father's "darling little daughter." Although he allowed her to merge with his idealized strength and wisdom, it was for his own needs. From her mother, whom she also idealized, she could not expect protection and comforting enfolding in response to her struggles with her two younger brothers. What her mother mirrored and reported in letters to the family was her patient endurance. It was this she confirmed—uncomplaining resignation. A healthy, vigorous child, who could romp and play with her brothers until school age, she was overlooked in her father's restless search for the perfect education for his sons. William, writing from school to his family when Alice was 12, describes the scene in his imagination of "Alice, the *widow* (italics supplied), sitting and reading a novel while eating some rich fruit father has brought her, mother and aunt in armchairs with hands crossed in front of them listen[ing] to father who is walking up and down speaking of the superiority of America to these countries, and how much better that we should go home" (Matthiessen, 1980, p. 91).

Once home, Henry, Sr., though aware of Alice's lack of social, intellectual, and physical stimulation in Europe, still centers his interests and his efforts on his sons. There were now beginning to be some intimations of Alice's vulnerability to fragmentation. She struggled to maintain cohesion in the face of traumatically unrealized needs for mirroring, for being allowed to formulate goals which proceeded from her self as a center of initiative and perception. Closeted in the library with her ambivalently loved father, whose pate she would like to batter, she struggles with narcissistic rage at being so little noticed in her own right as a creature with ambitions and the desperate need to express these in realizable goals. It was not the incestuous longing of an adolescent for the love of her father; it was the driven wish of an adolescent for confirmation as a developing young woman who needed to experience her femininity in her own way, according to the dictates of her own being. As one outlet for this she turned to marriage, a goal many of her friends were pursuing and finding. In numerous letters to her girl friends, she described first with anticipation, then with longing, gradually with narcissistic spite, and finally with resignation, her dashed hopes for marriage. With terms of endearment typical of the manner in which women addressed each other, she described all the alarums and excursions of any young woman as she encountered marriageable men in her social life. In a letter written when she was 26 she confided, "I came near having an offer . . . escaping mortification of descending to the grave a spinster, not for choice of the sweet lot but from dire necessity. My fate which if he had only spoken I should look upon as rapturous is as burdensome and hopeless as ever. My own turn will never come this side of the grave" (Strouse, 1980, p. 168).

To a friend rumored to have a suitor, she wrote, "nail him . . . I am becoming ardently matrimonial and if I could get any sort of man matrimonally impassioned about me I should not let him escape" (Strouse, 1980, p. 164).

Strouse, in describing Alice's dilemma, suggests that to turn to intellectual activity, to use her mind productively would have meant entering the lists in competition with Henry, Sr., William, and Henry, Jr. But Alice's struggles and illness did not proceed from penis envy; rather, they proceeded from her desperate efforts for confirmation of her own unique worth and skills, the opportunity to define and pursue these with appropriate response from those selfobjects most necessary to her. When she humorously advised her brothers in her excited response to her only publication, a ten-line letter in the European Edition of the *Nation*, "to arm themselves against [her] dawn," it was not penis envy which dictated these feelings. It was the stimulation of her grandiosity to even this bit of mirroring affirmation to her intellectual potential, and the reawakened longing to be admired, to continue the thrust of her own development.

Further, it was not, as Strouse suggests, that turning to the womanly sphere would put her into competition with her mother and aunt. " . . . And since being a woman meant being mindless, selfless and effortlessly good, turning in that direction would have required Alice to relinquish her sense of superior intelligence and her desire to be something more than her mother and aunt" (1980, p. 121). Alice's desperate longings were to find *her own* way, to respond to *her own* perceptions, to undertake on *her own* initiative a course through which her own ambitions could be realized.

For brief periods Alice would find cohesive fulfillment in her work as a correspondence teacher of history for the "Society to Encourage Studies at Home." But her enthusiasm in her work was highly vulnerable to teasing and ridicule. Even Henry, Jr., the most dependable and responsive member of the family, with whom she had shared her interest in the works of two historians, ridiculed her. He described them as "two . . . grotesque specimens . . . and if Alice could see in the flesh her little wizened, Crawling Green with eyes like ill-made buttonholes, she would take to her bed for a month and renounce her 'historic-reveries'" (Strouse, 1980, p. 175).

But her work as a correspondence instructor under Katherine Loring gave her purpose and goal. That she had to defend her activities even to her friends is reflected in a letter to one: "I was deeply hurt at your ridicule of my professional character . . . [I] assure you it is not a thing to be laughed at. . . . You may as much as you please . . . I have to write between thirty and forty letters a month . . . it is what I care most about just now and I didn't want you to judge it without a hearing" (Strouse, 1980, p. 175–6).

As Strouse points out, William, the usual teaser, in this instance recognized the importance of this work to her. "Alice has got her historical professorship which will no doubt be an immense thing for her" (Strouse, 1980, p. 175). This period of vitality and harmony enabled Alice to travel, to ride and drive horses, to keep a greenhouse, and to organize a women's luncheon club for intellectual discussion. She appeared to be in charge of herself; yet she could not maintain cohesion. We cannot know with certainty, but the change in relationship with several important selfobjects—her last two friends had married, William had become engaged, and she passed the milestone of her thirtieth birthday—may have been a factor in bringing about her total collapse. Increasingly, she endured discontinuity, repeated, prolonged fragmentation in mysterious illnesses and in organic distress.

Throughout her *Diary* Alice describes the sudden fragmentation to which she was subject:

I had towed my stomach and heart back to harbor, they having broken loose.

Henry hangs on to whatever organ may be in eruption and gives me calm and patience. . . .

How strange it would be not to be under the domination of that mighty organ save digestively. No fiat of the faithful three was ever more immutable than the decrees sent forth by that pivot of my being. Mentally, no fate appals me; but morally no crawling worm was ever so abject as I am before the convolutions of that nest of snakes, coiling and uncoiling themselves. What pain remotely approaches the horror of those hours which may swamp one at any moment, passed second by second, hanging as it were by a cobweb of sanity. (A. James, 1964, p. 101)

We do not do justice to Alice's efforts to achieve her unique femininity if we describe her difficulties in terms of a retreat to preoedipal structure.

Nor was it, as Strouse suggests, her oedipally motivated wish not to compete with her mother and aunt that kept her from turning to the womanly sphere. It was not that being a woman meant "being mindless, selfless, and effortlessly good," relinquishing her sense of superior intelligence and her desire to become something more than her mother and aunt. It was not that the "feminine" alternative was as fraught with hazard as the "masculine" (Strouse, 1980, p. 121). Self psychology allows us empathic understanding of her narcissistic injury, the accompanying rage secondary to her ineffectual efforts to achieve a cohesive self through the appropriate mirroring of her earlier selfobjects and her maturing selfobject needs for a response to her developing femininity and her fine mind. She ultimately found in Katherine Loring a selfobject who could exquisitely provide the unequivocal affirmation which she so desperately sought:

> Katherine has the most inestimable habit of paying one compliments and delicately embroidering any outside reference to one's humble personality which may occur. I make it a rule always to believe the compliments implicitly for five minutes and to simmer gently for twenty minutes more. That insures a solid gain of 25 m[inutes] out of the 24 h[ours] in which one is at peace and charity with all mankind. (A. James, 1964, pp. 59–60)

Katherine Loring performed the mirroring selfobject function which enabled Alice to restore cohesiveness, but she could not retain a sense of pleasure in the attributes of her body and her mind more than briefly. The inappropriate and overstimulating use of her as a selfobject by her father and William to bolster their own self-esteem deprived her of transmuting the necessary psychic structure of regulating her own self-esteem. Their exaggerated compliments, embedded in teasing humor, stimulated her grandiosity and as quickly punctured it. Her mother's response fell far short of her needs, in that she emphasized resignation and fortitude. Alice poignantly described her sense of missing structure; indeed, the opening words of her *Diary* state that its purpose was to overcome "the sense of loneliness and desolation which abide in me" (A. James, 1964, p. 25). There is a striking transformation of Alice, from a vigorous, energetic 12-year-old into a 14-year-old who is resigned to "clothing (herself) in neutral colors and possessing [her] soul in silence." Some of what contributed to this transformation may be gleaned from a passage in her *Diary* quoted earlier, recalling her young self sitting in her father's study " . . . immovable, reading in the library with waves of violent inclination invading my muscles taking some of their varied forms such as throwing myself out of the window or knocking off the head of the benignant pater as he sat writing at his table."

Implicit in this report is her desperate longing for response to herself as a loveable, loving, intelligent young woman. Her father's behavior, by turns seductive and teasing if not sadistic, thwarted her oedipal strivings and did not permit their resolution and maturation. She was to be his "darling daughter who could be sure that never was daughter so loved." His need of and response to her were for a much younger child. William by turns exalted her to a lofty pinnacle as the object of his greatest desire, but in teasing fashion so that she was quickly catapulted to embarrassed, silent confusion.

Although Mrs. James was viewed by all her children as saintly, it was for her patient, uncomplaining, tireless performance that she was extolled. In an entry in her *Diary*, Alice recalls her father "ringing the changes on Mother's perfections" (A. James, 1964, p. 79). But it was also from her mother that she "learned to give all and ask nothing for herself," which does not suggest a vibrant pleasure in femininity.

Alice required a response from her parents to her developing femininity, which would have enabled her to traverse the oedipal phase and resolve its storms and passions. For her, the oedipal experience seemed to have been confusing and conflicted. Instead of vigorous, cohesive wholeness, for her the unresolved oedipal phase found expression and form in periodic fragmentation and the storms and passions of physical suffering.

Strouse points out that Alice drew a direct parallel between being patient and being a woman, quoting her as thinking that her difficulty lay in being unable "to assume the receptive attitude, that cardinal virtue in women, the absence of which has always made me so uncharming and uncharmed by the male sex" (1980, pp. 236, 237). Yet, as we have seen, Alice was not uncharmed by the male sex. Her difficulty arose from doubts about herself as an attractive, loveable, and loving young woman.

Alice's struggles with sexuality were inchoate and inarticulate. It is only from her *Diary*, begun when she had passed 40 and was a confirmed invalid, that we have even a remote intimation of her feelings. Commenting on the birth of a fifth baby to some unknown mother, she wrote, "I wonder if it is not indelicate in a flaccid virgin to be so preoccupied with the multiplication of the species *but it fairly haunts me*" (Emphasis supplied; A. James, 1964, p. 36).

Strouse considers that Alice had a highly emotional reaction to whatever doctor treated her. "First she adored him—time after time she reported on 'the best,' the 'finest,' the 'first' doctor she had ever liked; then inevitably, something went wrong. Each doctor failed to live up to her hope of perfect understanding and care." Strouse further suggests that since doctors were in all likelihood the only men who touched her adult body, in addition to whatever excitement or shame she may have felt in being physically examined, "she brought extraordinarily high expectations to these encounters" (1980, p. 236).

Strouse concludes that, although "Alice did not know any more than her doctors just what ailed her, she sensed its relation to her sexuality and the ideals of 19th century womanhood." Obviously, we cannot know from this distance what her menstrual experiences were and whether they had any relationship to her repeated prostrations. But certain comments arouse our curiosity. Upon the prediction of one doctor that her health would improve when she reached menopause, a commonly held view of women's troubles, Alice wrote to William, that "this seems highly probable since I have had sixteen periods the last year" (Strouse, 1980, p. 237). We cannot know the significance for her of this frequency or what her typical experiences may have been. Strouse suggests that Alice cast herself both as frail receptacle and as explosive force, "expressive of continuing conflicts about her sexual identity. She wanted to be chaste, pure, innocent, delicate (which would have been her father's ideal) as well as angry, imperial, vital . . . " (1980, p. 238). These conflicting feelings suggest that joyous sexual feelings remained split off from the central core of herself. Nor was she able to find confirmation for a program of action which arose from the center of her own perception and initiative. This was more clearly achieved in her relationship with Katherine Loring, who seemed to be able to mirror and confirm Alice's strivings most completely.

Alice's intense relationship with Loring both troubled and relieved Henry, Jr. She had first met Loring in her mid-twenties when she was an assistant teacher to Loring, head of the history unit of the *Society to Encourage Studies at Home*. The relationship intensified following Alice's most severe, year-long breakdown at age 30, at the time of William's engagement. Alice's own description, written to a friend, serves us best in characterizing this relationship. "She is a most wonderful being. She has all the mere brute superiority which distinguishes man from woman combined with all the distinctly feminine virtues. There is nothing she cannot do from hewing wood (and) drawing water to driving run-away horses (and) educating all the women in North America" (Strouse, 1980, p. 191).

Her capacity to be exquisitely in tune with Alice's wide-ranging episodes of physical distress seemed even greater than Henry's. Henry recognized that, but for Katherine Loring's willingness to be companion and nurse to his sister, he would have been unable to travel and to carry on his own activities freely. Periodically, at times when Katherine's own family responsibilities required her presence, even a temporary loss of Katherine's presence would bring on severe bouts of prostration. Yet, as Henry noted,

Katherine's return did not mean that Alice would get well, but rather that the intense and exclusive relationship could once again resume uninterrupted. Although, as Strouse notes, that kind of intense relationship between women in the nineteenth century was called a "Boston marriage" (p. 200), its uniquely unphysical nature is characterized by Alice in a note in her *Diary*. "K. says this is a shocking hotel; she is always coming, at the turn of the stairs, upon a waiter and chambermaid, rebounding from the sound of her, from osculatory relaxations. How different their life from ours! We toil not to be sure, but do we ever attain the Ideal as they must in the surreptitious kiss?" (A. James, 1964, p. 148). Perhaps the physical nature of Alice's needs provided its own gratification in the form of the ministrations it required.

Edel suggests that if Alice was too ill to be an active lesbian, she was nevertheless finding fulfillment in being ill. Her relationship with Loring may well have been at a much earlier level of nurturing and being nurtured. Through her illness she sought Katherine Loring's exclusive attention as she had earlier required her father's. Edel suggests that she was intensely jealous of Loring's sister, Louise, who, for a time, had equal claim on Loring's time. Long after her invalidism was well-established, Alice confided to Henry that if she might have Katherine's presence quietly and uninterruptedly for a year to relieve her of all responsibility she would get well (Edel, 1964, p. 12). Though Henry was skeptical, he noted that there was as much chance of her giving up Katherine as of having her legs sawed off.

After her death, Henry pointed out that "in our family group, girls seem hardly to have had a chance. . . . Alice's tragic health was, in a manner, the only solution for her of the practical problem of life . . . " (Edel, 1964, p. 8). That he was early aware of the function her illness played is implicit in a letter to his father in which he asked him to tell Alice that the worse her health was the more he cared for her, but that she "must not take it as an encouragement to sickliness" (Strouse, 1980, p. 184).

We may speculate that deficits in her capacity to feel good about her physical and mental attributes arose from the selfobject failures to which she was exposed at the time of her forming self. Disappointed in her mother, she turned to her father for confirmation. But his confirmation was dictated more by his own needs for an adoring response to his wit and verve. He was at times aware of the maturing needs of his daughter but only most inconsistently, subjecting her to repeated fragmentation. William compounded the difficulty in that by turns he raised her to the pinnacle of perfection and beauty and as rapidly punctured this inflated version of herself. For her, the oedipal phase was conflicted; though she longed for confirmation of herself as a loveable, loving and intelligent young woman, her aspirations were subjected to repeated failures. That her father was aware of his daughter's damaged self is implicit in his comment in a letter congratulating Emerson on his daughter's engagement, adding that he could only hope that his "poor bird" might find as safe a nest (Strouse, 1980, p. 94). It was through her illness that Alice could bind others to her with unquestioning, unteasing tenderness. Indeed, one of the earliest manifestations of this was her insistence that her father be at her bedside at all times to allay her night terrors (A. James, 1964, p. 6). Later Loring noted that the use of a modified form of hypnosis provided calmness which enabled Alice to drop off to sleep "without the sensations of terror which have accompanied the process for so many years" (A. James, 1964, p. 15).

There were periods in which Alice pursued normal activities. Even at the time of her mother's illness and death, when everyone anticipated a severe breakdown, she rose to managing the house and caring for her father with great verve and competence. Can this be viewed as a belated oedipal victory, taking her mother's place? It seems unlikely. Although concerned about her daughter, puzzled, troubled and pitying of her many breakdowns, pleased when Alice seemed to recover and become active again, Mrs. James epitomized abnegation and self-sacrifice. Alice idealized these qualities in her, and for a time could emulate them. But with her father's approaching death, Alice, ministering to his needs during the day, would collapse at night, bringing the ever faithful Katherine to her side.

Although Strouse described the final year of her father's life as a conjugal one, and the following year with Henry, Jr., another such, neither performed for her the intensely calming and soothing selfobject functions which Katherine was able to perform. Katherine Loring became for Alice a selfobject through whom she overcame repeated and prolonged episodes of fragmentation, a selfobject who provided missing structure, without whom she could not function. Until the end of Alice's life and beyond, since it was Loring who brought about publication of the *Diary* despite Henry, Jr.'s objections, Loring remained a dominant selfobject. In the end it was she who allowed Alice to speak to the world.

For Alice's brothers, the struggle to achieve cohesion was beset with less difficulty, but difficulty nevertheless. That they were children of a maternal father and a gubernatorial mother was not in itself productive of self pathology. Tenderness is deployed across the sexes and so is the power to function as an effective administrator. What was distorting was the intrusion of their father's needs into the forming selves of his sons. As we have seen, he repeatedly uprooted them from various schools and various countries. The very number and succession startled Henry, Jr., who wrote, "We couldn't have been changed oftener . . . if our presence had been objected to" (H. James, 1913, p. 16). Their father's strenuous efforts to provide the ideal education, and presumably the realization of their talents, seemed rather to serve his own great needs: to have them close by, to sustain him.

Typical is Henry, Sr.'s note to a friend in which he describes their returning to Europe when William was 15, largely because he believed that

> (William) was too much attracted to painting which he was studying at the time—as I supposed from the contiguity to Mr. Hunt (the artist); let us break that up we said, at all events. . . . I thought and still think that the true bent of his genius was towards the acquisition of knowledge: and to give up this hope without a struggle and allow him to *tumble down into a mere painter* was impossible. Let us go abroad then and bring him into contact with books and teachers. (Emphasis supplied; Strouse, 1980, p. 58)

Yet, when advised that the best source for such learning was Paris, he did not follow through. What this seems to indicate, then, was that Henry, Sr., was unable to endure his son's attraction to a selfobject mentor who might supplant him. As we have seen, when finally disillusioned with what Europe had to offer in the way of education for his sons and arranging to return to the States, he certainly gave lip service to his hope that his sons would "go it strongly" in finding "friends among their own sex and sweethearts in the other." At the same time, with his younger sons he wondered how much they would be able to study in a coeducational school in which they would be distracted "by the rosebud lips" of the girls. These comments from their father, in the absence of their own comments in letters or vignettes embedded in the family lexicon, suggest the difficulty they encountered in defining and claiming their own masculinity arising from their own perceptions and subject to their own initiative.

The James children did not suffer the trauma of abrupt withdrawal or emotional inaccessibility: their trauma arose from their father's being so everlastingly *there* and of using their feelings and experiences to discharge his own. The result was a merger enmeshment rather than a step-by-step process of transmuting internalization of selfobject functions into self-functions. The sons would struggle long in their efforts to define and pursue a program of action based on their own profoundly examined perceptions and initiative.

The two younger boys were free from their father's intrusion at an earlier age, both because of his intense involvement with their older brothers and because, while still in late adolescence, they took part in the Civil War. Wilky returned home wounded and a hero whom his father described as "manly and exalted in the tone of his mind. . . . It is really quite incomprehensible to me to see so much manhood so suddenly achieved" (Strouse, 1980, p. 76).

Bob, the youngest, wrote of his homesickness and his wish to resign from the military but was urged by his father not to yield to this temptation "which your manhood is called upon to resist." He further characterizes it as a "passing effeminacy," and "unmanly project," urging him "to be a man" and "to force himself like a man to do your whole duty" (Strouse, 1980, p. 77).

He suggests that Bob may be suffering guilt over unnamed "conduct which may not have been irreproachable in your own eyes" (Strouse, 1980, p. 77). Although offering to explain the "physiology of this," he resorts to vague references to moral life which is dependent on a balance between good and evil. In the Jamesian tongue, indirection and vagueness seemed to hold sway in relation to sexual matters but intellectual matters and theological discussion are detailed and explicit.

Perhaps the most explicit of their father's views about what one infers to be lusty sexual longings appears in a letter to Bob in answer not to a letter Bob had written to his father but to one he had written to his oldest brother William, again an indication not only of the intense family relationship but of Henry, Sr.'s inability to allow his sons a private relationship. Bob had referred to being in the "suburbs of hell" in his sufferings. Henry, Sr. wrote:

> I [too] feel at one moment as if all hell were let loose in me, envy, hatred, contempt of others, ill will, lasciviousness, memories, unchaste nay unclean desires; and then again such humility, such tenderness, such burning love to all mankind, and such ineffable delight in the marriage sentiment . . . [that] I used . . . to feel a great horror of myself when the infernal stage prevailed and great joy in myself when the heavenly flux was uppermost. . . . I should however be . . . terribly tossed and wrenched if I were not a married man . . . if I were not able when the celestial powers were *in force* to lavish tenderness . . . upon my wife and children, and when they were in flight to run to the bosom of your mother, the home of all truth and purity and deafen my ears to everything but her spotless worth till the pitiless inflowing infamy had spent itself. . . . Such is the explanation of your troubles of the mind. Your bosom like mine is the arena of a hot conflict between heaven and hell. . . . (A. James, 1934, p. 53)

At the same time, when Bob apparently was feeling confident, his father hastened to write, " . . . I lose no time in saying you must be on your guard. Your sense of power is very likely illusory. I do not say it is so necessarily but that it is likely" (A. James, 1934, p. 54). In the same letter he urges Bob to return home: "This thing is necessary to my happiness. I can't stand this tremendous separation from you . . . " (A. James, 1934, p. 52). His letters may open with a salutation such as "My darling Bobbins," and close with protestations of love which all "the family send, bushels full pressed down and running over" (A. James, 1934, p. 78).

That their father was a warm, tender individual, voluptuously expressive of his feelings for his children, need not have interfered with the achievement of core gender identity and of the integration of genitality in maturity. Both Bob and Wilky married in their mid-twenties and founded families. For William the struggle was more extended. He later wrote in a chapter on "Instincts" that "love" is an "anti-sexual instinct. . . . The sexual impulse . . . this strongest passion of all, so far from being the most 'irresistible' may be the *hardest one to give rein to*" (Emphasis added; Strouse, 1980, p. 54).

His diffidence and discomfort in writing about sexuality are further indicated in his discussion of "the primacy of personal isolation and the actual repulsiveness of the idea of intimate contact with most of the persons we meet, especially those of our own sex. . . . To most of us, it is even unpleasant to sit down in a chair still warm from occupancy by another person's body. . . . " He apologized in a footnote for having to discuss "these unpleasant matters" (Strouse, 1980, p. 54).

Written three years after his marriage, his attitude contrasts with the gaiety he enjoyed in his teasing "courting" of his sister Alice. As we have seen, his engagement to another Alice seemed to have propelled his sister into a breakdown. William was the oldest son, but the last to enter the matrimonial waters; some indication of his overpowering and overshadowing importance in the family is reflected caustically by Wilky, who had been married for six years and was the father of a family, when he wrote congratulating William: "It is certainly the greatest piece of news you have ever inflicted upon the world, and I suppose the greatest event that has ever transpired in the family" (Strouse, 1980, p. 182).

William's marriage culminated a tortured two-year engagement in which he was besieged by doubt, difficulty with his back and his eyes, and questions about inflicting himself upon a wife and family. He wrote to Wilky, when he finally decided upon the plunge, "Every doctor I have ever spoken to has said marriage ought to be the best possible mode of life for me. . . . " Like his father and his brothers, William would characterize his wife as an angel, "straight and true," he "the sinner," and would attribute to her his rescue from his difficulties. Like his father, and like Wilky and Bob, he would write, "I take [my wife] more for her moral than her intellectual qualities" (Strouse, 1980, p. 180).

Of the four brothers, Henry alone never married. In youth, Henry incurred an injury under circumstances not unlike his father's accident which had resulted in leg amputation. Henry's injury remains a mystery, clouded in uncertainty. There is no sound basis for an assumption that his injury incapacitated him for marriage. Edel, (1985, p. 58) examining Henry, Jr.'s life in detail, believed that the evidence pointed rather to a back injury.

His mother urged marriage upon him, as a panacea for many of his difficulties. Still, at age 26, abroad in "this blasted Europe," he confesses that he is homesick. He sympathizes now with his father's similar episodes, which he now regrets jeering about since he suffers from the same feelings. "(I am) abjectly, fatally homesick. If to think and to feel and to long were to act and to be—wouldn't I just be lolling on that . . . sofa . . . with my head on mother's lap and my feet on Alice's" (Matthiesen, p. 253). Spinster Alice and bachelor Henry were most exquisitely in tune with each other throughout their childhood and adult lives. William's efforts to comfort Alice were met "with shrieks of laughter," but she described the manner in which Henry would "cling to each organ" when in upheaval as akin to their having the same skin. In this capacity to merge with her suffering, she included her father. Upon his death, when, for a few months Alice kept house and Henry settled family affairs, he wrote, "My sister and I make an harmonious little menage, and I feel a good deal as if I were married." Edel (1964) refers to Henry's notes for an unwritten story: "two lives, two beings and *one* experience" (p. 9). In his novels and stories, Henry would embed his manifold insights in the complexity of relationships between parent and child, between the sexes in courtship and marriage, and within the same sex in friendship and rivalry. But he would never marry.

We undertook an examination of the James family in order to consider the vicissitudes of self formation and cohesion. Only Henry and William were alive (William would die the following year) when Freud wrote in 1909 that the freeing of an individual as he grows up from the authority of his parents is one of the most necessary, though one of the most painful, results brought about by the course of his development:

It is quite essential that the liberation should occur and it may be presumed that it has been to some extent achieved by everyone who has reached a normal state. Indeed, the whole progress of society rests upon the opposition between successive generations. On the other hand, there is a class of neurotics whose condition is recognizably determined by their having failed in this task.

For a small child his parents are at first the only authority and the source of all belief. The child's most intense and momentous wish during these early years is to be like his parents (that is, the parent of his own sex) and to be big like his father and mother. But as intellectual growth increases, the child cannot help discovering by degrees the category to which his parents belong. He gets to know other parents and compares them with his own, and so comes to doubt the incomparable and unique quality which he has attributed to them. (Freud, 1909)

Freud continues in this essay to elaborate his theory of the family romance and the child's conflict and rivalry with the parent of the same sex.

In the theory of human development which Kohut formulated, the "liberation" of the individual from his parents is viewed differently. It is not separation and individuation, the opposition of the generations, upon which the whole progress of civilization is based. It is that the cohesive nuclear self of the child is created in the interplay of natural endowment and responsive selfobject functions of the empathic parental milieu. Appropriately in tune with the child's developing needs at each phase, parents then facilitate the child's entrance into the widening world of selfobjects, allowing for the consolidation of a nuclear self, metaphorically bipolar. Grandiose fantasies and ambitions in one pole are modulated and expressed through the elaboration of skills and talents in realizable goals with which the second pole is imbued. The child, through transmuting internalization, continues to consolidate a self in which the pattern of ambitions and goals, the tensions between them, the program of action undertaken toward their realization are experienced as continuous in time and space. The individual now has transmuted the capacity for "self-righting," for regulating self-esteem. From his ability to find a continuing and ever more sophisticated array of selfobjects, he achieves sustenance of the self throughout the life cycle. Bit by bit parents relinquish their central role; optimal frustration, minimal "loss" of a selfobject function, stimulates transmuting internalization, which facilitates the firming and deepening of the nuclear self-function. It is thus not a self which stands alone, separate and free from the authority of the parents, but one which "spontaneously moves toward new modes of sustenance by an increasing array of selfobjects outside" the parental milieu (Kohut, 1984). It is thus not the *opposition* of the generations but the *dialogue* between the generations, as well as the encouragement and the freedom the older generation provides, that allows the individual to undertake new ways, new ideas, and new approaches to the vicissitudes of living and of societal change.

All the James children wrote of their father's capacity to pour forth his personal sufferings in vivid description and to intrude these in a manner that sought out his children as selfobjects to support his fragmenting self.

The reader senses a zest in these confidences and a resignation on the part of the children to being so used. The resulting merger enmeshment created difficulty for each of the children.

The gendered self, masculine or feminine, seeks a program of action through which to express ambitions and aspirations, to identify talents, to elaborate supporting skills, and through these to define vocation. Both William and Henry struggled to free themselves from a merger with their father as they sought to define their own goals, their own life work. For a prolonged period, both lived at home rather than asserting and pursuing their own life course. Both suffered from vague illnesses, William with his back, eyes, and digestive disorders, Henry with his back and constipation. William struggled to define a program of action, a profession, through which he could realize his unique gifts. "Much I would give," he wrote at age 26, "for a constructive passion of some kind" (Matthiessen, 1980, p. 209). We have seen how, as children, an interest would be fostered for a time but then interrupted according to their father's needs. Stimulated by the emerging interests and talents of his sons, Henry, Sr., intruded his own needs and interests. He maintained a merger with his children which made it difficult for them to define and pursue a meaningful life from the centrality of their own vision.

In a prolonged pursuit of a profession, with many interruptions, William studied physiology, medicine, and ultimately became a distinguished psychologist and philosopher. But he was a tense, self-doubting young man who suffered numerous periods of fragmentation expressed in hypochondriacal concerns, suicidal ideation, and work inhibition. He felt disgusted with his life and paralyzed. Everyone else seemed productive, he alone a waste. He longed for some guide to action. He suffered a vastation similar to his father's, experiencing dread, insecurity, insomnia, fear of going out alone. Although he had, by the time of his marriage at age 36, achieved a purpose and direction, he would describe his wife as having "taken him from the dust and transformed him, a diseased boy, into a man" (Strouse, 1980, p. 180). Implicit in this description is her importance to him as a selfobject through whom cohesion could be restored and sustained.

Henry also groped toward his ultimate course as a writer; he too suffered intervals of loss of purpose and hypochondriacal concerns, in which his quiet suffering and uncomplaining demeanor were the source of his mother's admiration and the subject of her praise. She viewed his behavior as exemplary, unlike William's (and his father's) importunate bewailings. Henry could not, however, move toward marriage though his mother urged this upon him. Marriage would "harmonize the discordant elements in your life—you would make . . . the most loving and loveable and the happiest of husbands. I wish I could see you in a favorable attitude of heart towards the divine institution of marriage." Henry responded that he would do so if she would provide the wife, the fortune and the *"inclination"* (Emphasis supplied; Strouse, 1980, p. 25). Edel suggests that his androgynous psychic structure gave him exquisite sensitivity in describing the interaction between men and women.

As we have seen, the two younger brothers left home earlier, probably freed initially by enlistment in the Union Army. Wilky returned seriously wounded and required a long period of convalescence. Upon his recovery, he and his younger brother attempted to found a plantation manned by freed slaves, but this, like many other ventures, failed. Each married and founded families earlier than their oldest brother and unlike Henry who remained unmarried; but Wilky was plagued by severe illnesses, and Robertson, who looked upon children as on guard in more or less hostile surroundings, by alcoholism, a later breakdown, and marital difficulties.

My purpose in reviewing the vicissitudes of the James brothers is to demonstrate how self psychology can illuminate our understanding of their struggles to achieve unity and maintain cohesion. Their tribulations are vitalized by an understanding of the importance of parents as selfobjects in the creation and consolidation of a cohesive nuclear self. As children, they were vigorous, lively, curious, and competitive. Their competitiveness centered in their strivings to secure response to their lively wit and intellect, their unique qualities, their own aspirations. But they needed, as well, affirmation and pride in their manliness. Surely their father's avowed purpose was to facilitate such a development. Indeed, as we have seen, he wrote understandingly that his sons were "getting to the age when the heart craves a little wider expansion than is furnished by domestic affections. They want friends among their own sex and sweethearts in the other, and my hope for their own salvation temporal and spiritual is that they go it strongly in both lines when they get home" (Strouse, 1980, p. 59). His own struggles with sexuality made him less capable of mirroring their efforts to achieve pride in their masculinity, to make a joyous assertion of their sexuality.

We may well speculate whether William and Henry did not reflect retreat from the oedipal phase and regression to the preoedipal phase reflected in their focus on the nurturing relationship both with their mother and with Alice. Both wrote, when abroad, of their longing for this. William, after an illness, wrote that he had been "crying all the time for to have you [Alice] sitting by me stroking my brow. . . . " Henry, in describing his homesickness, yearned to be at home with his mother and Alice, "lying on the sofa with [his] head in the lap of one and [his] feet in that of the other."

To be nostalgic for an earlier period certainly need not be regarded as regressive as long as an individual engages in shaping his ambitions and striving toward heterosexual object choice, professional, vocational, or social goals. But we have seen that both William and Henry were beset by long periods of inactivity and hypochondriacal concerns. Their mother responded to her sons with genuine concern, but to Henry she complained that the trouble with William is that he must

> . . . express every fluctuation of feeling, and especially every unfavorable symptom without reference to the effect on those about him. . . . He keeps his good looks but whenever he speaks of himself says he is no better. This I cannot believe to be the true state of the case, but his temperament is a morbidly hopeless one, and with this he has to contend all the time, as well as his physical disability. . . . If, dear Harry, you could only have imparted to him a few grains of your own blessed hopefulness, he would have been well long ago. (Matthiessen, 1980, p. 221)

Yet William genuinely suffered from insomnia, digestive troubles, eye trouble, back weakness, and deep periods of suicidal depression. Henry also suffered from hypochondriacal concerns, but patience and forbearance from troubling his mother with the state of his health won her praise and Henry welcomed this. We have seen how with Alice as well, patience and forbearance won her approval. It is not that their mother was unsympathetic. If anything, Henry himself characterized her as "living in her children so exclusively, with a want of anything in her consciousness that was not about and for us; that I think we almost contested her being separate enough to be proud of us—it was too like our being proud of ourselves." Her selflessness was "so consistently and unabatedly active" that she had nothing left to offer "*acutely*" (Matthiessen, 1980, p. 202). Henry's comments suggest that their mother's response was so all-encompassing as to render it powerless at times of specific difficulty. At this distant time we can only speculate that in her interaction with her sons and her daughter, her equanimity, patience and forbearance did not perform a selfobject function which would permit transmuting internalization into their capacity to soothe and calm themselves, to monitor their own anxiety as they sought and undertook the requirements of maturity. Something about their relationship with her, and with their father, maintained a merger from which they could not free themselves adequately.

Henry refers to his father's gaiety, which attracted the children to him and which also "invited free jokes and other familiarities at his expense" (Matthiessen, 1980, p. 194). We have seen how important both his wife and his children were in maintaining Henry, Sr.'s cohesion, in helping him to fend off fragmentation. And though the children idealized him, they found his difference from their friends' fathers troubling and discomforting. He had no concrete occupation that they could describe, other than vaguely as student and scholar, and William and Henry both struggled against their de-idealization of his writings and beliefs. William in particular, as we have seen, referred to his father's entire life as being "devoted to the *monotonous* elaboration of one single bundle of truths . . . the true relationship between mankind and its creator. What he had to say on this point was the burden of his whole life, and its *only* burden" (Emphasis supplied; Matthiessen, 1980, p. 139).

Henry, Sr., had arrived at his vocation as a writer and lecturer in theology only after severe struggles in early adulthood and a breakdown during William's and Henry's early years. He was able to sustain himself as a student and scholar because of independent means secured through inheritance. He was generous with his children and could support their own prolonged struggles to find a way of life consistent with their abilities. His many uprootings of the children in their early years, as he sought the perfect education for them, made their own efforts to elaborate standards and goals for themselves constantly subject to fragmentation and reworking. His own early struggles to define a vocation and (as became increasingly apparent to them) the sterile nature of his choice weakened his ability to function as a reliable, idealized selfobject with whose greatness, strength, and calmness they could merge.

As they entered the adolescent phase, Henry, Sr., continually extolled womanhood as naturally sweet, pure, and virtuous, whereas man must constantly struggle with his evil nature. As his sons grew into young adulthood, their struggles to integrate sexuality were intruded upon by their father in his intense reliving of his own experiences at similar periods. This is at variance with a father who is available and who empathically supports the normal strivings of his offspring so that sexuality becomes integrated and coherent rather than split off.

Robertson, the youngest son, suffered greatly with self-loathing because of his "lustful appetite"; he extolled the virtues of his father even though Henry, Sr., shared with him his own difficulties. There have been few more poignant descriptions of the driven attempt to retrieve a sense of wholeness and perfection by union with an archaic selfobject than Robertson revealed in the following:

> . . . Since father died, who was the only being on earth I ever cared for deeply, that loss has built up in me out of the ignominy of drink and debauchery what seems to me of late to be becoming one long day. . . . Dead affections and decencies long forgotten seem to be calling from afar off, and there are

moments in which my heart is wrung, as if with a sort of pain of bliss. . . . (Matthiessen, 1980, p 262)

This revelation of his inner state helps us also to understand substance abuse and sexual drivenness as disintegration products with which the fragmenting self, weakened and chaotic, seeks to restore a sense of wholeness and perfection. What Robertson sought from his father was not the intrusion of his own struggles with sexuality but recognition of his manliness.

But it was not only his father's failure as a selfobject that brought about Robertson's fragmentation-prone self. From his earliest childhood his subjective experience was of being little appreciated by his overburdened mother. As we have seen, some 50 years later he commented, "I never see infants now without discerning in their usually solemn countenances a conviction that they are on their guard in more or less hostile surroundings" (Matthiessen, 1980, p. 24). His mother's advice to him at the birth of his son was "not to let the little tyrants rule too soon." The understimulated, unmirrored child feels himself to be unsupported, and it would appear that, for Robertson, his deficits in self cohesion occurred early. In young adulthood he suffered, like his brothers, from back trouble, digestive upsets, and, as he confided in a letter to William, nocturnal emissions and fear of impotence. Instead of pride and zest in his masculinity, Robertson resorted to driven behavior in an endless, unavailing attempt to soothe and calm himself. His union with an archaic selfobject appeared then to be the only solution to his difficulties.

William, too, suffered from anxieties and fears about sexual expression, but they may have been masked by his overzealous concern about the "probable risk of generating unhealthy offspring." In answer to a letter Robertson had written, telling him that he had fallen in love, William responded:

For myself I have long since fully determined never to marry with anyone, were she as healthy as the Venus of Milo, for the dorsal trouble is evidently s'thing (sic) in the blood. I confess that the flesh is weak and passion will overthrow strong reasons, and I may fail in keeping such a resolve; but I mean not to fail. I want to feel on my deathbed when I look back that whatever evil I was born with I kept to myself, and did so much toward extinguishing it from the world. (Strouse, 1980, p. 126)

However, it would be another seven years, after a tortured self-doubting engagement and numerous consultations, that he finally overcame his inhibitions and married, as we have seen, at age 36. His frequent teasing of Alice in extravagant romantic tones suggests his use of her as a target for his fantasies to postpone development of romantic relationships outside the family.

For Alice, the goals of sweetness, purity and virtue forced her to disavow the passions and rivalries evoked by family relationships. The narcissistic rage kindled by her inability to secure responses to her whole self as a loveable, loving, intelligent young woman was discharged in numerous periods of prostration. Until the diagnosis of terminal breast cancer in her final year, no organic basis for these periods of illness was ever determined.

Henry, Sr., and Mary were devoted and loving parents to their children, deeply concerned with their physical and emotional health and eager to support their ventures. But the very nature of their personalities, and the manner in which these impinged on each of their children, resulted in certain selfobject failures which left deficits in self cohesion for each of the children. For the James children, the process of shaping their own ambitions toward longed-for goals through skills and talents uniquely theirs exposed weaknesses in their nuclear selves. Attempts to enact their own agenda entailed repeated fragmentation, psychological and physical suffering. William and Henry achieved distinguished and productive lives. William was able to marry and to found a family in addition to a professional career. Although Henry did not marry, he produced a body of writing which continues to inform and delight generations of readers. The two younger brothers, although they did marry and establish families, continued to struggle throughout their lives with business failures as well as illness. They could not establish a continuum between their ambitions and ideals that would permit them to sustain joyful and meaningful lives. Alice, an energetic and lively child until adolescence, struggled to the end of her days with repeated episodes of fragmentation and invalidism.

15

Future Directions

IN THE FOREGOING CHAPTERS we have explored individual therapy across the life cycle, from childhood through old age. A study of self psychology in relation to the treatment of families, groups, and community action has not been attempted. Yet self psychology offers us a broad vision of human striving which social work methods seek to enhance. It is not my purpose to offer a comprehensive view of the various methods of intervention but rather to consider how our work may become more purposeful and direct, how the social worker's use of herself in these methods can become more flexible and insightful because of the enlarged vision offered by self psychology. My concern here is less with the particular method of family or community intervention than with the dynamics of structure building which, set in motion by the therapist as new selfobject, rekindle or build anew the capacity to forge and strive to reach goals that confirm purpose and worth.

Kohut did not ignore the role of psychosocial factors in the etiology of self disorders and in the possibility of remedy through community action (Kohut, 1977). What is significant in our consideration of the applicability of self psychology to this process is that there is now available an expanded understanding of human striving to feel whole and worthwhile. Beyond treatment of individuals, there exists the possibility of bringing new light to bear on our work with families, with groups formed for the purpose of therapy, and with groups which seek to fulfill a community purpose. It is the task of those actively engaged in such methods to test the strength and applicability of the concepts of self psychology, but I will briefly offer some impressionistic views.

FAMILY THERAPY

Let us consider, even though briefly, the manner in which the concepts of self psychology may be employed in family intervention. There are indices which family therapists and theorists recognize in determining

239

whether an approach employing individual or family therapy is appropriate (Hollis and Woods, 1981; Walsh, 1983). Walsh has described major models of family therapy, categorizing these according to *growth-oriented approaches*—psychodynamic, systems, or experiential therapy—and *problem-solving approaches*—structural, strategic, or behavioral models. She has pointed out that, regardless of differences in particular strategies and techniques employed in various models of family therapy, " . . . all approaches focus on direct assessment and change of the relationship among individuals, rather than problems 'inside' the individual symptombearer or derivatives of transference phenomena." She regards this as the "major distinction of the family systems orientation from traditional individual treatment models." She believes that "therapeutic transference, an essential vehicle for assessment and change in individual models, plays a diminished role in family therapy because the therapist can observe patterns and promote change directly among key family members. Transference reactions do occur in family therapy but are redirected for expression and change back into the natural relationship network" (Walsh, 1983, p. 484).

We must emphasize that whatever the method, whatever the approach, the key factor in treatment is the manner in which the social worker uses herself in freeing the family for growth, in bringing about a shift toward mutually sustaining and productive relationships. In determining how a therapist uses herself, transference issues are as vital in family therapy as they are in individual therapy. The transference needs to be comforted, admired, stimulated, preferred, and forgiven arise within family therapy and individual therapy alike, and it is not that they are redirected for expression and change back into the natural relationship network, but that there is set in motion a process which allows the individual to acquire, to take into the self, a new function. By reason of the response of the therapist to the particular transference need in ascendance, a family member may acquire a bit of the psychic structure of self-soothing, of monitoring anxiety as he undertakes mastery of a particular emotional response or behavior. In the process of structure building, empathy is enhanced since disavowal of emotional stress is relinquished as a defense, and cognition and affect are united—the individual knows that he hurts and why; moreoever, he may be able to alter the behavior that has elicited the painful feeling state or behavior. He becomes more empathically in touch with other members of the family, and from this increase in the capacity for empathy he can respond more appropriately to their specific needs and can elicit more sustaining response to his own.

To illustrate, the Jones family is one in which the mother feels lonely and isolated, the father hardworking and unappreciated, and the two adolescent children surly and uncommunicative. The listening presence of the social worker provides an opportunity for them to feel heard and responded to empathically. To immerse oneself in a family system arouses countertransference reactions which can themselves then serve as a diagnostic tool for assessing deficits in particular family members and areas of appropriate intervention. The therapist can savor the need of the adolescent son to free himself by semi-delinquent behavior from too controlling and joyless a relationship with his father. She can sense an alliance with the rebellious daughter who is seeking to form an attachment that will reverberate to her own needs rather than to those of her mother. She can vicariously experience the isolation of the mother, bound down by household tasks with little recognition from family members of the way in which she manages their complex needs. She can understand the father's wish to have his authority recognized and, in his fatigue, explosions in narcissistic rage commanding immediate obedience.

These countertransference reactions, freed from her personal agenda, become available for assessing the counterproductive behavior of the family members, whose unmet mirroring and idealizing needs result in their driven behavior and thought. It is not the system of intervention that is crucial but the therapist's understanding of the particular unmet need in the present. She is more than a listening presence; she is a source of calmness; her focused empathic attention is a center of strength. Although, initially, the comments of family members labeling and condemning each other may be to her directly, they begin to hear each other's comments. They begin to speak directly to each other, in anger, in regret, in concern, in remorse, in appreciation, in affection.

Without detailing the long process of therapy in which these four family members are engaged, let us say that it is their unexpressed longings which emerge. These lie underneath the depressive state of the mother, the raging demands of the father, the semi-delinquent behavior of the son, the failed relationships of the daughter. In a rekindled process that overcomes the sense of depletion and emptiness with which this mother pursues her tasks, she is able to present herself first to the therapist and then to her husband and children for the nourishment of their appreciation and love. As the father can openly share with the therapist and then with his family the difficulties of his work and his realistic anxieties about the economic future, their understanding restores and invigorates his capacity to function productively and creatively. When both parents can understand and accept the importance for their children of being permitted to take on greater responsibility for themselves and for monitoring their own behavior, they are able to perform the important selfobject function of withdrawing step-by-step from too close supervision but remaining available as needed. Although the son ultimately asked for and received individual therapy as he strove to heal the deficit in self-esteem which led him to undertake daredevil (semi-delinquent) behavior, his relationship with the family was involved and concerned. The mother became less intrusive and supervisory in her response to her daughter's dating patterns; she appeared more genuinely supportive as the daughter at the same time became aware of the methods by which, through the externalization of her own fears, she had kept her mother actively engaged and apprehensive.

In stepwise fashion, the family members, together and as individuals, became more empathically in tune with each other. Their use of the therapist reflected the manner in which her selfobject functions had "gone inside," had become their own self-functions. They were more alert to each other's needs and better able to cue each other to these needs. A time for termination was discussed; as it drew close, the family expressed genuine regret at the loss of this important period of their lives. They shared reminiscences of stormy times they had passed through, both in and outside of therapy, and philosophically reflected that such times could come again but that they felt better equipped to meet them.

We recognize that this family revealed many strengths and that these strengths could be drawn into the process of structure building and firming. In the more seriously damaged families who come on their own or are mandated to family and children's agencies, the treatment process will be more concretely structured, specific educational tasks will be undertaken, narrower goals will be described. But if we examine these interventions we can recognize them as the mirroring, affirming, and guiding selfobject functions so necessary to the early period of the forming of the self. A further mode of intervention will provide the opportunity for appropriate merging with an idealized figure who may provide the prestructural selfobject needs of these severely deficited individuals. For some families such selfobject functions may have to be continued indefinitely and may have to be supplemented by a variety of institutionalized services.

May we then speak, in general, of a family self, structurally cohesive, functioning with vigor and harmony? The family self, like the individual self, monitors anxiety, provides soothing and calming functions, and can aid by that response which enables the individual to continue the path toward the creation of his own program of action. Individual family members, subject to fragmentation, will turn to the family, to one another, for that support which enables them to reintegrate their temporarily weakened self and to be restored in their functioning. The family self, or its individual members, can offer mirroring affirmation or guidance for a specific need required by a temporarily impaired self. Being enfolded in the idealized strength and wisdom of the family as selfobject may re-invigorate the individual member to renew his efforts toward mastery of a particular task or phase. This is not to suggest that the family, as in certain maladaptive instances, holds the individual captive in a merger. The selfobject functions performed by the family self, in tune with the developmental needs of the children and the mutual sustainment of its adult members, fosters a gradual expansion of the selfobject world to peers and mentors in the vocational community and in intimate personal relationships through which the sustenance of the self is maintained in adulthood. Individual members may now engage in the active pursuit and achievement of a meaningful and purposeful life. The capacity to regulate self-esteem becomes a reliable tool for self-righting at times of narcissistic vulnerability, and this includes the capacity to seek response from appropriate selfobjects, including the family self when necessary.

This is an essentially impressionistic view of the manner in which self psychology may illuminate the process of family therapy. It remains for those engaged in such work to experience the enlarged vision of human striving to feel whole and worthwhile which self psychology offers. An understanding of driven behavior, originating not in the unruly drives but in earlier failures to elicit responses to mirroring and idealizing needs and wishes, enables the caseworker to use herself as a new selfobject through whom the family self can now acquire new self-functions: mutual sustainment through which individual members may forge and pursue attainable and valued goals. In addition, the family self fosters differentiation not for the sterile end of autonomy, but for the enrichment which varied and mature selfobject choices in the larger world can now provide.

GROUP THERAPY

Family therapy addresses a natural relationship unit that has a shared past, ongoing interaction, and a future, as well as its own values, goals, language (verbal and nonverbal), and loyalties (Walsh, 1983, p. 484). A determination of whether an individual, family, or group method of intervention is to be undertaken will depend sometimes on chance, i.e., the particular pattern of service delivery of the agency which is approached for service. The decision of which method to employ depends on the knowledge, skills, and biases of the practitioner making the assessment (Goldstein, 1984, p. 184). Although this may be true, the client's need, level of functioning, and specific problem must become the major determinant.

Group therapy has been increasingly employed in a variety of settings, for a variety of needs, and across the life cycle. To name a few: treatment of teenage pregnant girls, treatment of mothers with high-risk infants, treatment of teenage or adult substance abusers, treatment of isolated adolescents lacking social skills, treatment of parents in need of parenting skills and of child-abusing parents, treatment centering on problems of aging or on specific physical handicaps or illnesses. Within the past few years, Harwood (1983) has examined the application of self psychology to group psychotherapy; Leszcz, Feigenbaum, Sadavoy, and Robinson have employed the insights of self psychology to psychotherapy with elderly men (1985); and Kriegman and Solomon have described cult groups and the narcissistic personality, viewing the phenomenon as an offer to heal defects in the self (1985). The target problems and the client populations are as varied as the gamut of human suffering and deficit.

Kohut did not directly address group therapy as a mode of treatment. His interest in group dynamics arose in the context of the impact of charismatic leaders on society, with its potential both for constructive and destructive consequences (Kohut, 1971, 1977, 1978). He was also keenly interested in the study by means of empathy and introspection of group process which led to the clustering and cleavages in various schools of analytic thought. In his reflections, he used the concept of a "group self" analogous to the self of the individual. He believed that we could learn much from observations of the group self as it is formed, as it is held together, as it oscillates between fragmentation and reintegration, and from the regressive behavior exhibited when it moves toward fragmentation (Kohut, 1984, p. 838; 1985).

Although Kohut did not, as we have said above, address group treatment for the variety of human ills we have listed, the explanatory system of human behavior which he formulated enables us to think creatively about its application to such a mode of intervention. Further, it may assist the practitioner in understanding how the use of her mature psychic structure, functioning through a professional self, provides new selfobject functions for the group as a whole and for its members.

Whatever the unifying concept which orders the formation of a particular group, the response of the group self to the individual member and the opportunity for the individual member to experience and observe the reactive impact of the group upon himself exert a powerful force. At a dynamic moment, in the listening presence of the practitioner, needs and wishes which are initially inchoate and unexpressed may find form and expression. And if the search of the individual for confirmation and guidance (mirroring) or for an opportunity to be enfolded in the understanding of group self or figure (idealizing) meets with failure but with failure which is not traumatically intense, the individual has an opportunity to build structure. The calmness and strength of the practitioner, her responses or silence, enable the group self to become more empathic to the individual, and individuals to each other. It is not one such moment but many, and it is not a single intervention but an aggregate, which enables the group and its members to experience human relatedness, partnering. Raging conduct, silence, or withdrawal can now come under the powerful focus of understanding in the context of a group in which one has membership. Kohut pointed out that " . . . wounded self-esteem, deflated fantasies of importance . . . lead to the most dangerous form of group tension . . . readiness for aggressive action" (1984, pp. 530–31). It is this which will account for group attacks on an individual member and his response in narcissistic rage, silence, or withdrawal. The eddying experience of group cohesion and group disintegration can be observed, studied, and understood with an increase of that capacity to monitor anxiety, to calm and soothe an individual group member as he seeks mastery through appropriate, meaningful dialogue. Through this process, group members acquire the ability to restore cohesion, to function as human beings in partnership with other group members, and ultimately, in the external world with members of their own choosing.

In the matrix of self/group self, the practitioner provides the conditions under which healing may take place. She offers herself as missing structure, empathically in tune with the ascending transference need reflected in the group or in its individual members. She does not model or engage in role-playing; she offers selfobject functions which, through optimal frustration, may be transmuted into the self-function of increased empathy of group members for each other's needs and of group response to those needs.

The many problem-laden individuals around which groups are assembled for the purpose of therapy include those with very severe deficit in self structure. We do not mean to suggest, in simplistic fashion, that such individuals can be restored to cohesive functioning, or that they will be engaged in structure building which will lead to the belated acquisition of a cohesive, vigorous self. Some individuals will require additional institutional settings; others will require individual treatment in addition to group therapy. Indeed, even better structured individuals may benefit from a combined approach. But it is my belief that in the broad reach of group treatment, practitioners may find their capacity to use themselves flexibly and purposefully increased through an understanding of human striving. That striving, in well-functioning individuals as well as those who seek help because they do not function adequately, is to find a mirroring response from the selfobject world, to be able to merge, even briefly with the wisdom and competence of an idealized figure, and to be viewed and accepted as a worthwhile member of humankind.

COMMUNITY ACTION PROGRAMS

It is in community action programs that the profession of social work had its earliest beginnings. Though the first social workers were volunteers, their empathic response to overburdened mothers, to unsavory living conditions, to children lost in the criminal justice system, to workers locked into unhealthy job conditions, gave rise to clinics and fresh air camps, to provision of city services such as garbage collection, to the Juvenile Court, to factory inspection, to the creation of agencies focusing on the needs of children and families—to list only a few community responses. The efforts of a caring society to respond to the needs of disadvantaged populations gave rise to the professionalization of social work. As the profession matured, differentiation and specialization of services proliferated. But the theme running through the evolution of the profession continues: Do the problems we are seeking to solve arise because of individual pathology or social ills? If the two are inextricable, from which direction shall we undertake our interventions? Will individual treatment enable the individual to navigate the social system more effectively or will a community-based approach overcome maladaptive behavior and provide a milieu which enhances coherent functioning of large numbers of individuals?

Kohut employed the concept of experience-near and experience-distant theory building in attempting to understand the human condition. By experience-distant he meant the use of theoretical formulations distilled from broad clinical experience over time and then employed in seeking to understand the needs of given groups of patients. By experience-near he meant the knowledge gleaned by means of introspection and empathy from depth immersion in the psychological life of a patient. The interaction between these two types of experience may be understood by using an analogy from the natural world. On a dark night in which the moon is obscured, the landscape will be illuminated now here, now there, when the moon pierces through various cloud formations. For the most part we see only a fragment of the landscape, but occasionally the entire scene is brightly lit. Through practice-based research (experience-near), social work sought to gather data which would illuminate a particular area of human suffering and the interventions which might alleviate it. Through exploration and research into the conditions which cut off broad populations from the mainstream of opportunity and fulfillment (experience-distant), social work sought data which could lead to informed social policy and community intervention.

Kohut did not ignore the role of psychosocial factors in the etiology of self disorders. He recognized the indivisibility of nature and nurture, of endowment and environment, of psychosocial factors in historical time. It was his belief that the frequency of self disorders, of fragmentation-prone individuals seen in increasing numbers in analytic practice and in other treatment modalities, generally reflected a changing society. The proliferation of single-parent families and working mothers has brought about the delegation to institutions and community organizations of many of the caretaking functions formerly performed within the family, the extended kinship, and the church. In fact, it is not by means of delegation but rather by reason of neglect that educational institutions, correctional institutions, church and community groups have been drawn in to serve an escalating vortex of need. For large groups of individuals, and particularly for youth, human attachments required for growth, for maturation, and for well-being have been weakened (Holzman, 1980).

It is not difficult to understand then the intense search for connectedness which individuals of all ages undertake to overcome their sense of isolation and distance. Substance abuse, sexual abuse, and perversion of all kinds occur in the context of a desperate need to stimulate a deadened self, to dull an aching void, to still the mounting fear of worthlessness, abandonment, and annihilation. Clusters of such individuals may come together for human closeness. In such spontaneously arising clusters, immersion in group life and group pressure may lead to primitivization of mental processes, a lowering of standards (Kohut, 1984, p. 838). Acting-out, enactment rather than reflection, delay, and purposeful planning, may become the order of the day. Diffuse rage and helplessness may lead to senseless outbreaks of violence.

The myriad and varied responses which society must provide to deal with such wide-ranging disorder call into play the creative potential of government, school, church, policy-setters, and mental health professionals of every persuasion. But it is on the social work professional that a large share of the burden of day-to-day response to target populations falls. We can more effectively manage that burden if we view human striving through the lens of an explanatory system of human behavior that makes basic human needs lucid to us.

For example, a gang of adolescents, caught trashing a neighborhood clubhouse, obviously must be disciplined. But in our response, shall we regard this simply as an expression of the aggressive, destructive drive or shall we attempt to understand the unexpressed needs which erupted in violence? A response to their needs may suggest many forms of intervention: treatment for substance abuse, an approach through school outreach, an assessment of readiness for vocational training, to name a few. If we can understand, for example, the adolescents' need for activities which enhance bodily skills, and if we can provide them with programs in which competent instructors are available for guiding, confirming, idealizing, and working together in partnership, we offer an opportunity for the restoration of cohesion, for filling in of deficits in a potentially cohesive self. Our further work must be in assisting these adolescents to recognize early premonitory symptoms of anxiety and tension which threaten to erupt in narcissistic rage. We may then help them to acquire language and the ability to reach out preventively to appropriate others, to selfobjects, for help.

Another example of a community approach may be that of a neighborhood poorly serviced or neglected. Joined in an effort to bring a necessary response from governmental agencies, the members of the community experience a sense of heightened self-esteem from the availability of a community worker. That worker, although more knowledgeable and articulate, does not impose values and standards. Rather, she provides an opportunity for the neighborhood residents, meeting together to express views, to arrive at judgments, undertake action in which essentially she serves as a guide to the larger selfobject world. When their needs are mirrored, their strengths confirmed and directed, they may then undertake a program of action with goals which can be achieved. If setbacks are encountered, the community worker absorbs their hurt and disappointment, and this experience of being enfolded in understanding allows them to feel strengthened to continue their attempts.

As a further example of community intervention, a group of older adult dropouts, seeking to acquire skills which they failed to acquire at an earlier phase, experience the shame of not knowing at an age when one should know. With the affirming presence of the community worker, such feelings can be understood and absorbed. Many individuals have had earlier experiences of being ridiculed or shamed, of reaching out and being rebuffed. They may have had earlier experiences in which the level of performance expected of them was beyond their ability. Their efforts may have been demeaned, leaving a sense of helplessness and shame in their wake. Since our earliest learning arises in the intimate relationship of parent and child, each new effort reawakens the earliest need to have a target of idealization and to have one's efforts admired. Though age may dim its intensity, the capacity to be so aroused and the ability to quicken and mobilize this capacity for the pursuit of new skills, new goals, and new relationships are the essence of structure building.

The unifying theme in the gamut of social work methods, from work with the internal world of individuals to the external world of the community, is that of the self of the social worker. If we can understand the search for cohesion, the universal longing to feel whole and worthwhile, and the availability of these early longings to be rekindled, we can make ourselves more flexibly and purposefully available.

The theory of self psychology offers us an understanding of the part we, as social workers employing various practice methods, play in restoring or freeing the thrust to complete growth present in all human beings. Moreover, it clarifies what practitioners have long observed and known, that is, the manner in which those we work with use our mature psychic structure to provide for their missing structure and, in the process, transmute the functions we perform into self structure. In so doing, empathic resonance with the therapist provides the basis for experiencing empathic resonance in their social and work world.

The present work is intended only as an introduction to self psychology and leads the way to further study of Kohut's publications. His colleagues have continued to expand his theories in psychoanalysis and in psychotherapy and their publications constitute a growing body of knowledge. A thorough study of this literature provides us with an explanatory system of human behavior congruent with what actually takes place in social work, whether we are engaged with those whose inner world is in disarray or with their larger world, the family, institutions, and the community. Through the expanded vision which the concepts of self psychology provide us, we can be more vitally in tune with their strivings to feel whole and worthwhile.

Appendix:
Definitions of Terms
From Self Psychology

These descriptive terms and their brief definitions have been drawn from the publications of Kohut and a paper he co-authored with Ernest Wolf (1978).

Nuclear self: The central sector of the personality, cohesive and enduring, with the correlated set of talents and skills it attracts or develops in response to demands of ambitions and ideals, forms the *nuclear self*. This structure is basis for sense of self as independent center of initiative and perception; integrated with most central ambitions and ideals and with experience of body and mind as unit in space and continuum in time.

Bipolar self: Three major constituents:
   (a) pole from which emanate basic strivings for power and success.
   (b) pole that harbors basic idealized goals.
   (c) intermediate area of basic talents and skills activated by tension arc established between ambitions and ideals.

Tension arc: Abiding flow of actual psychological activity that is established between two poles of self; basic pursuits toward which one is driven by ambitions and led by ideals.

Tension gradient: Relationship in which constituents of self (ambitions, goals, skills, and talents) stand to each other; specific for individual self even in absence of specific activity between two poles; presence of action-promoting condition that arises "between" person's ambitions and ideals.

Selfobject:
  (a) Mirroring selfobject: those who respond to and confirm child's innate sense of vigor, greatness and perfection.
  (b) Idealized parent imago: those with whom child can merge as image of calmness, infallibility and omnipotence.
  (c) Alter-ego or partnering selfobject: those with whom one feels essential likeness.

Transmuting internalization: The process through which a function formerly performed by another (selfobject) is taken into the self through optimal mirroring, interaction, and frustration. Selfobjects and their functions replaced gradually by self and its functions. Healthy functioning self is not a replica of selfobjects but a unique self.

Damaged or weakened self: Result of faulty, unempathic interaction between child and selfobjects of childhood. May be diffuse, may affect one or other pole of self but in the great majority of instances not due to single event or specific events. There do exist events of such impact that even in adult life permanent damage to the self may ensue. In general most often may result from faulty intrusions of parental selfobject whose own incompleteness or fears of fragmentation maintained archaic merger with child, not providing mirroring admiration in steps towards more mature forms of self-selfobject relationships.

Pathology of self:
I. *Primary disorders*
  (a) As in psychoses; permanent or protracted breakup or enfeeblement results in non-cohesive self. May be due partly to biological tendency or because nuclear self in totality and continuity not responded to by minimally effective mirroring in early life. May result from interplay between or convergence of biological and environmental factors. Tendency toward uncurbed spreading of unrealistically heightened self-acceptance (mania) or self-rejection and self-blame (guilty depression).
  (b) *Borderline states*: Breakup, enfeeblement or functional chaos of nuclear self; may be permanent or protracted but experiential and behavioral evidence of central defect covered over by complex defenses.
  (c) *Narcissistic behavior disorders*: Temporary breakup, enfeeblement and serious distortion of self; symptoms are perversions, delinquency, addictions; may expose individual to serious social and physical

damage but self more resilient than in (a) or (b) and can be treated by analysis.

(d) *Narcissistic personality disorders.* Temporary breakup, enfeeblement and serious distortion of the self with symptoms of hypochondria, depression, hypersensitivity to slights, lack of zest. Involves *psychological state* rather than *actions and interactions of individual.* Can be treated by analysis.

II. *Secondary disturbances of the self*
(a) Reactions of structurally undamaged self to vicissitudes of life. Strong self can experience and tolerate wide swings of self-esteem in response to victory or defeat, success or failure. Various emotions —triumph, joy, despair—accompany these changes in the state of the self. Firmly established self will not fear dejection following failure or expansive fantasies following success.

(b) May also include reactions of strong self to physical illness, incapacities of structural neurosis, depression or anger over incurable paralysis, or chronic neurotic anxiety which inhibits persons from pursuing central self-enhancing goals. Includes dejection over vulnerability of self which leads to social isolation.

Psychopathology and symptomatology (Frequently occurring clusters of symptoms):
(a) *Understimulated self:* Occurs because of prolonged lack of stimulating responsiveness from selfobjects of childhood. Will attempt to create pseudo-excitement to ward off painful feelings of deadness (head-banging in infancy; compulsive masturbation in latency; daredevil activities in adolescence; addictive promiscuity, sexual perversions, gambling, drugs, alcohol, and hypersociability in nonsexual sphere in adulthood).

(b) *Fragmenting self:* Chronic or recurrent; may be of short duration when self-esteem is taxed, but in pathology minor rebuffs trigger profound loss of cohesiveness: *in space* via concern over body parts, hypochondria; *in time* via loss of purpose, goals.

(c) *Overstimulated self:* Propensity to recurrent state of overstimulation as result of excessive or phase-inappropriate responses from selfobjects of childhood either to grandiose exhibitionistic pole of child's forming self, or to activities of pole that harbors guiding ideals, or to both. If grandiose exhibitionistic pole of self exposed to unempathic overstimulation, then no healthy glow of enjoyment from external success. Subject to being flooded by unrealistic archaic greatness fantasies; experience painful tension and anxiety and avoid opportunities to be appropriately center of attention. If pole harboring ideals overstimulated by unempathically intense and prolonged display of parental selfobject in need of admiration, there will be persisting intense need for merger with external ideal. Contact with idealized selfobject experienced as danger to be avoided—healthy capacity for enthusiasm lost.

(d) *Overburdened self*: Unlike overstimulated self whose ambitions and ideals unempathically responded to *in isolation* without regard to *whole* self in forming state, overburdened self was not provided with opportunity to merge with calmness of omnipotent selfobject. Trauma is unshared emotionality. Result is absence of self-soothing capacity that protects normal individuals from being traumatized by spreading of emotions, especially anxiety. World, experienced as lacking in such selfobjects, is dangerous; overburdened self views environments as unfriendly, menacing.

Character types:
I. *These three types are common in everyday life and are not pathological but rather variations of normal human personality with assets and defects.* They represent direction needs take to fill in circumscribed weakness of self rather than intensity of needs.

(a) *Mirror-hungry*: Search for mirroring selfobjects in attempt to overcome inner sense of worthlessness, lack of self-esteem. Search for reliably mirroring selfobject may be successful for a time, but relationship will ultimately fail to perform function of responding to needs to display selves either because selfobject tires of demands or archaic grandiose needs of mirror-hungry cannot be satisfied and search for new object resumes.

(b) *Ideal-hungry*: Constant search for others they can admire for such idealizable qualities as prestige, power, beauty, intelligence, moral stature. Feel worthwhile only as long as can relate to such selfobject. Relationship may last long while and of benefit to admired and admirer, but structural defect persists and reality flaws inevitably bring about renewed search for another selfobject through which idealizing relationship can be repeated.

(c) *Alter-ego*: Seek relationship with selfobject which conforms to self in appearance, opinions, values, thus confirming reality and existence of self. Relationships effective for long periods in which each experiences feelings of other as if experienced by self. Structural defect will again be felt as missing part, and search for another twin ensues.

II. These two types are considered pathological narcissism because of the extent rather than location of the structural defect.

   (a) *Merger-hungry*: Seriously enfeebled or defective self needs selfobjects in lieu of self structure. Type of merger less important than fact that selfobject must perform as if it had no independent self. Boundaries between self and selfobject fluid. Cannot effectively discriminate own wishes and needs from those of selfobject. Uniquely sensitive to separations. Expects selfobject to be continually available.
   (b) *Contact-shunning*: Because of intensity of need, extremely sensitive to rejection; on unconscious level fearful that nuclear self will be swallowed up and destroyed by desperate longing for merger. Shuns contact with others or avoids it in variety of ways.

Terms encountered in case illustrations: These are best described when applied to specific cases in context of the nature of the pathology of the individual.

Mirror transference: Insufficiently responded-to childhood need for source of accepting, confirming mirroring revived in treatment situation; reactivation in form of selfobject transferences of structure building attempts thwarted in child. Structure building through transmuting internalizatons is new edition of relation between self and selfobjects in early life.

Idealizing transference: Insufficiently responded-to childhood need for merger with source of idealized strength and calmness revived in treatment situation; structure building in therapy proceeds through transmuting internalizations via empathic interpretation and optimal frustration, through temporary empathic failures and/or nongratification of the need except for the acceptance as legitimate.

Twinship or alter-ego transference: Has developmental line earliest precursors: experience of being human among humans. Maturing forms expressed in partnering, working together, etc. Insufficiently responded to by early archaic selfobjects; twinship, alter-ego need reactivated in treatment with structure building transmuting of selfobject functions performed by therapist.

Vertical split: Because of archaic merger with selfobject of childhood, nuclear ambitions are blocked from achieving, through talents and skills, the nuclear ideals and goals formed through internalization of idealized omnipotent selfobject.

Horizontal split: Nuclear greatness acquired through merger with idealized selfobject walled off by repression (horizontal split) from contact with consciously perceived self. Unconscious, buried self derived from idealized selfobject, when appropriately analyzed, will bring about cohesion of self via organizing influence of the now available goals and ideals.

Defensive structures: Activities (in narcissistic behavior disorders), fantasies (in narcissistic personality disorders) which cover over structural defect in self. Undertaken to improve low self-esteem; ineffective but still endlessly pursued.

Disintegration products: Fixation on or regression to aspects of oral, urethral, anal, phallic drives better explained through psychology of self. Deepest analysis leads to narcissistic injury and depression, not to bedrock of drives. Sexual perversions, for example, are sexualized replica of original healthy strivings; contain elements of healthy grandiose self (exhibition of one's body) or elements of healthy idealization of selfobject (voyeuristic interest in parts or body of others). Thus, parental failure to perceive and mirror child's forming self at time when drives are maturing (and only a part of whole self) leads to fragmentation, depression, and preoccupation with body parts or products.

Compensatory structures: Filling in of earlier structural defects through later developmental successes in childhood or, belatedly, via treatment leads to increased functional vitality; strengthened self becomes organizing center of skills and talents which improves exercise of these functions; success in this exercise of skills and talents increases cohesion and vigor of self. Rather than simply covering over defect in self, compensatory structures bring about functional rehabilitation, making up for weakness of one pole of self through strengthening other pole. Example: Weakness in area of exhibition and ambition compensated for by vigorous pursuit of ideals, or weakness in pole of self carrying guiding ideals compensated for by activities more directly gratifying exhibitionism and ambition.

Guilty man: Id (sexual and destructive) and superego (inhibiting and prohibiting) are constituents of mental apparatus of guilty man. Conflictual aspect of oedipus complex is genetic focus of development of guilty man and genesis of psychoneuroses. Mental-apparatus psychology adequate to explain psychic disturbances and conflicts of guilty man. Lives within pleasure principle, seeks to satisfy pleasure-seeking drives, to lessen tension arising in erogenous zones. Because of inner conflict and environmental pressure often unable to achieve goals, hence "guilty man."

Tragic man: Nuclear ambitions and ideals are poles of self, with tension arc stretching between which forms center of pursuits of tragic man. Not a conflict psychology focusing on the oedipus complex but the psychology of self explains pathology of fragmented self (from schizophrenia to narcissistic personality disorder), of depleted self (empty depression, world of unmirrored ambitions, devoid of ideals), and the struggles of tragic man. Man seeks to express pattern of nuclear self; his endeavors are beyond pleasure principle. Since his failures overshadow successes, called "tragic man" rather than self-expressive or creative man.

References

Atkins, R. N. (1984). Finding one's father: The mother's contribution to early father represen- tation. *Journal of the American Academy of Psychoanalysis, 9,* 534–559.

Austin, L. N. (1956). Qualifications for psychotherapists: Social caseworkers. *American Journal of Orthopsychiatry, 26,* 47–57.

Barglow, P., & Schaefer, M. (1976). Toward a new female psychology. *Journal of the American Psychoanalytic Association, Supplement, 24,* 305–330.

Basch, M. F. (1980). *Doing psychotherapy.* New York: Basic Books.

Basch, M. F. (1981). Selfobject disorders and psychoanalytic theory: A historical perspec- tive. *Journal of Psychoanalysis, 29,* 337–351.

Basch, M. F. (1983a). Empathic understanding: A view of the concept and some theoretical considerations. *Journal of the American Psychoanalytic Association, 31,* 101–127.

Basch, M. F. (1983b). The perception of reality and the disavowal of meaning. *Annual of Psychoanalysis, 11,* 125–153.

Basch, M. F. (1983c). The significance of self psychology for a theory of psychotherapy. In J. Lichtenberg & S. Kaplan (Eds.), *Reflections in self psychology* (pp. 223–238). New York: International Universities Press.

Basch, M. F. (1984). Selfobjects, development and psychotherapy. In P. Stepansky & A. Goldberg (Eds.), *Kohut's legacy* (pp. 157–169). Hillsdale, NJ: Analytic Press.

Beebe, B. (1985). *Mother-infant mutual influence and precursors of psychic structure.* Presented at the New York meeting, Frontiers of Self Psychology.

Benedek, T. (1959). Parenthood as a developmental phase: A contribution to the libido theory. *Journal of the American Psychoanalytic Association, 7,* 389–417.

Benedek, T. (1975). Discussion of parenthood as a developmental phase. *Journal of the American Psychoanalytic Association, 7,* 389–417.

Bibring, G. (1959). Some considerations of the psychological processes in pregnancy. *The Psychoanalytic Study of the Child, 14,* 113–121.

Bibring, G. (1947). Psychiatry and social work. In *Social case work, selected articles 1940-1950.* New York: Family Service Association.

Blanck, G., & Blanck, R. (1974). *Ego psychology in theory and practice.* New York: Columbia University Press.

Blos, P. (1954). Prolonged adolescence: The formation of a syndrome and its therapeutic implications. *Journal of the American Orthopsychiatric Association, 34,* 733–742.

Blos, P. (1965). The initial stage of male adolescence. *The Psychoanalytic Study of the Child, 20,* 145–164.

Blos, P. (1972). The ego ideal in adolescence. *The Psychoanalytic Study of the Child, 27,* 93–98.

Brazelton, T. B., & Als, H. (1979). Four early stages in the development of mother and in- fant interaction. *The Psychoanalytic Study of the Child, 34,* 349–371.

Brent, P. L. (1981). *Charles Darwin: A man of enlarged curiosity.* New York: Harper and Row.

259

Brockman, D. D. (1985). *Late adolescence: Psychoanalytic studies.* New York: International Universities Press.

Broucek, F. (1979). Efficacy in infancy: A review of some experimental studies and their possible implications for clinical theory. *International Journal of Psycho-analysis, 60,* 311–316.

Burling, T. (1934). The value of explicit acknowledgement of the transference. *American Journal of Orthopsychiatry, 4,* 518–523.

Cohen, R., Cohler, B., & Weissman, S. (1984). *Parenthood: A psychodynamic perspective.* New York: Guilford.

Cohler, B. (1980). Adult developmental psychology and reconstruction in psychoanalysis. In S. I. Greenspan & G. H. Pollock (Eds.), *The course of life,* Vol. III:149-200. Bethesda: NIMH.

Cohler, B. (1982). Personal narrative and life course. In P. Baltes & O. G. Brim (Eds.), *Life span and development.* New York: Academic Press. Vol. 4:205–241.

Demos, V. (1985). *Affect and the development of the self.* Presented at the New York meeting, Frontiers of Self Psychology.

Edel, L. (Ed.). (1964). Introduction. *The diary of Alice James.* New York: Dodd, Mead.

Edel, L. (1985). *Henry James: A life.* New York: Harper and Row.

Edgcumbe, R. (1976). The negative oedipal phase in girls. *The Psychoanalytic Study of the Child, 31,* 35–59.

Elson, M. (1964). The reactive impact of adolescent and family upon each other in separation. *Journal of the American Academy of Child Psychiatry, 3,* 697–708.

Elson, M. (1984). Parenthood and the transformation of narcissism in parenthood. In R. Cohen, B. Cohler, & S. Weissman (Eds.), *Parenthood: A psychodynamic perspective* (pp. 297–314). New York: Guilford.

Emde, R. N., & Robinson, J. (1979). The first two months: Recent research in developmental psychobiology and the changing view of the newborn. In J. D. Noshpitz (Ed.), *Basic Handbook of Child Psychiatry* (Vol. 1:72:105). New York: Basic Books.

Emerson, R. W. (1885). *First and second essays.* Boston: Houghton Mifflin.

Encyclopedia Brittanica (1941). Adolescence, Vol. 1.

Erikson, E. H. (1950). *Childhood and society.* New York: W. W. Norton.

Erikson, E. H. (1956). The problem of ego identity. *Journal of the American Psychoanalytic Association, 4,* 56–121.

Erikson, E. H. (1959). *Identity and the life cycle. Psychological issues, 1,* 1. New York: International Universities Press.

Fairbairn, W. R. D. (1952). *An object relations theory of the personality.* New York: Basic Books.

Freud, A. (1946). *The ego and the mechanisms of defense.* New York: International Universities Press.

Freud, A. (1958). Adolescence. *The Psychoanalytic Study of the Child, 13,* 255–278.

Freud, A. (1965). *Normality and pathology in childhood: Assessments of development.* New York: International Universities Press.

Freud, S. (1893). On the psychical mechanism of hysterical phenomena: Preliminary communication. *Standard Edition, 2,* 3–17. New York: W. W. Norton.

Freud, S. (1905). Three essays on the theory of sexuality. *Standard Edition, 7,* 125–245. New York: W. W. Norton.

Freud, S. (1909). Notes upon a case of obsessional neurosis. *Standard Edition, 10,* 115–138. New York: W. W. Norton.

Freud, S. (1914). On narcissism: An introduction. *Standard Edition, 14,* 67–102. New York: W. W. Norton.

Freud, S. (1917). Mourning and melancholia. *Standard Edition, 14,* 237–258. New York: W. W. Norton.

Galenson, E., & Roiphe, H. (1976). Some suggested revisions concerning early feminine development. *Journal of the American Psychoanalytic Association, Supplement, 24,* 5: 24–58.

Garrett, A. (1949). The worker client relationship. In H. J. Parad (Ed.), *Ego psychology and dynamic casework.* New York: Family Service Association.

Garrett, A. (1950). Transference in casework. *Social casework: Selected articles, 1940-1950*. New York: Family Service Association.

Garrett, A. (1958). Modern casework: The contribution of ego psychology. In H. J. Parad (Ed.), *Ego psychology and dynamic casework* (pp. 53-72). New York: Family Service Association of America.

Gedo, J., & Goldberg, A. (1973). *Models of the mind: A psychoanalytic theory*. Chicago: University of Chicago Press.

Gill, M. M. (1982). *Analysis of transference*, Vol. 1 & 2. New York: International Universities Press.

Gill, M. M. (1983). The interpersonal paradigm and the degree of the therapist's involvement. *Contemporary Psychoanalysis*, 19(2).

Gilligan, C. (1982). *In a different voice: Psychological theory and women's development*. Cambridge: Harvard University Press.

Goldberg, A. (1972). On the incapacity to love: A psychotherapeutic approach to the problems in adolescence. *Archives of General Psychiatry, 26*, 3-7.

Goldberg, A. (1975). Narcissism and the readiness for psychotherapy termination, *Archives of General Psychiatry, 29*, 695-704.

Goldberg, A. (1977). *Psychoanalysis and the distinctiveness of psychotherapy*. The Franz Alexander Lecture. Los Angeles, California, unpublished.

Goldberg, A. (1978a). A shift in emphasis: Adolescent psychotherapy and the psychology of the self. *Journal of Youth and Adolescence, 7*, 119-132.

Goldberg, A. (Ed.). (1978b). *Psychology of the self: A casebook*. New York: International Universities Press.

Goldberg, A. (Ed.). (1980). *Advances in self psychology*. New York: International Universities Press.

Goldberg, A. (Ed.). (1983). *The future of psychoanalysis*. New York: International Universities Press.

Goldberg, A. & Stepansky, P. (Eds.). (1984). *Kohut's legacy*. Hillsdale, NJ: Analytic Press.

Goldstein, E. (1984). *Ego psychology and social work practice*. New York: Free Press.

Grunes, J. M. (1981a). Reminiscences, regression and empathy. In S. I. Greenspan & G. H. Pollock (Eds.), *The course of life*, Vol. III:545-548. Bethesda: NIMH.

Grunes, J. M. (1981b). Parenthood issues in the aging process. In R. Cohen, B. Cohler, & S. Weissman (Eds.), *Parenthood: A psychodynamic perspective* (pp. 103-112). New York: Guilford.

Gunderson, J. & Singer, M. (1975). Defining borderline patients. *American Journal of Psychiatry, 132*, 1-10.

Guntrip, H. (1969). *Schizoid phenomena, object relations and the self*. New York: International Universities Press.

Gustafson, E. E., Green, J. A., & West, M. A. (1979). The infant's changing role in mother-infant games. *Infant Behavior Development, 2:4*, 301-308.

Gutman, D. L. (1981). Psychoanalysis and aging: A developmental view. In S. I. Greenspan & G. H. Pollock (Eds.), *The course of life*, Vol. III:545-548. Bethesda: NIMH.

Hamilton, G. (1951). *Theory and practice of social casework*, 2nd ed. New York: Columbia University Press.

Hamilton, G. (1958). A theory of personality: Freud's contribution to social work. In H. J. Parad (Ed.), *Ego psychology and dynamic casework* (pp. 11-37). New York: Family Service Association of America.

Hartmann, H. (1939). *Ego psychology and the problem of adaptation*. New York: International Universities Press, 1958.

Harwood, I. M. (1983). The application of self psychology concepts to group psychotherapy. *International Journal of Group Psychotherapy, 33*, 469-486.

Hollis, F. (1964). *Casework: A psychosocial therapy*. New York: Random House.

Hollis, F. and Woods, M. E. (1981). *Casework: A psychosocial therapy*. New York: Random House.

Holzman, P. (1980). Discussion, vulnerable youth: Hope, despair and renewal. In S. Feinstein & P. L.Giovacchini (Eds.), *Adolescent psychiatry*, Vol. 8:309–316. Chicago: University of Chicago Press.

Jacobson, E. (1964). *The self and the object world*. New York: International Universities Press.

James, A. (1934). *Alice James: Her brothers—her journal.* Anna Robeson Barr, Ed. New York: Dodd Mead.

James, A. (1964). *The diary of Alice James.* Edited and with an introduction by Leon Edel. New York: Dodd, Mead.

James, H. (1913). A small boy and others. In *Henry James Autobiography*, edited and with an introduction by F. W. Dupee. New York: Criterion Books, 1956.

James, H. (1914). Notes of a son and brother. In *Henry James Autobiography*, edited and with an introduction by F. W. Dupee. New York: Criterion Books, 1956.

James, W. (1980). *The selected letters of William James.* Boston: David R. Godine.

Kohut, H. (1956). Discussion of Annette Garrett's paper: Modern casework: The contribution of ego psychology. In P. Ornstein (Ed.), *The Search for the Self*, Chapter 10. New York: International Universities Press, 1978.

Kohut, H. (1959). Introspection, empathy and psychoanalysis. In P. Ornstein (Ed.), *The Search for the Self*, Chapter 12. New York: International Universities Press, 1978.

Kohut, H. (1966). Forms and transformations of narcissism. In P. Ornstein (Ed.) *The Search for the Self*, Chapter 32. New York: International Universities Press.

Kohut, H. (1970). *Self esteem and ideals*, M. Elson (Ed.). Unpublished seminars presented at the University of Chicago Student Mental Health Clinic.

Kohut, H. (1971). *Analysis of the self.* New York: International Universities Press.

Kohut, H. (1974). The self in history. In P. Ornstein (Ed.), *Search for the Self*, Chapter 46. New York: International Universities Press.

Kohut, H. (1975). A note on female sexuality. In P. Ornstein (Ed.), *Search for the Self*, Chapter 47. New York: International Universities Press.

Kohut, H. (1977). *Restoration of the Self.* New York: International Universities Press.

Kohut, H. (1978). *The Search for the Self: Selected Writings of Heinz Kohut, 1950–1978*, P. Ornstein (Ed.), Vol. I & II. New York: International Universities Press.

Kohut, H. (1984). *How Does Analysis Cure?* A. Goldberg and P. Stepansky (Eds.). Chicago: University of Chicago Press.

Kohut, H. (1985). *Self psychology and the humanities.* Edited with an introduction by Charles B. Strozier. New York: W. W. Norton.

Kohut, H., & Tolpin, M. (1980). The disorders of the self: The psychopathology of the first year of life. In S. I. Greenspan & G. H. Pollock (Eds.), *The course of life*, Vol. I:425–442. Bethesda: NIMH.

Kohut, H., & Wolf, E. S. (1978). Disorders of the self and their treatment. *International Journal of Psycho-analysis, 59*, 413–425.

Kopit, A. (1978). *Wings: A play.* New York: Hill and Wang.

Kriegman, D., & Solomon, L. (1985). Cult groups and the narcissistic personality: The offer to heal defects in the self. *International Journal of Group Psychotherapy, 35*, 239–261.

Lachmann, F. M. (1984). Self psychology and psychotherapy: Discussion of "Selfobjects: Development and Psychotherapy" by M. F. Basch, and "Psychoanalytic Psychotherapy: A Contemporary Perspective," by A. Ornstein. In A. Goldberg & P. Stepansky (Eds.), *Kohut's legacy* (pp. 183–190). Hillsdale, NJ: Analytic Press.

Lachmann, F. M. (1982). Narcissistic development. In D. Mendell (Ed.), *Early female development: Current psychoanalytic views* (pp. 227–248). New York: Spectrum Publications.

Lang, J. A. (1984). Notes toward a psychology of the feminine self. In P. Stepansky & A. Goldberg (Eds.), *Kohut's legacy* (pp. 51–70). Hillsdale, NJ: Analytic Press.

Leszcz, M., Feigenbaum, E., Sadavoy, J., & Robinson, A. (1985). A men's group: Psychotherapy of elderly men. *International Journal of Group Psychotherapy, 35*, 177–195.

Lichtenberg, J., & Kaplan, N. S. (Eds.) (1983). *Reflections in self psychology.* Hillsdale, NJ: Analytic Press.

Mahler, M., Pine, F., & Bergman, A. (1975). *The psychological birth of the human infant: Symbiosis and individuation.* New York: Basic Books.

Markus, R. (1984). I've lost a real close friend. *Chicago Tribune*, Sec. 4:1.
Matthiessen, F. O. (1980). *The James family: A group biography*. New York: Vintage Press, Random House.
New York Times (1984). Sunday Magazine Section, April 1, p. 25.
Offer, D., & Offer, J. B. (1975). *From teen-age to young manhood: A psychological study*. New York: Basic Books.
Offer, D. & Sabshin, M. (1974). *Normality: Theoretical and clinical concepts of mental health* (2nd ed.). New York: Basic Books.
Ornstein, P., & Ornstein, A. (1977). On the continuing evolution of psychoanalytic psychotherapy: Reflections and predictions. *The annual of psychoanalysis*, 5, 329–370.
Ornstein, P. (Ed.) (1978). *The Search for the Self*, Vol. 1 & 2. New York: International Universities Press.
Ornstein, P. (1982). On the psychoanalytic psychotherapy of self pathology. *Psychiatry*, 42, 498–531.
Parens, H. (1975). Discussion of parenthood as a developmental phase. *Journal of the American Psychoanalytic Association*, 23, 154–165.
Perlman, H. H. (1957). *Social casework: A problem solving process*. Chicago: University of Chicago Press.
Perlman, H. H. (1968). *Persona: Social role and personality*. Chicago: University of Chicago Press.
Perlman, H. H. (Ed.) (1969). *Helping: Charlotte Towle on social work and social casework*. Chicago: University of Chicago Press.
Perlman, H. H. (1979). *Relationship: The heart of helping people*. Chicago: University of Chicago Press.
Person, E., & Ovesey, L. (1983). Psychoanalytic theories of gender identity, *Journal of the American Academy of Psychoanalysis*, 11, 203–226.
Piaget, J. (1940). The mental development of the child. In *Six psychological studies*. New York: Vintage Press, 1968.
Rangell, L. (1981). From insight to change. *Journal of the American Psychoanalytic Association*, 29, 119–141.
Richmond, M. (1917). *Social diagnosis*. New York: Russell Sage Foundation.
Ritvo, S. (1976). Adolescent to woman. *Journal of the American Psychoanalytic Association*, 24:5, 127–138.
Robinson, V. C. (1930). *A changing psychology in social case work*. Chapel Hill: University of North Carolina Press.
Schafer, R. (1974). Problems in Freud's psychology of women. *Journal of the American Psychoanalytic Association*, 22, 459–485.
Silverman, M. A. (1981). Cognitive development and female psychology. *Journal of the American Psychoanalytic Association*, 29, 581–605.
Simon, B. K. (1970). Social casework theory: An overview. In R. W. Roberts & R. H. Nee (Eds.), *Theories of social casework* (pp. 353–396). Chicago: University of Chicago Press.
Simon, B. K. (1977). Diversity and unity in the social work profession. *Social Work: Journal of the National Association of Social Workers*, 22, 394–401.
Solomon, B. C. (1985). Discussion of Dr. Phyllis Tyson's paper, Female psychological development. Presented to the Chicago Psychoanalytic Society, Scientific Meeting, January 22.
Stern, D. (1977). *The first relationship: Infant and mother*. Cambridge: Harvard University Press.
Stern, D. (1983). The early development of schemas of self, other, and "self with other." In A. Goldberg & P. Stepansky (Eds.), *Kohut's legacy* (pp. 49–84). Hillsdale, NJ: Analytic Press.
Stoller, R. J. (1968). The source of femaleness. *Psychoanalytic Quarterly*, 37, 1: 42–55.
Strean, H. (1978). *Clinical social work*. New York: Free Press.
Strouse, J. (1980). *Alice James: A Biography*. Boston: Houghton Mifflin.
Tolpin, M. (1971). On the beginnings of a cohesive self. *The Psychoanalytic Study of the Child*, 26, 316–352.
Tolpin, M. (1978). Self objects and oedipal objects: A crucial developmental distinction. *The Psychoanalytic Study of the Child*, 33, 167–184.
Tolpin, M. & Kohut, H. (1980). The disorders of the self: The psychopathology of the first

years of life. In S. I. Greenspan & G. H. Pollock (Eds.), *The course of life*. Bethesda: NIMH.
Tolpin, M. (1980). Discussion of "Psychoanalytic developmental theories of the self: An integration" by M. Shane and E. Shane. In A. Goldberg (Ed.), *Advances in self psychology* (pp. 47–68). New York: International Universities Press.
Tolpin, M. (1982). *Injured self cohesion: Developmental, clinical and theoretical perspectives; A contribution to understanding narcissistic and personality disorders*. Unpublished paper given to the University of California Symposium on Narcissistic and Borderline Disorders: Current Perspectives, October 2–3.
Tolpin, M. (1983a). Discussion of papers by Drs. Sander and Stern. In J. D. Lichtenberg & S. Kaplan (Eds.), *Reflections on self psychology* (pp. 113–127). Hillsdale, NJ: Analytic Press.
Tolpin, M. (1983b). Corrective emotional experience: A self psychological reevaluation. In A. Goldberg (Ed.), *The future of psychoanalysis* (pp. 363–380). New York: International Universities Press.
Tolpin, P. (1980). The borderline personality: Its makeup and analyzability. In A. Goldberg (Ed.), *Advances in self psychology* (pp. 299–316). New York: International Universities Press.
Tolpin, P. (1984). Discussion of "A current perspective on difficult patients" by Bernard Brandchaft and R. D. Stolorow, and "Issues in the treatment of the borderline patient" by Gerald Adler. In A. Goldberg & P. Stepansky (Eds.), *Kohut's legacy* (pp. 138–142). Hillsdale, NJ: Analytic Press.
Towle, C. (1935). The mental hygiene of the social worker. In H. H. Perlman (Ed.) *Helping: Charlotte Towle on social work and social casework* (pp. 27–46). Chicago: University of Chicago Press.
Towle, C. (1945). *Common human needs*. New York: National Association of Social Workers.
Towle, C. (1946). Social casework in modern society. In H. H. Perlman (Ed.), *Helping: Charlotte Towle on social work and social casework* (pp. 97–119). Chicago: University of Chicago Press.
Tyson, P. (1982). A developmental line of gender identity, gender role and choice of love object. *Journal of the American Psychoanalytic Association, 30,* 59–84.
Tyson, P. (1985). *Female psychological development as relived in the interaction between patient and analyst*. Unpublished paper presented at the Chicago Psychoanalytic Society Scientific Meeting, January, 22.
U.S. Department of Commerce: Bureau of the Census (1984). *Statistical Abstract of the United States,* 104th edition.
Walsh, F. (1983). Family therapy: A systematic orientation to treatment. In A. Rosenblatt & D. Waldfogel (Eds.), *Handbook of clinical social work*. Chapter 22. San Francisco: Jossey-Bass.
Watson, A. S. (1966). Reality testing and transference in psychotherapy. *Smith College Studies in Social Work, 37,* 191–201.
Weissman, S., & Barglow, P. (1980). Recent contributions to the theory of female adolescent psychological development. In S. Feinstein & P. L. Giovacchini (Eds.), *Adolescent psychiatry,* Vol. 8, pp. 213–240. Chicago: University of Chicago Press.
Winnicott, D. W. (1951). Transitional objects and transitional phenomena. *Through paediatrics to psychoanalysis.* Chapter 18. London: Hogarth Press, 1958.
Winnicott, D. W. (1957). *Mother and child*. New York: Basic Books.
Winnicott, D. W. (1965). *The maturational process and the facilitating environment*. New York: Basic Books.
Wolf, E. S., Gedo, J., & Terman, D. (1972). On the adolescent process as a transformation of the self. *Journal of Youth and Adolescence, 1:*252–272.
Wolf, E. S. (1979). Transference and countertransference in the analysis of the disorders of the self. *Contemporary Psychoanalysis, 15*(3):577–594.
Wolf, E. S. (1980a). On the developmental line of selfobject relations. In A. Goldberg (Ed.), *Advances in self psychology* (pp. 117–132). New York: International Universities Press.
Wolf, E. S. (1980b). Tomorrow's self: Heinz Kohut's contribution to adolescent psychiatry. In S. Feinstein & P. L. Giovacchini (Eds.), *Adolescent psychiatry,* Vol. 8:48–50. Chicago: University of Chicago Press.
Wolf, E. S. (1981). *Empathic resonance: A panel discussion*. Fourth conference on self psychology. Berkeley, California, October 4.

Wolf, E. S. (1982). *Do adolescents need selfobjects?* Plenary address to 1982 Institute of Self Psychology in Adolescent Treatment and Development. Los Angeles, California.

Wolf, E. S. (1984a). Discussion of papers by Drs. Lichtenberg and Ornstein. In J. D. Lichtenberg & S. Kaplan (Eds.), *Reflections on self psychology* (pp. 203–215). Hillsdale, NJ: Analytic Press.

Wolf, E. S. (1984b). Disruptions in the psychoanalytic treatment of disorders of the self. In A. Goldberg & P. Stepansky (Eds.), *Kohut's Legacy* (pp. 143–156). Hillsdale, NJ: Analytic Press.

Index